THE SHAKESPEAREAN STAGE SPACE

How did Renaissance theatre create its powerful effects with so few resources? In *The Shakespearean Stage Space*, Mariko Ichikawa explores the original staging of plays by Shakespeare and his contemporaries to build a new picture of the artistry of the Renaissance stage. Dealing with problematic scenes and stage directions, Ichikawa closely examines the playing conditions in early modern playhouses to reveal the ways in which the structure of the stage was used to ensure the audibility of offstage sounds, to control the visibility of characters, to convey fictional locales, to create specific moods and atmospheres and to maintain a frequently shifting balance between fictional and theatrical realities. She argues that basic theatrical terms were used in a much broader and more flexible way than we usually assume and demonstrates that, rather than imposing limitations, the bare stage of the Shakespearean theatre offered dramatists and actors a variety of imaginative possibilities.

MARIKO ICHIKAWA is Professor of English at the University of Tohoku, Japan. Her previous publications include *Staging in Shakespeare's Theatres* (co-authored with Andrew Gurr, 2000) and *Shakespearean Entrances* (2002).

THE SHAKESPEAREAN STAGE SPACE

MARIKO ICHIKAWA

CAMBRIDGE UNIVERSITY PRESS
Cambridge, New York, Melbourne, Madrid, Cape Town,
Singapore, São Paulo, Delhi, Mexico City

Cambridge University Press
The Edinburgh Building, Cambridge CB2 8RU, UK

Published in the United States of America by Cambridge University Press, New York

www.cambridge.org
Information on this title: www.cambridge.org/9781107020351

© Mariko Ichikawa 2013

This publication is in copyright. Subject to statutory exception
and to the provisions of relevant collective licensing agreements,
no reproduction of any part may take place without the written
permission of Cambridge University Press.

First published 2013

Printed and bound in the United Kingdom by the MPG Books Group

A catalogue record for this publication is available from the British Library

Library of Congress Cataloguing in Publication data
Ichikawa, Mariko.
The Shakespearean stage space / Mariko Ichikawa.
pages cm
ISBN 978-1-107-02035-1
1. Shakespeare, William, 1564–1616 – Stage history – To 1625. 2. Shakespeare, William, 1564–1616 – Stage history – England – London. 3. Theaters – Stage-setting and scenery – England – History – 16th century. 4. Theaters – Stage-setting and scenery – England – History – 17th century. 5. Theater – England – London – History – 16th century. 6. Theater – England – London – History – 17th century. 7. English drama – Early modern and Elizabethan, 1500–1600 – History and criticism 8. English drama – 17th century – History and criticism. I. Title.
PR3095.I28 2012
792.0942′09031–dc23
2012018845

ISBN 978-1-107-02035-1 Hardback

Cambridge University Press has no responsibility for the persistence or
accuracy of URLs for external or third-party internet websites referred to
in this publication, and does not guarantee that any content on such
websites is, or will remain, accurate or appropriate.

To Andy Gurr, Alan Dessen and Ray Powell

Contents

List of figures and table   *page* viii
Acknowledgements   ix
Note on texts and old spelling; system of dating   xi
Editorial abbreviations   xiii

1. Playhouses, play texts and the theatrical language   1
2. '*Maluolio within*'   29
3. '*Music within*' and '*Music above*'   52
4. Were the doors open or closed?   72
5. '*Enter Brutus in his Orchard*'   100
6. What to do with onstage corpses?   129
   Conclusion: the Shakespearean stage space and stage directions   151

Notes   158
Plays cited   194
Other works cited   204
Index   217

Figures and Table

FIGURES

1a. The Rose Theatre: Phase 1 (by permission of Museum of London Archaeology)	*page* 2
1b. The Rose Theatre: Phase 2 (by permission of Museum of London Archaeology)	3
2. De Witt's sketch of the Swan Theatre (by permission of Utrecht University Library. MS 842, fol. 132r)	5
3a. Inigo Jones/John Webb drawings: elevation and plan for an indoor playhouse (by permission of the Provost and Fellows of Worcester College, Oxford. Harris and Tait 10 (Gotch 1/7B))	10
3b. Inigo Jones/John Webb drawings: two transverse sections of the same playhouse (by permission of the Provost and Fellows of Worcester College, Oxford. Harris and Tait 11 (Gotch 1/7C))	11
4. The new Globe Theatre, Bankside, London (photo by Mariko Ichikawa)	36
5. The frontispiece to Francis Kirkman's *The Wits, or Sport upon Sport* (by permission of the Folger Shakespeare Library. Wing W3218)	54
6. A woodcut from Thomas Hill's *The Gardener's Labyrinth* (by permission of the Folger Shakespeare Library. STC 13483, sig. G3r)	102

TABLE

1. Positions which might be referred to by the stage directions '*enter*', '*within*' and '*above*'	155

Acknowledgements

I have received help and support from many individuals and institutions in the process of writing and rewriting the manuscript. It is a great pleasure to acknowledge my indebtedness and express my gratitude.

This book is mainly based upon my essays that have been published in journals and collections of essays. I wish to thank the editors and the publishers for their permission to use revised versions of these essays:

'What to do with a Corpse?: Physical Reality and the Fictional World in the Shakespearean Theatre', *Theatre Research International*, Volume 29(3), pp. 201–15, (2004) © International Federation for Theatre Research, published by Cambridge University Press, reproduced with permission.

'"*Maluolio within*": Acting on the Threshold between Onstage and Offstage Spaces', in S. P. Cerasano (ed.), *Medieval and Renaissance Drama in England*, vol. 18 (Fairleigh Dickinson University Press, 2005), pp. 123–45.

'"*Music Within*" and "*Music Above*"', *Shakespearean International Yearbook*, Volume 5, ed. Graham Bradshaw and Tom Bishop (Aldershot: Ashgate, 2005), pp. 314–35. Copyright © 2005, reproduced by permission of the publishers.

'Were the Doors Open or Closed?: The Use of the Stage Doors in the Shakespearean Theatre', *Theatre Notebook*, 60 (2006), 5–29.

'"*Enter Brutus in his Orchard*": Garden Scenes in Early Modern English Plays', *Shakespearean International Yearbook*, Volume 9, ed. Graham Bradshaw, Tom Bishop and Laurence Wright (Aldershot: Ashgate, 2009), pp. 214–47. Copyright © 2009, reproduced by permission of the publishers.

'A Special Meaning of "*Within*"?', in Frank Occhiogrosso (ed.), *Shakespeare Closely Read: A Collection of Essays* (Fairleigh Dickinson University Press, 2011), pp. 9–17.

'Shakespearean Speeches: The Physical Reality of the Playhouse and the Fictional Reality of the Dramatic World', in *Shakespeare and Theatre Culture: A Collection of Essays in Commemoration of the 50th Anniversary of the Founding of the Shakespeare Society of Japan* (Tokyo: Kenkyusha, 2012), pp. 180–95 [written in Japanese].

The award of a scholarship from the Fulbright Program in the academic year 2004–5 made possible a substantial period of research at the Folger

Shakespeare Library that proved crucial to the development of this project. In 2010–11 the Folger Shakespeare Library itself granted me a short-term fellowship, which enabled me to finish this book. I am particularly grateful for the expert help and support provided at the Folger by Carol Brobeck, Fellowships Administrator, Georgianna Ziegler, Head of Reference, Betsy Walsh, Head of Reader Services and her staff including Rosalind Larry, Camille Seerattan, LuEllen DeHaven, Harold Batie and Alan Katz. My debt to the British Library is also immense and profound. I am especially thankful to the helpful staff in the Manuscripts and Rare Books Rooms.

At Cambridge University Press, Sarah Stanton, Rebecca Taylor, Fleur Jones and Christina Sarigiannidou have provided encouragement and expert guidance, for which I am most grateful. I am also deeply indebted to the two anonymous readers for their insightful comments. I have sought help and advice from many scholars and received very warm and kind responses to my requests. I am especially grateful to John Astington, Julian Bowsher, David Carnegie, Susan Cerasano, John Cox, Frank Hildy, Bernice Kliman, Joanna Parker, Soko Tomita, Laetitia Yeandle and Georgianna Ziegler. It has been a privilege at all times to enjoy their professional expertise. My special thanks are due, as always, to Andrew Gurr, Alan Dessen and Raymond Powell. Andrew Gurr offered me wise counsel and valuable assistance at every stage of this project. Alan Dessen read earlier versions of all the chapters and provided productive suggestions. Raymond Powell read both earlier and later versions of the manuscript, responding fully and helpfully to both. For unfailing help and encouragement I owe these mentors more than I can express. The remaining errors and inadequacies are, of course, all my own.

Finally, I wish to thank my parents and sister and her family, who have always been supportive in loving ways.

Note on texts and old spelling; system of dating

Quotations from Shakespeare are taken from *The Norton Facsimile: The First Folio of Shakespeare*, prepared by Charlton Hinman, with a new introduction by Peter W. M. Blayney, 2nd edn (New York: W. W. Norton, 1996) and *Shakespeare's Plays in Quarto: A Facsimile Edition of Copies Mainly from the Henry E. Huntington Library*, edited by Michael J. B. Allen and Kenneth Muir (University of California Press, 1981). Folio texts are cited by the through-line numbers provided in *The Norton Facsimile*; Quarto texts are cited by signatures. Act-scene-line references are those of *The Riverside Shakespeare*, edited by G. Blakemore Evans with the assistance of J. J. M. Tobin, 2nd edn (Boston: Houghton Mifflin, 1997). For non-Shakespearean plays, I consulted the early printed texts and the surviving manuscripts (either in the original form or in facsimile). The printed texts are cited by signatures, and act-scene-line references or through-line numbers are also supplied from modern editions only when they are necessary for the discussion of the passages.

I have retained the original typographical conventions of the use of *i, j, u* and *v*, but have not preserved the long *s* or indicated ligatures. As for typeface and layout, various kinds of setting practice and strategy can be observed in early modern printed texts. The following are typical examples: the initial words of act-opening speeches are set in capitals, and the first letters are set in 2-line capitals; the initial letters of characters' names are printed in a different typeface from the rest; turn-ups and turn-downs are used for saving lines; and it is not uncommon for two very short speeches to be set in the same line. I have not preserved these and similar compositorial practices and strategies, although for the most part I have retained the original use of italic and roman type, capitalisation and punctuation. In some play texts, the majority of speeches are printed in black letter while stage directions and speech prefixes are usually set in roman. For these texts both black letter and roman have been transcribed as roman.

SYSTEM OF DATING

The old-style system of dating, which began the calendar year on 25 March instead of on 1 January, has been silently adjusted to the modern dating.

Editorial abbreviations

D	Duodecimo
F	Folio
MS	Manuscript
O	Octavo
Q	Quarto
r	recto (right page)
TLN	Through-line number(s)
v	verso (left page)

CHAPTER 1

Playhouses, play texts and the theatrical language

This book explores the original staging of plays by Shakespeare and his contemporaries in London's professional playhouses, with special attention focused on the relation between onstage and offstage spaces and on the audience's awareness both of the imaginative world created by the play and the wood, lath and plaster reality of the playhouse itself – that is to say, the balance between fiction and theatre. The play texts themselves are almost the sole evidence as to how they were staged, apart from a few surviving playhouse documents, such as theatrical 'plots' and Philip Henslowe's papers. In this introductory chapter I set out to do four things. First, I survey the structure of the playhouses. Second, I consider the nature of the play texts in relation to the performances of the plays. Third, I turn to the nature of the language in which the play texts are written. Finally, I summarise the particular questions I address in the chapters that follow.

PLAYHOUSES

In order to deal with questions concerning the staging of early modern plays, it is necessary to understand the structure of the original stages and to be as clear as possible about the nature of the acting space in which the actors performed the plays. Important basic features include: shape and size; facilities; the nature of the division between the stage and the backstage area; and the physical relationship between the stage and the auditorium.

In Shakespeare's time, there were two kinds of playhouse: 'public' outdoor theatres where plays were performed in daylight; and 'private' indoor theatres where candles were used to supplement the light from the windows of the auditorium. The public playhouses built in this period were the Red Lion (1567); the playhouse at Newington Butts (1575, closed in 1594); the Theatre (1576, dismantled in 1598); the Curtain (1577); the Rose (1587, enlarged in 1592, demolished by 1606); the Swan (1595); the Globe (1599, rebuilt in 1614, operated until 1642); the Boar's Head (converted from an inn in 1599, the leases expired in 1616); the Fortune (1600, rebuilt in 1622, operated until 1642); the Red Bull (converted from an inn, c.1605, operated until 1642); and the Hope (1613, after 1617 mainly used for bear baiting). Although John Brayne's Red Lion did not last long, there is not much doubt that this project had an influence on the design of the Theatre, which he was to build jointly with his brother-in-law James Burbage nine years later. According to the records of disputes between Brayne and his carpenters, the Red Lion consisted of 'skaffoldes' for spectators and a 'stage' with a 'turrett' on it. The stage was large – 40 feet (12.2 metres) wide, 30 feet (9.1 metres) deep and 5 feet (1.5 metres) high – with a 'voyde parte' in it, apparently for a trap.[1]

The 1989 archaeological excavations of the Rose site have revealed that the original structure of the playhouse was a regular fourteen-sided polygon about 22 metres across. The depth of each bay, that is, the distance between the outer and inner walls of the building was 3.5 metres (measured centre to centre). The

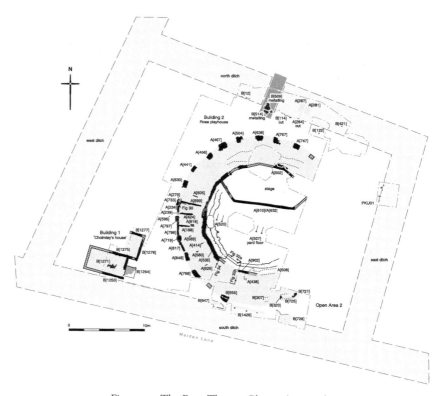

Figure 1a. The Rose Theatre: Phase 1 (1587–92).

enlargement of the playhouse in 1592 entailed dismantling the northern half of the building and reconstructing it farther north (see Figures 1a and 1b). Its stage was surprisingly small both in its original form and even after the enlargement of the playhouse. The original stage projected a maximum of 5.0 metres into the yard, tapering towards the front, where it had an estimated maximum width of 8.2 metres. The new stage was built 2.0 metres north of the first one and its size was much the same as its predecessor's.[2] The angled *frons scenae*, or tiring-house wall, of the first Rose stage indicates the presence of three doorways in the *frons*. A central opening, covered by hangings, would have been used for 'discoveries' such as the ones in the following stage directions: '*A charge, the cable cut, A Caldron discouered*' (Marlowe, *The Jew of Malta* Q1, K2r); 'Curtaines open, *Robin Hoode* sleepes on a greene banke, and *Marian* strewing flowers on him' (Chettle and Munday, *The Downfall of Robert, Earl of*

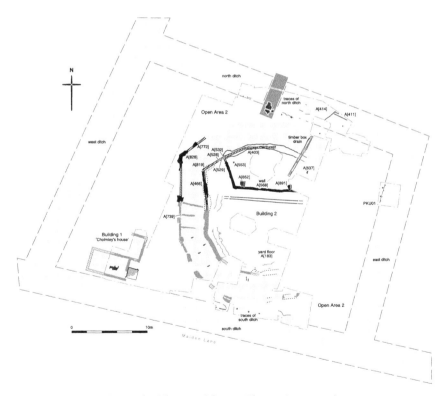

Figure 1b. The Rose Theatre: Phase 2 (1592–1606).

Huntingdon Q1, F3v).³ The earliest documentary evidence for a stage roof is Philip Henslowe's record of payment in 1595 for installation of a descent machine at the Rose: 'Itm pd for carpenters worke & mackinge the throne In the heuenes the 4 of June 1595'.⁴ But there is clear archaeological evidence that the stage 'heavens' appeared in the 1592 rebuild. In the excavated Rose site there was no sign of any means of supporting a roof over the early form of the stage, while the remains of two pillar bases were found just inside the foundation wall of the later stage front. As a result, the Rose's archaeologist, Julian Bowsher, was convinced that its original stage had no permanent roof, although there might have been awnings or even a small cantilevered cover.⁵ Given that the Rose seems, on archaeological evidence, to have been built in 1587 without any permanent stage cover, it is scarcely reasonable to think that a good ten years earlier, 1576/1577, the Theatre and the Curtain might have originally had a stage roof complete with a descent machine.⁶ In his most recent article, Bowsher reports new discoveries from excavations at the Theatre site. He writes: 'the limited evidence for its size and layout was a surprise. A surprise, because the Theatre remains appear to be very similar to the Rose remains. Its diameter is a similar 23 m, it had a similar *ingressus* feature and, very possibly, an angled stage like that of Rose Phase One. In other words, although the Theatre looks like the Rose, the converse is true; the Rose was modelled on the Theatre, which is itself not a surprise.'⁷ He assumes therefore that the Curtain, built between the two, was also similar, and thinks that there was an early playhouse form represented by these three.

What a public playhouse may have looked like from the inside is best seen in the well-known Swan sketch, which is a copy made by Arend van Buchell of the original drawn by Johannes de Witt around 1596 (see Figure 2). This is the only contemporary drawing we have of the interior of an amphitheatre, although it may be untrustworthy in many ways.⁸ The sketch shows a circular playhouse with three tiers of galleries for spectators. A large rectangular stage projects into a yard and is raised above the ground. The unroofed yard was occupied by standing spectators, or 'groundlings', although no such figures are present in the sketch. The stage has two massive posts, which support the roof over the stage, and above this roof there is a hut. At the rear of the stage is a tiring-house with two round-arched double doors in its façade. They are shut and their hinges clearly indicate that the doors opened on to the stage. Above these doors is a partitioned gallery containing several people who look like spectators. This may be the 'lords' room'. Jonson's *Every Man out of His Humour*, a Globe play, provides a speech that contains the phrase 'ouer the stage, i'the Lords roome' (Q1, F3r).⁹ We know that the tiring-house gallery, when required, served as a place for acting '*above*'. It has been much discussed

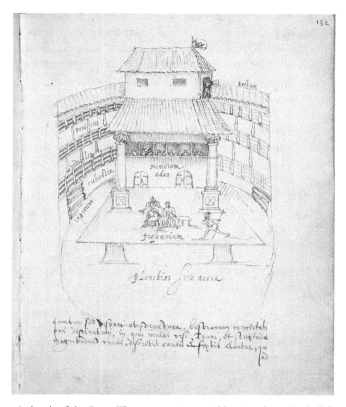

Figure 2. A sketch of the Swan Theatre, c.1596, copied by Arend van Buchell from a lost original by Johannes de Witt.

whether the Swan's stage had only two doors as de Witt drew it or whether it was equipped with a discovery space as well. Middleton's *A Chaste Maid in Cheapside*, which is the only extant play certainly acted at the Swan, provides '*Enter Maudline and Moll, a Shop being discouered*' (Q1, B1r) and '*A Bed thrust out vpon the Stage, Allwits Wife in it, Enter all the Gossips*' (E4r). These stage directions appear to suggest the existence of a central discovery space, although the two doorways shown in the Swan sketch might have served for the events described in these directions.

It has often been assumed that because the framework of the Theatre was reused for the Globe, the size and shape of the two playhouses must have been much the same. However, archaeological excavations at the Theatre and the Globe sites appear to reveal that the Globe was larger than the Theatre, and that, in short, 'the Globe was not merely The Theatre reassembled'.[10] In

1989 a section of the Globe site was dug by archaeologists, as a result of which John Orrell has suggested that the likeliest interpretation of the archaeological evidence is that the Globe was a twenty-sided polygon about 100 feet (30 metres) across.[11] In a book recently published as a report on the Rose and Globe excavations, Julian Bowsher and Patricia Miller observe: 'Theoretically the Globe may have had any number of bays but the 16-sided [25.76 metres in diameter] and 18-sided [*c.*29 metres across] versions appear to align most logically with the limited archaeological remains.'[12]

In 1600 the Lord Admiral's Men moved from the 'littell Roosse'[13] to the new Fortune. The building contract for the Fortune, between Philip Henslowe and Edward Alleyn on one side and the carpenter Peter Street on the other, shows that it was built square but that in other respects it was generally modelled on the round – or, to be more precise polygonal – Globe. (Street had been hired for the construction of the Globe by the Lord Chamberlain's Men.) The Fortune contract contains the following clauses:

The frame of the saide howse to be sett square and to conteine ffowerscore foote of lawfull assize everye waie square wthoute and fiftie fiue foote of like assize square everye waie wthin . . . And the saide fframe to conteine Three Stories in heighth . . . All which Stories shall conteine Twelue foote and a half of lawfull assize in breadth througheoute . . . Wth a Stadge and Tyreinge howse to be made erected & settupp wthin the saide fframe, wth a shadowe or cover over the saide Stadge . . . And wch Stadge shall conteine in length ffortie and Three foote of lawfull assize and in breadth to extende to the middle of the yarde of the saide howse . . .[14]

This information makes possible some provisional calculations, if we make the assumption that the tiring-house was effectively a continuation of the galleries along the back wall of the playhouse. Since the galleries were 12 feet 6 inches deep, the tiring-house would have been of an identical depth. We know that the stage projected forward from the tiring-house façade into the centre of the yard. Its width was 43 feet, and if we take the phrase, 'to extende to the middle of the yarde' to refer to the exact centre, the distance from the front of the stage to the back of the playhouse would have been 40 feet. If we subtract 12 feet 6 inches for the depth of the tiring-house, that leaves 27 feet 6 inches for the stage itself. On the basis of this calculation, therefore, the stage would have been 43 feet (13.1 metres) wide and 27 feet 6 inches (8.4 metres) deep. But this estimate has been questioned, particularly since the Rose excavations. John Orrell has suggested that the clause 'Wth a Stadge and Tyreinge howse to be made erected & settupp wthin the saide fframe' refers not to the outer walls of the playhouse, 80 feet by 80 feet, but to the inner framework formed by the galleries, that is, to the space within the yard, 55 feet by 55 feet. His view is that in large open-air playhouses like the Fortune and the Globe both the stages and the tiring-houses were commonly constructed inside the yards. If this were the case, the effect would have been to make the Fortune and the Globe stages wide but comparatively shallow.[15]

Analysis of plays that we think may have been written principally for performance at these playhouses suggests that their stages, like those of most other public playhouses, had two main entrance doors and a large opening for discoveries between them, together with a balcony, a trap-door, a roof supported by posts and a descent machine. The number of openings in the tiring-house façade at these and other playhouses is still, however, a matter of dispute.[16] Although Tim Fitzpatrick and some other scholars take the view that there were only two doors to the stage, some plays put on at the Fortune provide examples that seem to imply the presence of three doorways. One example is 'Enter Vrcenze and Onophrio at seuerall doores, and Farnezie in the mid'st' (Chettle, Dekker and Haughton, *Patient Grissil* Q1, E3r).[17] In addition, some Globe plays contain scenes that require the use of a central opening. Barnes's *The Devil's Charter*, 4.1 is such a scene. At the beginning of this scene Alexander is discovered '*in his studie beholding a Magicall glasse with other obseruations*' (Q1, F4v). He soon '*commeth vpon the Stage out of his study with a booke in his hand*' (G1r). Then he conjures up the Devil and charges him to present the man who has murdered Candy. The Devil descends and sends another devil from under the stage. The newly arrived devil '*goeth to one doore of the stage, from whence he bringeth the Ghost of* Candie *gastly haunted by* Caesar *persuing and stabing it, these vanish in at another doore*' (G2r). At the end of the scene, Alexander exits '*into the studie*' (G2v). In short, in this scene, while the central opening is serving as Alexander's study, containing a magic mirror and other instruments (probably on a desk), a devil presents the scene of Candy's murder through the use of two flanking doors.[18] During the early modern period, playhouse design became gradually more sophisticated, with the result that the stages of the Globe and Fortune were better equipped than those of earlier theatres. One sign of this process is that the Fortune contract calls for 'convenient windowes and lightes glazed' to the tiring-house.[19] If, as Orrell has suggested, the tiring-house was to be built within the gallery frame, these glass windows may well have been in the tiring-house wall facing the stage. R. A. Foakes observes: 'Later theatres certainly had practical windows at the rear or sides of the stage, and the Fortune contract would suggest that these were provided there, on the gallery level, along with "lights" or gratings in the stage doors.'[20] If, however, the tiring-house was a continuation of the galleries, the windows would have been in the outer wall of the playhouse.²¹

Some basic information is available about the size and shape of the Boar's Head in its legal documents. It was square in shape and its yard was about the same size as that of the Fortune, measuring 54 feet 6 inches (16.6 metres) by 55 feet 7 inches (16.9 metres). Above the yard were single galleries on the north and south and a double one on the west. Its stage was rectangular, 39 feet 7 inches (12.1 metres) wide and 25 feet (7.6 metres) deep, and equipped with a roof ('cou*er*inge ou*er* the stage'). There was a gallery over the stage on the east.²² In 1602, the combined company of the Earl of Worcester's Men and Lord Oxford's Men was admitted by the Privy Council as a third London company and allocated to the Boar's Head.²³ In 1605 the company, now Queen Anne's Men, left here, when the Red Bull became available for their use. The Red Bull was square in shape, and the requirements of plays acted there suggest that its stage had two doors, a discovery space between them, a balcony, a trap and a roof equipped with a descent machine and supported by posts, as in the following stage directions: '*At one end*' / '*At tother end*' / '*At the middle*' (Dekker and Massinger, *The Virgin Martyr* Q1, K4v)²⁴; '*Enter* Synon *with a torch aboue*' (Heywood, *2 The Iron Age* Q1, D4r); '*Earth riseth from vnder the stage*' (Heywood, *The Silver Age* Q1, H1v); '*Iuno and* Iris *descend from the heauens*' (*The Silver Age* Q1, F1r). Henslowe's contract for building the Hope stipulates the construction of a dual-purpose house doubling as a theatre and a bear- and bull-baiting arena 'of suche large compasse, fforme, widenes, and height as the Plaie house called the Swan in the libertie of Parris garden'. The Hope had a stage roof which was explicitly to be 'borne or carryed without any postes or supporters to be fixed or sett vppon the ... stage' so that the stage might be removable.²⁵

The private hall theatres built in Shakespeare's time were St Paul's (1575, used until *c*.1590, then again 1599–1606); the first Blackfriars (1576, operated until 1584); the second Blackfriars (1596, operated as a playhouse from 1600 until 1642); the Whitefriars (*c*.1606–07, the lease expired in 1614); Porter's Hall (1615, playing ceased there by 1617); the Cockpit in Drury Lane or the Phoenix (converted from a cockpit *c*.1616, operated until 1642); and the Salisbury Court (1629, operated until 1642). St Paul's playhouse was fitted up in a hall within the precincts of St Paul's Cathedral. The exact location of this hall has not been identified with certainty and some locations have been proposed. For example, Reavley Gair has suggested that the theatre was located in the north-west quadrant of the chapter house precinct,²⁶ and more recently, Herbert Berry has argued that it was in the almonry that was on the south wall of the nave between the lesser south door and the west wall of the chapter house cloister.²⁷ The playhouse, particularly its stage, seems to have been very small, since the Induction to *What You Will*, a Paul's Children play by Marston, provides a reference to the insufficiency of space for spectators to sit on the stage: 'Lets place our selues within the Curtaines, for good faith the Stage is so very little we shall wrong the generall eye els very much' (Q1, A3r). From the evidence supplied by plays staged at the playhouse, Gair thinks that the façade of the stage had three doors, with windows above the two side doors, and a curtained alcove above the central double doors.²⁸ I am rather dubious about the windows, because references to windows in stage directions, such as '*The Casement opens, and Katherine appeares*' (Marston, *Jack Drum's Entertainment* Q1, C2v) and '*Camelia from her window*' (*Jack Drum's Entertainment* Q1, D3r), do not necessarily indicate the existence of windows. The curtained alcove could well have served as the 'casement' and 'window' mentioned in these directions. *Antonio's Revenge*, another Paul's Children play by Marston, has the stage direction '*While the measure is dauncing, Andrugios ghost is placed betwixt the musick houses*' (Q1, K1v), which implies that the upper playing area was flanked by 'music houses'. This is the only stage direction including the term 'music house'. In early modern stage directions 'music room' is more common and this term is always used in the form '*the music room*', implying that there was only one music room in other theatres. The design of the upper level of Paul's playhouse may therefore have been unique.

The first Blackfriars was made by Richard Farrant, Deputy Master of the Children of the Chapel Royal for use by his boy actors, in a room at the old Dominican priory, measuring approximately 26 feet (7.9 metres) by 46 feet 6 inches (14.2 metres). The second Blackfriars was built by James Burbage in part of the Upper Frater of the monastery, the space measuring 46 feet (14 metres) by 66 feet (20.1 metres) internally.²⁹ It had at least two levels of galleries in the auditorium. Stage directions in plays performed at the second Blackfriars suggest that its stage had two doors, a discovery space between them, a balcony, a trap and a descent machine. Chapman, Jonson and Marston's *Eastward Ho*, for example, opens with a triple entrance: '*Enter Maister Touch-stone, and Quick-siluer at Seuerall dores, . . . At the middle dore, Enter Golding discouering a Gold-smiths shoppe, and walking short turns before it*' (Q1, A2r). This stage direction implies three doorways, the middle one large enough to conceal a shop. At first the residents of the Blackfriars area blocked the Lord Chamberlain's Men from playing there, and the playhouse was leased in 1600 to Henry Evans, who established a new Chapel Children boy company in Blackfriars. It was in August 1608 that the adult company, now the King's Men, regained the lease of the theatre, and it was probably in late 1609 or early

1610 that they finally began performing there.³⁰ Thereafter the company played at the Blackfriars³¹ during the winter months and at the Globe during the summer.³² The Whitefriars theatre was built in the refectory of the former Carmelite priory, the dimensions being about 35 feet (10.7 metres) by 85 feet (25.9 metres), longer and narrower than Blackfriars.³³ Staging demands of plays performed there suggest that the stage had two doors, a curtained discovery space, the upper acting level and a trapdoor. Jean MacIntyre observes: 'Because the stage was built in a smaller existing space than Blackfriars, the horizontal scale seems [to] have been reduced so as to maximize space for the paying audience, leading to what the scripts suggest were distinctive modifications: a smaller platform, a proportionately wider discovery space, entry doors set at the very edges of the stage, and a reduced upper playing area.'³⁴ Kelly Steele contends that Blackfriars and Whitefriars plays provide evidence indicating that the upper performance area in both playhouses projected out over the stage and was supported by posts.³⁵ If this conjecture were true, it could account for references to trees and posts in plays acted at these theatres and, more

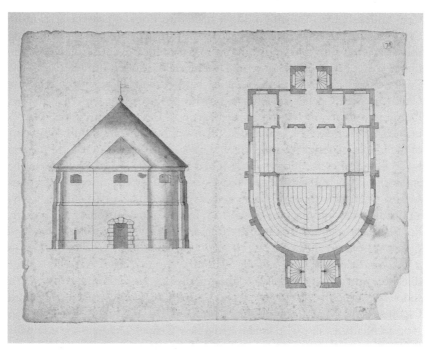

Figure 3a. Inigo Jones/John Webb drawings: elevation and plan for an indoor playhouse.

significantly, it would offer an explanation as to how acrobatic ascents to and descents from *above* were managed, such as the one in the following stage direction from a Blackfriars play: '*Tiberio climes the tree, and is receiued aboue by Dulcimel*' (Marston, *Parasitaster, or the Fawn* Q1, H3r). But it is far from clear that there was a need for such an elaborate structural addition, and whenever an onstage ascent to or descent from the upper level was required, either a property post or a ladder or one of the columns of the tiring-house façade would have adequately served the purpose.[36]

A set of drawings in the Worcester College collection provides an elevation, a plan and two transverse sections of an indoor playhouse (see Figures 3a and 3b). Iain Mackintosh had suggested that these drawings were made by Inigo Jones for the conversion of the Cockpit in Drury Lane to a theatre around 1616,[37] and this view had been reinforced by John Orrell's detailed analysis of the drawings.[38] But Gordon Higgott later argued on grounds of style that they were more likely to represent an unrealised playhouse projected by William Davenant in 1639.[39] He has more recently put forward his new view that the

Figure 3b. Inigo Jones/John Webb drawings: two transverse sections of the same playhouse.

Worcester College drawings were made around 1660 by Jones's assistant, John Webb.[40] Andrew Gurr finds Higgott's new dating plausible, while also thinking that features of the drawings do seem to offer more evidence for Renaissance design than Restoration work.[41] Gurr's latest view is that they were made for the repair of the Salisbury Court playhouse by William Beeston in 1660.[42] Franklin J. Hildy observes: 'If the drawings were done in the Restoration, it must have been during the first eighteen months of the period when the old actors from the King's Men and other companies of the pre-Civil War years were being called back into service, when the old repertory was being revived, and the old playhouses were being reopened, because these drawings show a theatre that harks back to a past age and only vaguely anticipates the future proscenium arch style theatres that began with the opening of the Lincoln's Inn Fields Theatre in June 1661.'[43] The drawings show a playhouse with a U-shaped galleried auditorium surrounding a railed rectangular stage. There are two tiers of galleries. All the audience were seated in the two galleries and in the pit. According to Orrell's calculations, the theatre measures 40 feet (12.2 metres) by 55 feet (16.8 metres) externally, excluding its attached stair-turrets, and the stage is 24 feet (7.3 metres) wide by 15 feet (4.6 metres) deep and 4 feet (1.2 metres) high.[44] The *frons scenae* has two rectangular doorways and a central arched doorway between them, and there is a railed balcony above these three openings. The stage balcony is fitted with 'degrees' (bench seats) for spectators, except for the central area, which is framed architecturally with terms and a broken pediment. This central area would have provided a music room when not used as an upper playing space. The second Blackfriars, the Cockpit in Drury Lane and the Salisbury Court seem to have been similar to each other in size and in substantial matters of design.[45] The stages of the hall theatres were markedly smaller than those of the open-air theatres.

Not only did the playhouses differ from one another in size, shape and architectural features but also many structural changes were introduced over the years. When discussing the staging of a particular play, we should of course take into consideration the physical features of the playhouse at which the play was (or may have been) performed. But in addition, we need now to consider how the treatment of play texts in the playhouses may have affected the texts themselves.

PLAY TEXTS

The majority of plays survive in printed texts. Various changes would have happened to the play after the completion of the manuscript – through the preparation of the playbook by the company book-keeper, the censorship of the playbook by the Master of the Revels, minimal rehearsal, actual performances and subsequent changes and modifications of the playbook by the author himself or other revisers. What stage of the play does a printed text represent? Does the text derive from the author's manuscript or from the company's official playbook? Does it represent the original or a later revised version? These have been and remain important questions. Recent research suggests, however, that a crucial assumption underlying all these questions is in fact invalid. It is the belief that the whole text would have been corrected or altered in a systematic way, either when it was annotated by the book-keeper or when the play was revised by the dramatist himself or other hands.

Through his investigation of the eighteen surviving manuscript playbooks, William B. Long has demonstrated that in general book-keepers seldom marked or changed playwrights' stage directions and speech prefixes, even when there was an obvious case for doing so in order to eradicate ambiguity and possible confusion.[46] The surviving evidence as a whole indicates that book-keepers did not concern themselves with clarifying or particularising imprecise and permissive directions. The manuscript playbook of Heywood's *The Captives*, for example, contains an unusually large number of markings and annotations by the Cockpit book-keeper, and Heywood's difficult handwriting made it necessary for the book-keeper to make such numerous annotations.[47] But even in this heavily marked manuscript one particularly notable unresolved contradiction survives. At one point the author's direction for the character of Friar Richard reads: '*Eather strykes him wth a staffe or Casts a stone*' (TLN 2432–4). Later in the play, in describing what he has done with the (unknown to him) already dead Friar John, Friar Richard says 'I hitt him wth a stone' (TLN 3187). When writing this speech for Friar Richard, Heywood appears to have either forgotten about the earlier permissive direction or he had decided eventually to resolve it. Long's observation about book-keepers' attitudes towards playwrights' directions is worth citing here: 'So infrequently do theatrical alterations occur that if a stage direction exists in a late sixteenth- or early seventeenth-century play text, manuscript or printed, it is most likely a playwright's.'[48] In many cases, what a stage direction represents may be no more than the form of staging which the author expected or imagined as he wrote it, and not necessarily the form that actually took place on the stage.

The discrepancy between the playing time given in contemporary references (two to three hours[49]) and the length of such plays as *Hamlet* and *Antony and Cleopatra* compels us to consider the relationship between the extant text and what the original players actually spoke. Michael J. Hirrel claims that plays were presented as parts of larger theatrical events that included additional forms of entertainment, with the result that these events regularly took almost four hours. The availability of this length of time, he argues, would have allowed long plays by Shakespeare and Jonson to be performed essentially as written; the time left by shorter plays would have been made up by adding more of these incidental entertainments, such as songs, dances and jigs.[50] Intriguing as it is, this argument runs against the contrary view, for which there is considerable evidence, that cutting plays was the norm. The title-pages of some printed texts include the claim by the authors, including Jonson himself, that the published versions contain more lines than were performed in the theatre: '*AS IT WAS FIRST COMPOSED* by the AUTHOR B. I. *Containing more than hath been Publickely Spoken or Acted*' (*Every Man out of His Humour* Q1, A2r); 'The perfect and exact Coppy, with diuerse *things Printed, that the length of the Play would* not beare in the Presentment' (Webster, *The Duchess of Malfi* Q1, A2r). Similarly, Humphrey Moseley's introductory epistle to the 1647 Beaumont and Fletcher Folio (F1) contains the following passage: 'When these *Comedies* and *Tragedies* were presented on the Stage, the *Actours* omitted some *Scenes* and Passages (with the *Authour's* consent) as occasion led them; ... But now you have both All that was *Acted*, and all that was not; even the perfect full Originalls without the least mutilation' (A4r). Certainly most surviving manuscript playbooks, including relatively short ones, contain more or less heavy cuttings by book-keepers, and printed texts annotated for performance by professional hands (such as the Folger Shakespeare Libray quarto of *The Two Merry Milkmaids* and the Padua folio texts of *Macbeth* and *Measure for Measure*) have what appear to be systematic cuts.[51] The length of the plays may not have been the only reason for cutting, but these pieces of evidence support Stephen Orgel's view that 'The text ... was not the play, and all plays would have been cut for performance', including plays by Shakespeare and Jonson.[52] His comment on the passage just cited from Moseley's prefatory epistle to the 1647 Beaumont and Fletcher Folio is worth quoting: 'The implication is that cuts were determined by occasion: actors varied their performances according to their sense of the audience; they might change from season to season, from playhouse to playhouse, even, if occasion required, from performance to performance.'[53]

Andrew Gurr, too, emphasises the instability of play texts. He suggests that the playbook licensed by the Master of the Revels was not the text that the company actually performed but that it was the 'maximal text' the company could perform. From the maximal text the company could make any number of cuts, but they could not make new additions to it.[54] Since the 'allowed book' bearing the Master's signature was the fully authoritative text in playing company terms, it was unlikely in his view ever to have gone to the printer.[55] The nature of some of the short texts labelled as 'memorially reconstructed texts' or 'bad quartos' has recently been reconsidered. For instance, Gurr takes the view that the manuscript behind the Q1 text of *Henry V* was based ultimately on the authorial manuscript printed as the F1 text, but that it was a copy which had been radically revised by the company for performance.[56] Richard Dutton, on the other hand, argues that *Henry V* Q1 represents a version of the play performed in 1599, while the F1 version dates from 1602.[57] Lukas Erne offers to explain the relationship between the long and short texts of *Romeo and Juliet*, *Henry V* and *Hamlet* by claiming that Shakespeare wrote plays as a literary dramatist in order to be published in print as well as having them performed onstage, and that the long and short versions represent literary and theatrical versions.[58] This may be so. It should, however, be pointed out that those 'literary versions' contain no scenes that are in principle unstageable.

On the matter of the instability of play texts, Tiffany Stern calls our attention to their literally fragmentary nature.[59] She argues that printed texts provide a variety of reasons for believing that prologues, epilogues, songs and letters were kept on separate pieces of paper. In the 1679 Beaumont and Fletcher Folio (F2), for example, the printers give thanks to a gentleman who has recently provided them with '*several Prologues and Epilogues, with the Songs appertaining to each Play, which were not in the former Edition*' (A1r). These elements were more extractable, movable and revisable units than the rest of the play. In particular, the connection of prologues and epilogues to the play would generally have been a one-day event, and some surviving prologues and epilogues were clearly written only for the first performance. (In Chapter 6, however, we shall see how a certain kind of epilogue would have been integral to the plays.) It is also an important fact that players did not have access to the whole play but that all they had was their own 'part' with the cue at the beginning of each speech. Stern argues that when plays were revised, the sites for revision were limited to the middle parts of speeches, so that cuts and changes would not disturb actors' cues. Her description of plays as 'patchworks' is illustrated by the observation that 'The dialogue and all that happens within that dialogue exchange was in performance made up of separate manuscripts: learnt actors' parts; backstage-plots; and songs, scrolls, prologues and epilogues all of which might be read onstage, and all of which have their own histories ... So the internal texts that make up a play had an oddly metatextual and perhaps paratextual relationship to the rest of the performed play: for the play onstage was not a manifestation of one book, but an aural and visual gathering of the contents of many scattered manuscripts.'[60] To take the example of *The Captives* mentioned above, the playbook has the permissive direction for Friar Richard, but the actor's part might well have contained a stage direction specifically calling for the use of a stone for attacking Friar John's body. Many authorial stage directions may have been changed in theatrical plots and actors' parts, if not in playbooks.

A play text may be a composite of material written by different people possibly at different times. It can also be a conflation of several versions. Furthermore it might lack explicit instructions and practical information which could have been found in a theatrical plot, actors' parts and other kinds of theatrical document. In short, as Gurr says, 'almost no play texts survive from Shakespearian time in a form that represents with much precision what was actually staged'.[61] What then can be done with surviving play texts? It would be vain to try to reconstruct any actual performance, let alone the première. However, any portion of a play text, whatever version it might reflect, does potentially provide information about routine moves and locations and other staging methods. The best we can do is to collect as many examples as possible, both those that occur frequently and those that are more unusual, so that we may establish those staging practices that are sufficiently common to be regarded as standard, together with other possible forms.

For plays surviving in two or more versions, I have therefore examined all available substantive texts.[62] It has to be granted, though, that the results of this procedure do not lend themselves to easy summary. We shall see that these texts not only provide different forms of staging for the same scene, they also, somewhat confusingly, at times offer different ways of indicating the same action or the same location. At the risk of adding a further layer of complexity, I also look at examples from academic and amateur plays of the period. Although this book's main focus is on plays by Shakespeare and his contemporaries in London's professional playhouses, it seemed to me worth seeing if non-professional plays reflected some of the issues present in the staging of the professional drama, particularly – to take one example – in their handling of the relationship between theatre and fiction.

Interpreting any single example of staging is always difficult, involving as it does factors such as the nature of the text under discussion and the particular conditions in the theatre where the version of the play was performed. There is consequently almost always more than one interpretation. Even when an interpretation seems on the face of it self-evidently correct, it is worth considering alternative possibilities because the discussion of that example may rest on assumptions that are not wholly secure. Since the texts are incomplete in themselves and the context in which they should be interpreted is not very certain, my conclusions cannot achieve the sharpness of definition one might ideally want and they must remain, to varying degrees, hypothetical and speculative, invoking frequent use of terms such as 'probably', 'possibly' and 'perhaps'.

THE THEATRICAL LANGUAGE

A play text consists mainly of stage directions and speeches. In order to treat them properly, it is important to understand the nature of the language in which they are written.

Stage directions

It cannot be over-emphasised that Shakespeare and his fellow playwrights supplied stage directions primarily for their actors. Both writers and readers of stage directions were familiar with the stage conditions and staging practices, because that was the very basis for their communication. On this point, Gary Taylor, in the General Introduction to the Oxford *Textual Companion*, provides an important observation regarding the paucity of early modern stage directions: 'The written text of any such [theatrical] manuscript thus depended upon an unwritten para-text which always accompanied it: an invisible life-support system of stage directions, which Shakespeare could either expect his first readers [the players] to supply, or which those first readers would expect Shakespeare himself to supply orally.'[63] The unwritten para-text, precisely because it was never written down, has been irrecoverably lost. Interpreting surviving stage directions therefore necessarily involves conjectures, a hazardous process but one we must try to make as sound as possible.

Stage directions are instructions written for actors and backstage people. They should therefore, in theory, be entirely functional in theatrical terms. But, as Richard Hosley observes, some stage directions are technical while others are rather literary. Although the distinction between technical and literary directions is often blurred, Hosley's terms and concepts are still useful for our discussion.

18   *Playhouses, play texts and the theatrical language*

Elizabethan stage-directions are of two essential kinds. Some are 'theatrical' in that they usually refer not to dramatic fiction but rather to theatrical structure or equipment: *upon the stage, at another door, within, a curtain being drawn, a scaffold thrust out, the throne descends, arising in the midst of the stage*. Others, conversely, are 'fictional' in that they usually refer not to theatrical structure or equipment but rather to dramatic fiction: *upon the walls, before the gates, within the prison, on shipboard, from the bay, in the Tower, forth of the castle, enter the town*.[64]

In brief, theatrical directions are written from a theatrical point of view, while fictional directions are written from a fictional point of view. When one is seeking information and evidence about the stage structure and ways of staging from stage directions, it is important to try to distinguish between these two kinds.

The problem is that it is no easy task. It is sometimes almost impossible to determine whether a direction is theatrical or fictional. What appears to be a fictional direction may actually have been a theatrical direction. It is certainly true that *'on/upon the walls'* refers to the fictional world, but in theatre practice this phrase would have been functional and therefore theatrical, indicating always the use of the upper playing area.[65] It is perhaps noteworthy that the surviving theatrical plots offer *'upon the walls'* (*Frederick and Basilea* plot, TLN 36–7); *'on the walls'* (Chettle and Dekker, *Troilus and Cressida* plot, TLN 15–16); *'on the walls'* (*Troilus and Cressida* plot, TLN 47); *'on the wall'* (*Troilus and Cressida* plot, TLN 50), although these may have derived from authorial papers.[66] The same point might be made about the phrase *'at the/a window'*.[67]

Consider *'Enter in prison'* directions. Although Hosley's examples of fictional directions include *'within the prison'*, the early play texts, so far as they have been examined up to now, do not provide any stage direction containing this exact phrase. Instead, *'in prison'* frequently occurs in entry stage directions, as in the following example:

Enter in prison Iunior *Brother.* (Middleton, *The Revenger's Tragedy* Q1, E3v)

On the face of it, this appears to be a fictional direction: the phrase *'in prison'* may simply specify that the scene is located in a prison. At the very beginning of the scene, the entering Junior Brother calls a keeper and asks if there is any news from his brothers: *'Iuni.* Keeper'; *'Keep.* My Lord'; *'Iuni.* No newes lately from our brothers?' (E3v). Although no entry direction is provided for the keeper, he would probably make a slightly delayed entrance from a different doorway, answering Junior Brother's call. The keeper's arrival would immediately establish the prison setting. Did Junior Brother, then, need to do nothing more specific to suggest the locale of the scene? It may be that he was intended to appear in a special part of the stage. Just as some '*Enter in his study*' directions indicate the discovery of a character sitting in the curtained space,[68] so '*Enter in prison*' might sometimes involve the same use of the discovery space, which could appropriately represent a place of confinement as well as a study. But, as Alan C. Dessen argues, '*Enter in prison*' directions may be understood as '*Enter as [if] in prison*',[69] and, perhaps to make matters clearer for the actor, some '*Enter in prison*' directions contain quite vividly explicit instructions:

Enter Sir Charles in prison with yrons, his face bare, his garments al ragged and torne. (Heywood, *A Woman Killed with Kindness* Q1, E3r)

Enter Appius, and Marcus Clodius in prison, fettered and gyved. (Webster and Heywood, *Appius and Virginia* Q1, I1r)

These stage directions indicate that an entering character, not being attended by a keeper or jailer, could establish a prison setting visually, by being dressed in a distinctive costume and/or being bound in chains, shackles or the like. If there was such a conventional way of suggesting a prison setting, the locution '*Enter in prison*' would have worked in theatrical terms. In *The Revenger's Tragedy*, Junior Brother might well have looked like a prisoner, being dressed in a prisoner's costume and/or being shackled.[70]

Certain nouns also pose problems. Take, for example, 'tent'. A considerable number of early modern stage directions contain references to tents. Some directions are certainly theatrical, while others are probably fictional, as Dessen's detailed comments make clear.[71] I should, however, like to present some instances which may help to distinguish between theatrical and fictional stage directions. The extant theatrical plot of *2 The Seven Deadly Sins* offers a reference to a tent: '*A tent being plast one the stage for Henry the sixt. he in it A sleepe . . .*' (TLN 3–4).[72] As this direction specifically indicates, a property tent would have been erected on the stage, so that King Henry could have remained asleep in the tent onstage throughout the action.[73] The prologue to *The Devil's Charter* involves a dumb show requiring two 'tents':

At one doore betwixt two other Cardinals, Roderigo *in his purple habit close in conference with them, one of which hee guideth to a Tent, where a Table is furnished with divers bagges of money, which that Cardinall all beareth away: and to another Tent the other Cardinall, where hee delivereth him a great quantity of rich Plate, imbraces, with ioyning of hands.* Exeunt *Card.* Manet Roderigo. *To whome from an other place a Moncke with a magical booke and rod . . .* (Q1, A2r–v)

The flanking doors, referred to as '*one doore*' and '*an other place*', are both used for entrances. It is unlikely that the central discovery space would serve as '*a Tent*', requiring the use of a property tent for '*another Tent*'. Bernard Beckerman observes that this is the only Globe play requiring the use of property tents,[74] and clearly the symmetrical arrangement of two property tents on the stage would be appropriate for the dumb show. In the stage direction cited above, both '*a Tent*' and '*another Tent*' would probably work theatrically, each referring to a removable structure named 'tent'. It is however also possible that, as Andrew Gurr suggests, the discovery space might be used for both tents; a table with several bags of money on it and a great quantity of rich plate (presumably on another table) could be placed separately behind the pair of curtains covering the central space.[75] Although maybe less likely than the use of actual property tents, we cannot entirely dismiss the possibility that in this context '*a Tent*' and '*another Tent*' are fictional rather than theatrical terms.

There are a fair number of stage directions calling for a discovery or entrance from a 'tent', as in the following examples:

Alarme: Amyras & Celebinus, issues from the tent where Caliphas sits a sleepe. (Marlowe, *2 Tamburlaine the Great* O1, I2v)

Enter Achilles *and* Patroclus *in their Tent.* (Shakespeare, *Troilus and Cressida* F1, TLN 1888; 3.3.37)

He discouereth his Tent where her two sonnes were at Cardes. (*The Devil's Charter* Q1, I1v)

Achilles discouered in his Tent, about him his bleeding Mermidons, himselfe wounded, and with him Vlysses. (Heywood, *1 The Iron Age* Q1, H4v)

While the entry direction taken from *Troilus* F1 may well indicate the use of a stage door as the 'tent',[76] the other three directions very likely refer to a discovery space as the 'tent'. In these four directions, 'tent' therefore seems to be a fictional term.

The F1 text of Shakespeare's *3 Henry VI* also provides a stage direction reference to a tent:

Enter three Watchmen to guard the Kings Tent. (TLN 2220; 4.3.0)

The staging of this tent scene is a problem. While the watchmen are on guard, Warwick, Clarence, Oxford and Somerset arrive quietly with French soldiers. When they surprise King Edward in his tent, they exit, chasing the guard, and then re-enter, bringing the King onstage:

Warwicke and the rest cry all, Warwicke, Warwicke, and set vpon the Guard, who flye, crying, Arme, Arme, Warwicke and the rest following them.
The Drumme playing, and Trumpet sounding. Enter Warwicke, Somerset, and the rest, bringing the King out in his Gowne, sitting in a Chaire: Richard and Hastings flyes ouer the Stage. (TLN 2253–9; 4.3.27)

What is actually shown onstage is the beginning of the surprise attack (Warwick and his men's arrival and their exit chasing the guard) and its result (their re-entrance with the captured King, and Richard's and Hastings's flight over the stage); the attack on the King is imagined to take place offstage while the battle sound is being heard.[77] It is therefore unlikely that a property tent would have been erected on the stage. What seems fairly certain is that both the chase and the flight would have involved the use of both flanking doors: Warwick and his men would have entered by one flanking door and exited, chasing the guard, by the other flanking door; the surprised Richard and Hastings would have entered from one of the flanking doors – perhaps the door by which Warwick and others had exited – run across the stage, and exited by the other door.[78] If this were the case, and if there were a third opening between the two doors in the tiring-house façade of the theatre, Warwick and his men would probably have used the central opening for carrying on the captured King sitting in a chair, so that they could have avoided clashing with Richard and Hastings. The exit and re-entrance of Warwick and others suggest two possibilities. It is certainly possible that '*the Kings Tent*' was supposed to be offstage, accessible only from the door by which they exit, running after the King's guard. If, however, the King was brought on through the central opening, the discovery space itself might have represented '*the Kings Tent*'. Either way, it seems that the phrase '*the Kings Tent*' must be understood fictionally rather than theatrically.

Even if a particular term occurs in a fair number of stage directions, its usage may not always be the same. It might sometimes indicate the use of the named property or structure onstage; it might sometimes be a fictional term for a particular part of the stage; and it might sometimes refer to a thing that has to be imagined to be there in the theatrical space, onstage or off.

Speeches

The majority of stage directions are brief entry and exit directions. Antony Hammond writes: 'ninety percent of what actually happened on stage in their performance is not to be found in the stage-directions of any manuscript or printed text ... The actors' movements, quite apart from their body language, their positioning and grouping (what directors call "blocking"), and their business with props, is largely unrecoverable terra incognita'.[79] In considering what could have happened onstage we might sometimes have to seek evidence or information from characters' speeches alone. A verbal reference to a particular structure or thing might indicate that the structure or the thing is actually there, being visible to the audience. It is equally possible that the structure or the thing referred to is not physically present and has to be imagined.

Where the text refers to something physically imposing such as a bank, the question arises as to how literally it should be interpreted. It does not automatically follow that the object has to be there in view of the audience. Wood scenes in *A Midsummer Night's Dream* contain some references to banks. Do these references indicate the use of a property bank or banks? In a well-known instance, towards the end of Act 2, scene 1, Oberon describes a floral bank:

I know a banke where the wilde time blowes,
Where Oxlips, and the nodding Violet growes,
Quite ouercanopi'd with lushious woodbine,
With sweete muske roses, and with Eglantine:
There sleepes *Tytania*, sometime of the night,
Luld in these flowers, with daunces and delight:

(Q1, C2v; 2.1.249–54)

After his departure, Titania and her fairies arrive to begin the next scene (2.2). Peter Holland thinks that a property such as was listed by Henslowe in his inventory of properties in 1598 as 'ij mose banckes' would probably have been used for Titania's 'flowry bed' (D3r; 3.1.129) in the two continuous scenes usually referred to as 2.2 and 3.1.[80] However, as R. A. Foakes suggests, a great deal turns on whether Titania remained onstage asleep through the intervening action or whether she went into the curtained space which might well have represented her 'bower' (D3v; 3.1.197).[81] The F1 text, which reflects a later playbook used after the King's Men had adopted *entr'acte* music, gives no information about whether Titania is asleep onstage during the interval between Acts 2 and 3, whereas it indicates that the two pairs of lovers remain asleep during the interval between Acts 3 and 4: '*They sleepe all the Act*' (TLN 1507; 3.2.463). I am therefore inclined to think that Titania was intended to retire into the curtained space and that a property bank was not used for her bed. In 2.2, while Titania is sleeping, whether onstage or off, Lysander and Hermia arrive. Hermia says to Lysander, 'finde you out a bedde: / For I, vpon this banke, will rest my head' (Q1, C3v; 2.2.39–40). Despite her use of the determiner 'this', the 'banke' she is referring to need not be an actual property bank; later on, Puck merely alludes to finding Hermia 'sleeping sound, / On the danke and dirty ground' (C4r; 2.2.74–5). The last wood scene (4.1) begins with Titania's sweet words spoken to the ass-headed Bottom: 'Come sit thee downe vpon this flowry bed' (F2v; 4.1.1), and since their dalliance on the 'flowry bed' continues for a fairly long while (4.1.1–75), it is certainly the case that a property bank might have been brought on for this scene, although it is by no means an absolute requirement.

Similarly, a verbal reference to a 'rock' sometimes poses a question. For example, at the beginning of *Julius Caesar*, 5.5, Shakespeare clearly had a copy of Plutarch in front of him at this point, because it seems to have triggered Brutus's opening line as he enters with his followers, 'Come poore remaines of friends, rest on this Rocke' (F1, TLN 2640–1; 5.5.1).[82] Arthur Humphreys takes the speech as an indication of the use of a stage rock,[83] and no doubt the Globe company had a property similar to the one listed in Henslowe's inventory as 'j rocke'.[84] But there is no absolute need for the property rock to be brought on stage. After the brief allusion in the first line, neither Brutus nor anyone else makes further mention of it and there is no action that requires the use of a property rock, which suggests that its literal presence is hardly essential.[85] On the other hand, the fact that it is the subject of the first line spoken by the entering Brutus creates a certain impact, and even if it has to be imagined rather than viewed, it contributes both to the physical setting of the scene and to the general atmosphere, helping to establish the bleakly depressed mood in which Brutus and his followers now find themselves.

Other Shakespearean plays provide further examples. In *Cymbeline*, 3.3 Belarius refers to his cave as 'This Rocke' (F1, TLN 1629; 3.3.70) and in *The Tempest*, 1.2 Caliban describes his den as 'this hard Rocke' (F1, TLN 482; 1.2.343). For a 'Rocke' to serve theatrically as a cave would require the use of the discovery space, not least because these scenes involve characters' entrances from somewhere inside it: '*Enter Belarius, Guiderius, and Aruiragus*' (*Cymbeline* F1, TLN 1554; 3.3.0); '*Enter Caliban*' (*The Tempest* F1, TLN 458; 1.2.320).[86] The use of a property rocky cave seems unnecessary, but if one was used, it would have had to be erected either inside or immediately in front of the discovery area.[87]

One might assume that since speeches are supposed to be spoken in the dramatic world, they would always refer to that world. But the meanings of certain terms and phrases can sometimes be very ambiguous. Consider the meaning of the word 'within' in the phrase 'Who's within there!' and its variants. Usually, especially when the phrase is used in scenes taking place either outside or inside a house, the meaning of 'within' is clear, referring to the interior of the house. In *The Merchant of Venice*, 2.6, for example, Lorenzo, having just joined other characters already onstage, says to them 'approch / here dwels my father Iew' (Q1, D2r; 2.6.24–5) and then shouts 'Howe whose within?' (D2r; 2.6.25). Here 'within' refers to the inside of Shylock's house, and the house is represented by the tiring-house façade. On the other hand, when in *2 Henry VI*, 1.4 York uses the same phrase, the meaning of 'within' is not so evident. This scene appears to take place in Gloucester's garden. The witch Margery Jordan and two priests conjure a spirit on the main stage, while the Duchess is observing them from the upper level. Suddenly, York and Buckingham break in and arrest the Duchess and the conjurers. They are taken off, guarded, and Buckingham also departs. Then, just before the end of the scene, York calls in a servant in order to send him on an errand: 'Who's within there, hoe?' (F1, TLN 710; 1.4.78). Is York referring to the inside of Gloucester's house as 'within'? If so, is one of York's own servants waiting for him in Gloucester's house? Such a question is plainly absurd, but the real point is that it would have no relevance in the Shakespearean theatre. In the absence of scenery there was no need for the location of the scene to remain clear and fixed throughout. In the present instance, the scene's locality would probably become unspecific after the departure of the Duchess of Gloucester and others, so that when York cries 'Who's within there, hoe?', the meaning of 'within' would become uncertain and ambiguous. The phrase would work well enough in the theatre, as the servant enters from within the tiring-house, without making the audience question what is being referred to as 'within' in the fictional world.

A similar phenomenon can be observed around a character's exit. In *Richard III*, 1.4, the First Murderer stabs Clarence and carries him off the stage, saying as he does so, 'Take that, and that, if all this will not do, / Ile drowne you in the Malmesey-But within' (F1, TLN 1103–4; 1.4.269–70). However, earlier in the scene, just before Clarence woke from a sleep, the First Murderer, talking to the Second Murderer, had referred to the malmsey butt as in the next room and not as within: 'Take him on the Costard, with the hiltes of thy Sword, and then throw him into the Malmesey-Butte in the next roome' (TLN 986–8; 1.4.154–6).[88] In fictional terms it does not much matter whether the First Murderer goes in or out. Since the actor goes into the tiring-house, the word 'within' serves its purpose adequately enough in terms of the theatrical space.

The theatrical language

A reference to a door in the dialogue might not necessarily indicate that a stage door is representing a door in the fictional world. In the middle of the opening scene of *As You Like It*, Oliver calls in his servant Dennis and asks if the Duke's wrestler Charles is waiting for him. Dennis's reply contains a reference to a door: 'So please you, he is heere at the doore, and importunes accesse to you' (F1, TLN 92–3; 1.1.91–2). Earlier in the scene, through the exchange between Orlando and Oliver, the location was defined as Oliver's 'Orchard' (TLN 44; 1.1.41). Dennis may therefore be referring to the door of the orchard, whether it is imagined to be offstage or represented by an actual stage door.[89] The commonest meaning of 'orchard' was 'garden'.[90] Shakespeare followed his chief source, Thomas Lodge's prose romance *Rosalynde*, in locating the quarrel between Orlando and Oliver in the garden of Oliver's house.[91] Although he continued the scene by having Oliver remain onstage after Orlando's exit with Adam (TLN 84; 1.1.84), he may not have been concerned about the location of the second half of the scene. If the locality has become vague, the phrase 'heere at the doore' might work in predominantly theatrical terms.

This can be seen too if we look at similar speeches in the sheep-shearing scene in *The Winter's Tale*. This long scene, as a whole, gives the impression that it takes place in the open air, particularly towards the end of the scene in Autolycus's words to the Shepherd and his son, 'Walke before toward the Sea-side, goe on the right hand, I will but looke vpon the Hedge, and follow you' (F1, TLN 2705–7; 4.4.824–6). The scene, however, contains two occasions when the Shepherd's servant announces the arrivals of newcomers, mentioning their presence at a door: 'O Master: if you did but heare the Pedler at the doore, you would neuer dance againe after a Tabor and Pipe' (TLN 2006–8; 4.4.181–3); 'Why, they [twelve satyrs] stay at doore Sir' (TLN 2163; 4.4.342). Ernest Schanzer cites these lines as indicating an indoor setting for the scene,[92] while Stephen Orgel, more plausibly, suggests that the scene begins indoors and moves outdoors.[93] They are both trying to explain the speeches only at the fictional level. On the Shakespearean stage, the meaning of the phrase 'at the door' might not always have referred exclusively to the fictional world. Where the locality is ambiguous, when a character is referred to as 'at the door', especially before entering, as in *As You Like It*, 1.1 and *The Winter's Tale*, 4.4, 'the door' might be understood to refer simply and straightforwardly to the stage door behind which the actor is waiting for his entrance. Thus, some speeches might not make perfect sense in the dramatic world but the audience was perfectly capable of absorbing, without discomfort, this brief reference to the realities of the playhouse.

THE USE OF THE STAGE SPACE

As we have seen, there was no typical English Renaissance playhouse: the London commercial playhouses varied considerably in size, shape and architectural features. They were however similar in the spatial relationship between the stage and the auditorium and in the basic equipment of the stage. The stage projected into the auditorium. Although the five-feet-or-so height of the stage, whether railed off or not, physically separated itself from the audience, actors and spectators shared the same continuous light. As for the equipment of the stage, the internal evidence from the professional plays of this period suggests that Elizabethan, Jacobean and Caroline playwrights were able to expect almost identical facilities in the London playhouses: at the rear of the stage was a tiring-house; the tiring-house façade had three openings, that is, two flanking doors and a 'discovery space' between them; there was a balcony above the stage; and a trapdoor to the space below. In such a theatre, the playing space could extend above, below, beyond and behind the stage.

On the other hand, the stage was used by more than just the actors. In private hall theatres like the second Blackfriars and the Cockpit in Drury Lane, gallants sat on the stage itself, reducing the playing space. At St Paul's, as mentioned above, sitting on the stage was not permitted, and in 1639 Charles I banned this practice at the Salisbury Court.[94] In the First Folio of Shakespeare's plays, its prefatory epistle '*To the great Variety of Readers*' by John Heminges and Henry Condell refers to wits sitting 'on the Stage at *Black-Friers*, or the *Cock-pit*' (F1, A3r), implying that the Globe and other public theatres had no such practice. Similarly, in the Induction to the Globe version of *The Malcontent*, added by Webster, when a Tireman forbids Sly from sitting on the stage, Sly says 'Why? we may sit vpon the stage at the private house' (QC, A3r). However, there is also evidence for gallants sitting on the stage at public playhouses. Two epigrams by Sir John Davies, 'In Rufum' (no. 3) and 'In Sillam' (no. 28), composed 1594–95, when no private theatres were open, provide references to sitting on the stage: 'Rvfus the Courtier at the theatre, / Leauing the best and most conspicuous place, / Doth either to the stage himselfe transfer, / Or through a grate doth shew his doubtfull face' (Davies and Marlowe, *Epigrams and Elegies* O1, A4r); 'He that dares take Tabaco on the stage' (C2r).[95] A well-known passage in Dekker's *The Gull's Hornbook* (published 1609) appears to suggest that by 1609 sitting on the stage had become fashionable in public theatres as well: 'Whether therefore the gatherers of the publique or priuate Play-house stand to receiue the afternoones rent, let our Gallant (hauing paid it) presently aduance himselfe vp to the Throne of the Stage. I meane not into the Lords roome, (which is now but the Stages Suburbs)' (Q1, E2v). Some public playhouses including the Globe may well have, at least occasionally if not regularly, allowed gallants to sit on the stage.[96] In both public and private theatres, the stage gallery not only housed a performance area; it too accommodated spectators. The limits of the acting space in early modern theatres were elastic, and as a result the early modern concept of the stage was in no way fixed and determined. The chapters that follow concern questions relating to the ambiguous demarcation between onstage and offstage spaces and those relating to the inconspicuousness of the boundaries between the stage and the auditorium.

If the demarcation between onstage and offstage spaces was not fixed, it follows that the meanings of fundamental directions such as '*enter*', '*exit*'/ '*exeunt*' and '*within*' might in some cases be similarly ambiguous. It is especially necessary to examine the usage of '*within*', the most common theatrical term for 'offstage'. Chapter 2 deals with the staging of Malvolio's imprisonment in *Twelfth Night*, Act 4, scene 2, which involves the stage direction '*Maluolio within*' (F1, TLN 2005; 4.2.19). Chapter 3 reassesses the validity of the theory that the Globe theatre did not have a music room above the stage before 1609. This widely accepted view is based upon the occurrences of the stage directions '*Music within*' and '*Music above*' in play texts. When dealing with the relation between onstage and offstage spaces, the question of how the stage doors were disposed during the performance becomes particularly important. Chapter 4 considers if the doors were usually open or closed.

In a theatre where the stage was almost entirely surrounded by the audience and where the boundaries between the stage and the auditorium were not clear and sharp, the distinction between the dramatic fiction and the physical reality could become similarly blurred. In order to consider how the dramatic world was created in the theatrical space and how its reality was maintained, I deal with the locality of scenes and special exits from the stage. It is a curious fact that Shakespearean and contemporary plays have many scenes located in 'gardens' or 'orchards', including the two already mentioned. Chapter 5 considers how a garden setting was usually established on the stage and how a stage direction such as '*Enter Brutus in his Orchard*' (*Julius Caesar* F1, TLN 615; 2.1.0) was interpreted. One major characteristic of the drama of the early modern period is the way it allows the imaginative truth of the fictional world to intersect with, even interpenetrate, a recognition of the wood, lath and plaster reality of the playhouse itself. Maintaining that balance, and above all ensuring that the fictional world was never seriously disrupted, was always a matter of artistic concern, never more so perhaps than in the subject of Chapter 6: how to dispose of an onstage corpse. Dealing with these subjects, we shall see to what extent and in what manner the logic of the fictional world governed the theatrical space during the performance and in what way the physical limitations of the theatre could be accommodated.

CHAPTER 2

'Maluolio within'

Twelfth Night, Act 4, scene 2, which involves Malvolio's imprisonment, is one of the most problematic scenes in Shakespeare in terms of the original staging. In his article, 'Malvolio and the Dark House', John H. Astington deals with problems of staging this prison scene.[1] The 1623 Folio text, which is the sole authority for the play, places the stage direction '*Maluolio within*' before Malvolio's first speech in this scene:

CLOW. What hoa, I say, Peace in this prison.
TO.   The knaue counterfets well: a good knaue.
Maluolio within.
MAL.   Who cals there?
(F1, TLN 2003–6; 4.2.18–20)

Including the speech 'Who cals there?', he delivers a total of twenty-two speeches from *within*. The stage direction '*Maluolio within*' is usually thought to indicate that Malvolio is 'entirely out of sight and speaking from the tiring house, possibly from behind one of the stage doors', but such a staging, Astington believes, would involve practical problems of the following kind:

> on Shakespeare's stage Malvolio was not to be seen watching Feste in 4.2, or so the Folio implies, and although we must hear him, his voice would have reached an Elizabethan audience from 'within' the tiring house, through the thickness of a fairly substantial wooden door, and across the depth of the stage, thirty feet or so to the first rank of standing spectators in the yard . . . The central physical problems of the scene, therefore, are those of audibility and visibility. . .[2]

Considering this question further, Astington has concluded that the stage direction '*within*' does not always indicate that the character should remain unseen within the tiring-house, and, in his view, 'the house as dark as hell [i.e. Malvolio's prison] could quite appropriately have lain below the Elizabethan trapdoor'.[3]

Although I am not convinced by Astington's suggestion that the space below the stage could have been treated as *'within'*, I agree with him that the meaning of *'within'* was much broader than the way we usually understand it.[4] An examination of the use of *'within'* in other plays of the period will shed light on this somewhat slippery theatrical term, as will an analysis of various scenes in which a character clearly speaks from offstage, even in the absence of a stage direction to this effect. Both investigations will provide a wider perspective for evaluating the significance of *'Maluolio within'*.

AUDIBILITY

Some stage directions referring to *'within'* also contain an adverb or adverbial phrase that specifies a particular part of *'within'*. Some of these directions place a character behind a stage door. Not surprisingly, what they indicate is the character's pre-entry action, as in the following examples:

One knockes within at the doore. (Kyd, *The Spanish Tragedy* Q4, H3r)[5]

The Clowne bounce at the gate, within. (Marlowe, *Doctor Faustus* QB, G1r)

On the face of it, each of these stage directions indicates that the character waiting offstage should knock at the door from which he is to enter the stage. However, it is equally possible that, especially in the instance from *Doctor Faustus*, a stage attendant (not the actor himself) produced the required sound effect by beating on something with an iron bar or the like.[6] Since offstage knocking may have involved the use of sound-producing equipment, about which we know very little, it seems prudent not to rely very much on examples of offstage knocking but to confine ourselves to characters' offstage speeches, as in the following examples from *Othello*, performed at the Globe, and from *Richard II*, probably performed at the Theatre. When in *Othello*, 5.2 the unseen Emilia calls out to Othello to admit her, the Q1 text marks 'Emillia *calls within*' (M2r; 5.2.85), while the F1 text provides '*AEmilia at the doore*' (TLN 3343; 5.2.85) and '*AEmil. within*' (TLN 3350; 5.2.89). Similarly, when in *Richard II*, 5.3 York makes a plea to be admitted, in order to reveal Aumerle's treachery, the Q1 stage direction reads '*The Duke of Yorke knokes at the doore and crieth*' (I2r; 5.3.38), while F1's corresponding stage direction reads '*Yorke within*' (TLN 2535; 5.3.38). In such situations the obvious place for the character to stand is behind the door from which he is to enter.

The use of '*within*' is sometimes linked to a character's arrival or departure through the central opening covered by hangings. Fletcher's *Women Pleased*, acted by the King's Men, provides one such example. In Act 4, scene 3, a chimney-sweeping boy creeps into the chimney and then calls out from there. The stage directions for these actions read: '*Boy goes in behinde the Arras*' (F1, 6F1r); '*Boy within, Madam here be de Rat, de Rat Madam*' (6F1r). Here '*within*' clearly refers to the discovery area '*behind the Arras*'. A similar example occurs in Tourneur's *The Atheist's Tragedy*. In Act 5, scene 1, the dead body of Sebastian, the younger son of D'Amville, the atheist of the title, has scarcely been brought on when Rousard, his sickly elder son, is heard twice to groan from offstage: '*Rousa. Ooh. – Within*' (Q1, K2v); '*Rousa. Ooh. – Within*' (K2v).[7] The voice is described as coming 'from his chamber' (K2v). Then '*A Bed [is] drawne forth with Rousard*' (K2v) and, to D'Amville's evident distress, Rousard dies after groaning twice more onstage. The direction '*Within*', which accompanies the first groans, almost certainly refers to the curtained discovery space from which the bed is thrust on to the stage.[8] In Jonson's *Bartholomew Fair*, staged at the Hope by the Lady Elizabeth's Men, Ursla's pig booth, which is also referred to as her 'lodge' (F2, D4r), 'mansion' (E1r) or 'bower' (E1r), would probably have been represented by the central discovery space, even though there is no specific stage direction to this effect.[9] Ursla herself would have made her entrances and exits through the central opening, and so in 2.5 when the stage direction reads '*She calls within*', she would have cried from the curtained area, 'What *Moonecalfe*? you Rogue' (E1r).[10]

Dekker and Massinger's *The Virgin Martyr*, acted at the Red Bull, contains a scene where the stage direction '*within*' is used in the same scene to refer to three different positions. In 5.1, a Dekker scene,[11] the unseen devil Harpax is first directed to be heard from '*within*'/'*Within*' (Q1, K4r, K4v; 5.1.81, 86), laughing on each occasion. His voice then increases in volume; it is referred to as '*lowder*' (K4v; 5.1.94). He also changes location, first shouting '*At one end*' (K4v; 5.1.95), then '*At tother end*' (K4v; 5.1.97), and finally laughing '*At the middle*' (K4v; 5.1.100). After laughing '*Within*' for the last time (L1r; 5.1.119), he is directed to enter '*in a fearefull shape, fire flashing out of the study*' (L1r; 5.1.122). It is almost certain that the term '*end*' here denotes the two flanking doors,[12] and that '*the middle*' refers to the central discovery area serving as '*the study*'. While on the face of it there may seem no reason why he should not take various offstage positions including the specified three, in practice he may well have positioned himself behind the three openings in the *frons scenae*. In other words, when he laughs '*within*' for the first time at line 81, he would already be '*At one end*'. He would remain there for a while, laughing and shouting several more times from the same position (lines 83, 84, 85, 86, 94, 95). He would then race to '*tother end*' (line 97), before moving back to '*the middle*' (line 100), and when he laughs '*Within*' at line 119, he would still remain '*At the middle*' so that he could come '*out of the study*' three lines later. This example suggests that even when an offstage voice is not directly related to the character's entrance, it may have been usual for the actor to deliver the speech from behind one of the openings in the tiring-house façade, as opposed to behind the solid wall of the *frons scenae*. The advantages in terms of increased audibility are, of course, obvious.

In this connection consider two anticipatory directions marked by a book-keeper for singers and musicians, which can be seen in King's Men plays by Massinger, *Believe as You List* and *The City Madam*, even though neither of these warnings includes '*within*'. The manuscript playbook of *Believe as You List* bears Sir Henry Herbert's licence dated 6 May 1631. The play had been refused a licence on 11 January 1631 because it dealt with Spain's deposing of the king of Portugal.[13] Assuming that the original play was, therefore, completed by the end of 1630, it must have been written to be performed at the company's winter playhouse in Blackfriars rather than at the Globe. The revised version may also have been intended for the Blackfriars.[14] This is, however, not to say that the play was not performed at the Globe; most King's Men plays would have been performed at both theatres. This manuscript contains the anticipatory direction reading '*Harry: Willson: & Boy ready for the song at ye Arras:*' (TLN 1968–72), which is an annotation marked by the company book-keeper. (The hand has been identified as that of Edward Knight, who held the position of book-keeper in the King's company in the later 1620s and early 1630s.)[15] Later in the same scene, there are the book-keeper's instruction '*the Lute. strikes & then the Songe*' (TLN 2022–3) and the author's original direction '*musicq & a songe*' (TLN 2025). Another King's Men play, *The City Madam*, licensed for performance by Herbert on 25 May 1632,[16] was published in 1658 in quarto 'As it was acted at the private House in *Black friers* with great applause' (Q1, A1r). This play is also very likely to have been performed at the Globe, as well. As for the title-page's theatre attribution, Alan B. Farmer and Zachary Lesser have shown, by analysing the title-pages of early modern printed plays, that in the period after 1630 publishers evidently believed that an indoor-theatre attribution would sell more books than an outdoor-theatre attribution.[17] *The City Madam* Q1 contains '*Musicians come down to make ready for the song at Aras*' (K2r). This anticipatory direction, printed in the margin of the quarto, must have been originally written by the book-keeper (Knight) as he prepared the theatre playbook lying behind the Q1 text. This warning is related to the following two stage directions: '*Musick. At one door Cerberus, at the other, Charon, Orpheus, Chorus*' (L2v); '*Sad musick. Enter Goldwire, and Tradewell as from prison . . .*' (L3r). In these two anticipatory directions, '*at y*ᵉ *Arras*' and '*at Aras*' very likely refer to the central space immediately behind the stage hangings. In either case, it might be desirable that the music involved in the event taking place on the main stage be performed on the same level in the tiring-house, rather than in the music room above.[18] In neither play, however, does the dialogue provide any particular reason why the music and song should be delivered from the curtained space. In each case, the book-keeper's purpose of specifying the space behind the hangings must have been to ensure better audibility of the music, while also keeping both flanking doorways clear for entrances and exits by the actors. The acoustics of large open-air theatres and those of smaller hall theatres must have been very different,[19] but for the purpose of audibility, in both kinds of theatre, the central area behind the stage hangings, which served as a discovery space in many scenes, was no doubt preferable to any other places in the tiring-house, including the spaces behind flanking doors.

'*Within*' is a general stage direction, and it could refer to anywhere within the tiring-house. In practice, when used for offstage voices, it most commonly refers to one of the spaces behind the three openings in the *frons scenae*. It may be worth mentioning at this stage that in some examples '*within*' is accompanied by '*above*' or its equivalent, which suggests that '*within*' could also refer to the upper floor of the tiring-house. Since, however, it is most unlikely that Malvolio might have been positioned on the upper level, these examples will be saved until the next chapter.

VISIBILITY

When a character referred to as '*within*' is speaking from behind one of the three openings in the tiring-house façade, he may or may not be visible to the audience. It depends on whether the stage door or the stage curtain is open or closed at the time. Look at a passage taken from Fletcher's *Love's Pilgrimage*, a King's Men play.

> *Enter Alphonso and a Servant.*
> ALPH. Knock at the door.
> SER. 'Tis open Sir.
> ALPH. That's all one
> Knock when I bid you.
> ...
> 2.SER. *within*. Come in Sir.
> *Enter [2. Servant].*[20]
>
> (F1, 8A4r)

Alphonso and his servant would enter from one of the flanking doors and cross the stage to the other, which represents the entrance to Leonardo's house. As the dialogue indicates, this door has already been opened. Although Leonardo's servant (the second servant) is directed to speak from *within*, he is clearly intended to be visible through the doorway before making his entrance.

In most other cases involving '*within*', the text provides only indirect information at best about whether the stage door or the stage curtain is open or closed. Consider Shakespeare and Fletcher's *Henry VIII*, Act 5, scene 1. In this scene, usually attributed to Shakespeare,[21] an old lady presumptuously comes to the King with the news of his baby daughter's birth, and a gentleman tries to stop her by shouting from *within*, 'Come backe: what meane you?' (F1, TLN 2962; 5.1.157). As he speaks the words, he might well be visible through the doorway by which the lady has just entered. Some editors suggest that the gentleman was actually Lovell, who is addressed by the King a short time later in the scene (TLN 2977; 5.1.169), and if so, he would have entered the stage at this point in pursuit of the old lady.[22] In any event, the gentleman's fruitless words of prevention, 'Come backe: what meane you?' would have been delivered from just behind or, perhaps, on the threshold of the door.

Fletcher and Beaumont's *Cupid's Revenge*, performed by the Children of the Revels, provides the following passage:

> *Enter Leucippus and Ismenus: the people within stoppes.*
> LEU. Good friends goe home againe, there's not a man shall goe with me.
> ISME. Will you not take reuenge? Ile call them on.
> LEUC. All that loue me depart:
> I thanke you, and will serue you for your loues:
> But I will thanke you more to suffer me
> To gouerne em[:] once more, I doe beg yee,
> For my sake to your houses.
> ALL *within*. Gods preserue you.
>
> (Q1, I4v)

Visibility

The people would come to a halt immediately behind the doorway by which Leucippus and Ismenus have entered the stage. Leucippus asks them repeatedly to depart and go home. Since it is unlikely that either he or Ismenus would shut the door behind them, the people would remain at least partially visible, standing behind the doorway, until they leave after making their farewells to Leucippus from *within*.

Another intriguing example can be seen in the 1616 Quarto (B-text) of *Doctor Faustus*, which appears to contain additions made by William Bird and Samuel Rowley in 1602. Henslowe's *Diary* records the payment of four pounds on 22 November 1602 to these two playwrights for 'ther adicyones in docter fostes',[23] suggesting the play's revival soon after that date at the Fortune playhouse. In this version the magic grapes episode is followed by the fooling of the dupes. An offstage knocking is heard: 'The Clowne bounce at the gate, within' (QB, GII; TLN 1675). Even if the noise was produced by a stage attendant and not by the Clown himself, he and his company would have positioned themselves *within*, behind the door representing the gate. The Duke, who is onstage, orders a servant, also onstage, to go and ask the offstage dupes the reason why they disturb him. After more offstage knocking and shouting are heard ('They knocke againe, and call out to talke with Faustus' (GIv; TLN 1679)), the servant's response to this continuing uproar is spoken directly to those outside who are clamouring to enter: 'Why how now Maisters, what a coyle is there?' (GIv; TLN 1680). To enable him to address them in this manner, he has clearly had to open the stage door behind which the clowns are shouting, even though there is no stage direction to this effect. The servant continues to talk to the dupes and relays to his master what they want. Only after eighteen further lines, during which they have been in partial view of the audience, are they finally admitted ('Enter the Clowne, Dick, Carter, and Horse-courser' (GIv; TLN 1699)).

All these examples suggest the possibility that a character, or characters, who are directed to remain *within* the tiring-house are not necessarily intended to be unseen but, as in these cases, are likely to be framed in the doorway, so that the audience can both hear and see them. A photo of the new Globe Theatre shows the way they might have been visible (see Figure 4). As mentioned in the introductory chapter, in the theatres of the early modern period, public or private, the stage was almost entirely surrounded by the auditorium, and this fact had huge consequences for what the audience were then able to see. As with discoveries involving the use of the curtained space, characters positioned just behind doorways, even when the doors were open, would have been almost invisible to spectators

'Maluolio within'

Figure 4. The new Globe Theatre, Bankside, London, near the site of the original Globe. Note the actors standing just behind the doorways in the tiring-house façade.

sitting in the galleries on either side of the stage and to those sitting in the gallery over the stage. The proportion of these seats was by no means small. The evidence of the plays suggests that playwrights and players did not refrain from using positions in and around doorways when it suited their purpose, regardless of the varying problems of visibility this would create for some of their audience.

There are further examples where a character should or could be visible to the audience while remaining *within*. One is found in the surviving manuscript playbook of Fletcher and Massinger's tragedy of *Sir John van Olden Barnavelt*, first acted by the King's Men at the Globe. The chief hand in the manuscript is that of the professional scribe, Ralph Crane.[24] In Act 3, scene 6, Leidenberch sends his son offstage to go to bed, and then kills himself. While remaining offstage, the boy cries twice in his sleep: 'oh' (TLN 1671); 'now heaven blesse me: / ô me: ô me' (TLN 1674–5). What is noteworthy is the stage direction '*Son abed*' (TLN 1656), which was added by the King's company book-keeper (not Edward Knight) between the boy's exit ('*Ex^t Boy*' (TLN 1642)) and his first cry from *within* ('*Boy wth in* oh' (TLN 1671)). Clearly, the book-keeper meant the boy to be visible to the audience during his offstage presence. The added stage direction suggests that Leidenberch opens the stage hangings, revealing the son in bed, and finds that 'He is fast [asleep]' (TLN 1657). It is not certain whether the book-keeper intended the father to close the hangings before stabbing himself. Leidenberch could close them after or while saying 'Sleepe on sweet Child' (TLN 1658), but it is not essential that he do so. If he does not close the hangings, the boy would be visible when he cries in his sleep from *within*.

It may be useful to note here that '*within*' occurs in at least two stage directions for discoveries. Chapman's *The Widow's Tears*, acted at Blackfriars by the Children of the Queen's Revels, provides '*Tomb opens, and Lysander within lies along, Cynthia and Ero*' (Q1, I2v (I2 missigned 'K2')). Mayne's *The City Match*, performed at Blackfriars by the King's Men, has '*Draws the Curtaine within are discovered Bright. & Newcut*' (F1, R1r). What these directions specifically indicate is that the characters positioned *within* should be made visible to the audience.

Consider a scene in Jordan's *The Walks of Islington and Hogsdon*, a Red Bull company play. Its 1657 Quarto text (Q1) reproduces Henry Herbert's licence dated 2 August 1641 (H4r), suggesting that its official playbook was used as the printer's copy. In Act 1, scene 2 of the play, Splendora '*stands within the Arras*' (B3v) between her exit from the stage ('*Exit Splend.*' (B3v)) and re-entrance on to it ('*Enter Splend.*' (B4v)). The phrase '*within the Arras*' is most likely equivalent to '*behind the Arras*'. (When in *King John*, 4.1, the executioners are told to 'stand / Within the Arras' (F1, TLN 1571–2; 4.1.1–2), they should hide themselves behind the arras.)[25] During her presence '*within the Arras*', Splendora finds there a pen and paper, and writes a brief note to her lover Mercurio, while speaking aloud each word she writes. The Q1 text here gives her five stage directions: '*She writes*' (B3v); '*Writes agen*' (B4r); '*Writes agen*' (B4r); '*Writes*' (B4r); '*Writes agen*' (B4r). These actions should be visible to the audience, probably through a gap between the hangings.

Fletcher and Massinger's *The Little French Lawyer*, a King's Men play, offers a more suggestive stage direction:

> *Enter Dinant, and Lamira. A light within.*
>
> ...
>
> DIN. 'Pray' put your light out.
> LAM. No I'le hold it thus,
> That all chast eyes, may see thy lust, and scorne it,
>
> (F1, I4v)

This passage is in a scene commonly ascribed to Massinger.[26] Robert Kean Turner's edition of the play reads '*Enter* Dinant, *and* Lamira *with a light*' for '*Enter Dinant, and Lamira. A light within.*'[27] It is certainly possible that '*A light within*' is an error (conceivably for '*A light with her*') and if Lamira is holding a light, the dialogue might make better sense. But there are also reasons for accepting the original stage direction as it stands. For one thing, the F2 text of the play retains F1's reading: '*Enter* Dinant, *and* Lamira: *a light within*' (F2, 2Y4r). For another, the plays written or co-written by Fletcher provide a fair number of examples that suggest the necessity of reconsidering the early modern usage of '*within*', some of which have been mentioned above. In the present case, a servant holding a light may be visible through the doorway from which Dinant and Lamira have made their entrance. Even if there is no actual servant, and wherever might be referred to as '*within*', it is evident that the '*light within*' is intended to be visible to the audience. The light should continue to be visible for some time, because Dinant has to say to Lamira for the second time, 'Put out your light' (K1r), and this second instruction comes more than fifty lines after their entrance. In view of this example, I suggest that when a stage direction says that a character is positioned '*within*', we should be alive to the possibility that he may in fact be visible to the audience.

Some entry stage directions are phrased in such a way as to indicate that the character does not really enter the stage but is merely visible to the audience. Fletcher's plays provide many such stage directions. The following examples are taken from the surviving manuscript of *Bonduca*, which was evidently made for a private collector, and is the work of the King's company book-keeper Edward Knight '*from the fowle papers of the Authors*' (MS, TLN 2379).[28]

Enter: younger Daughter: & an Attendant: she shewes her selfe but at y^e *Doore.* (TLN 1046–9)

Enter Iudas: & his Company (peeping at the Doore:) (TLN 1850–2)

Enter: Drusus: Regulus: (stopping the Soldiers. At the Doore.)
Soldiers:/   kill him kill him kill him.
*w*th*in /*

(TLN 2108–10)

As W. W. Greg observes, these stage directions, which are more detailed and graphic than their equivalents in the text of *Bonduca* in the 1647 Beaumont and Fletcher Folio (F1),[29] might reflect 'amplifications by the scribe writing for readers and with recollections of actual performance in mind'.³⁰ These examples suggest that an actor could '*enter*' by showing himself '*at the door*', that is, either on or behind the threshold of the door, while an actor standing '*at the door*', even if visible to the audience, could be referred to as '*within*'. In other words, to *enter*, to stand *at the door* and to be *within* could sometimes be the same thing.

This notion may help to solve some problems involving the use of '*enter*' or '*within*'. In Act 4, scene 4 of *Troilus and Cressida*, a Globe play,³¹ when Aeneas calls to Troilus from offstage, the Q1 and F1 texts read as follows:

AENEAS *within*. My Lord is the Lady ready?
(Q1, H3v; 4.4.49)

Enter AEneus.
AENEAS *within*. My Lord, is the Lady ready?
(F1, TLN 2434–5; 4.4.49)

Although the textual situation in *Troilus and Cressida* is unusually complicated, it seems reasonably certain that F1 was printed from a copy of Q1 collated with a manuscript.³² F1 provides an entry direction for Aeneas, though it retains Q1's '*within*'. What the F1 entry direction indicates is probably that Aeneas merely peeps through a doorway but remains offstage. The Q1 staging would be much the same as the F1 staging, assuming that the door is open at the time. Later in the scene, Aeneas and Paris are directed to call from *within* in both versions at lines 98 and 99: '*Eneas within*' (Q1, H4r); '*Paris within*' (H4r); '*AEneas within*' (F1, TLN 2488); '*Paris within*' (TLN 2490). It may be that in these cases as well, they were visible through the doorway.³³

The Second Maiden's Tragedy, another King's Men play, now generally attributed to Middleton, survives in a theatre manuscript. This playbook bears Sir George Buc's licence of performance dated 31 October 1611: '*This second Maydens tragedy (for it hath no name inscribed) may wth the reformations bee acted publikely.*' The play's first performance in the winter of 1611–12 took place probably at the indoor Blackfriars.³⁴ This manuscript supplies:

Enter Votarius to the doore wthin (MS, TLN 2081–3)

This stage direction is the playwright's own, not the book-keeper's.³⁵ It occurs in the scene where Anselmus's wife attempts to convince her husband of her fidelity by deliberately making him observe her refusal of Votarius's advances. The dialogue around the stage direction suggests that Votarius shows himself through the doorway but does not really enter the stage; Leonella, who has been watching the door for her lady, stops him from coming forward: 'back, y'are to forward sir' (TLN 2081). It does not appear that she was meant to shut the door immediately; the words that Anselmus's wife speaks to Votarius ten lines later, 'whats ther, how now Sir, what yor busines?' (TLN 2093) seem to suggest that although Leonella does not admit Votarius straightway, he is visible while importunately asking her to let him in.

Several of the preceding examples have been taken from plays written or co-written by Fletcher for the post-1609 King's company for performance at the Blackfriars and/or the Globe. However, all the examples discussed are taken from a range of theatres and periods, some from pre-1609 Blackfriars plays and some from public-theatre plays including a Globe play by Shakespeare. All point to the conclusion that the stage direction *'within'* could refer to a position immediately behind, or almost on, the threshold of a doorway, and, if the door or the curtain was open, a character positioned there would have been visible to most of the audience.

ACTUALLY ONSTAGE?

In some cases characters referred to as *'within'* might have already crossed the threshold and therefore actually be onstage at that moment. In such examples the stage direction *'within'* may have been used with a special meaning. For instance, *The Little French Lawyer*, in a scene from Fletcher's share of the play, offers another intriguing example of *'enter'* and *'within'* occurring together in the same stage direction.

>   *Enter Monsieur la Writ within.*
> LA WRIT. I understand your causes.
>   Yours about corne, yours about pinnes and glasses,
>   Will you make me mad, have I not all the parcells?
>   And his Petition too, about Bell-founding?
>   . . .
>   Trouble me no more. I say, againe to you,
>   No more vexation: bid my wife send me some puddings;
>   I have a Cause to run through, requires puddings,
>   Puddings enough. Farewell.
> CLER.   God speed you, sir.
>
>   (F1, H4v–I1r)

This scene is located in the place appointed for the duel between Dinant and Cleremont on one side and Beaupre and Verdoone on the other. It is described as 'Nere to the vineyard eastward from the Citie' (H4r), and the presence of some passers-by reinforces the impression that it is an open space. The stage doors would therefore have been open throughout.³⁶ Dinant's failure to make the appointment forces Cleremont either to fight alone against two or to obtain a second. While he is trying to find a second, La-writ enters. This is La-writ's first appearance in the play. He speaks fifteen lines, as he dismisses his clients who are understood to be offstage. In this way the play's title character informs the audience of his occupation and of his humorous nature, before joining the characters already onstage. The entry direction, '*Enter Monsieur la Writ within*' may well indicate that La-writ shows himself, standing either on or just behind the threshold of the doorway, when he begins to speak. We may suspect that he starts his speech there but soon enters the stage to complete most of his leave-taking. It is just possible that he is meant to deliver the whole speech while remaining unseen, though given the length of the speech this is somewhat less likely.³⁷

There may be a third possibility involving a special usage of '*within*'. Robert Kean Turner's edition of the play reads '*Enter Monsieur* la Writ [*speaking to those*] *within*' for '*Enter Monsieur la Writ within*.'³⁸ Turner probably thought that the original direction would have made no sense; in the introduction to the edition, he describes some stage directions including '*Enter Monsieur la Writ within*' as harmless but imprecise.³⁹ Or he may have thought that '*Enter within*' was a shortened form of '*Enter speaking to those within*.' The locution '*Enter speaking to someone within*' can be found in some other early modern play texts. Marston's *The Dutch Courtesan*, performed at the Blackfriars by the Children of the Queen's Revels, has '*Enter Frevile, speaking to some within . . .*' (Q1, F2v). In William Warner's translation of Plautus's *Menaechmi*, which Shakespeare may possibly have used for *The Comedy of Errors*,⁴⁰ Menaechmus is directed to '*Enter talking backe to his wife within*' (Q1, A4v). Plays by Fletcher and close colleagues such as Beaumont include a fair number of instances where an entering character talks to another character who is understood to be offstage, although in these examples the entering character is given only a bare '*Enter*' direction. To cite some examples: in the opening scene of Fletcher's *Wit without Money*, Valentine enters, giving instructions to an offstage 'boy' who never appears: 'Bid the young Courtier repaire to me anon, Ile reade to him' (Q1, B2r); in Beaumont's *The Woman Hater*, a Paul's Children play, at the beginning of the scene designated in the quarto as 'ACTVS 3. SCENA. 4' – this scene may reflect casual revision by Fletcher⁴¹ – a Mercer enters, speaking to an apprentice who is again understood to be offstage: 'Looke to my shop, & if there come euer a

Scholler in blacke, let him speak with me' (Q1, F2r). If *'Enter within'* was a shortened form for *'Enter speaking to those within,'* then *'within'* could have been used in the sense of 'to direct a speech towards within the tiring-house.'

This possible special meaning could work in Fletcher's *Valentinian*, Act 4, scene 4,⁴² where Emperor Valentinian's loyal general, Aecius, commits suicide. Tricked by a false letter, the tyrannous Emperor doubts his loyalty and plots to kill him. But Aecius does not fly and prepares to meet his fate calmly at his own hand. Scarcely has he killed himself when Proculus, one of the Emperor's flatterers, arrives with others.

AEC.	...	
	There is no paine at all in dying well,	
	Nor none are lost, but those that make their hell	*kills himselfe.*
	Enter Proculus and two others.	
1. *Within.*	Hee's dead, draw in the Guard againe,	
PRO.	Hee's dead indeed,	
	And I am glad hee's gone; he was a devill:	
	His body, if his Eunuches come, is theirs;	
	The Emperor out of his love to vertue,	
	Has given 'em that: Let no man stop their entrance.	*Exit.*
	(F1, 7C3r)	

A short while ago in the same scene Proculus entered and exited with three others: *'Enter Proculus, and 3. others running over the Stage'* (7C3r); *'Exeunt'* (7C3r). It may therefore be that this time the character identified in the speech prefix as '1' remains offstage in order to deliver the speech 'Hee's dead, draw in the Guard againe' from there. However, despite the use of *'Within'*, one would imagine that the character '1' would have to enter the stage in order to view the body and confirm that Aecius is dead. At the very least, he would need to look in through the doorway.⁴³ He is therefore most likely one of the two characters who are directed to *'Enter'* with Proculus. Perhaps, only Proculus makes an actual entrance and the other two remain standing in the doorway. This might explain the use of *'Exit'* at the end of Proculus's speech, but, on the other hand, the singular direction may be used here to indicate his departure with the others. There is no particular reason why the other two should not come forward and the fact that Proculus agrees with what has just been said ('Hee's dead indeed') and then gives instructions concerning the dead body ('His body, if his Eunuches come, is theirs; / ... / Let no man stop their entrance') suggests that he has been accompanied on to the stage. The direction *'Within'* attached to '1' would therefore indicate that this unnamed character, having entered the stage, directs his call for the guard towards the door into the tiring-house.

Another possible example can be seen in the opening scene of *A Yorkshire Tragedy*, a Globe play originally assigned to Shakespeare but now generally considered to be by Middleton.[44]

RALPH. . . .
    Slidd I heare *Sam*, *Sam's* come, her's Tarry, come, yfaith now my nose itches for news
OLIUE, and so doe's mine elbowe.
    Sam calls within,   *where are you there?*
SAM. Boy look you walk my horse with discretion, I haue rid him simply, I warrand his skin sticks to his back with very heate, if a should catch cold & get the Cough of the Lunges I were well serued, were I not? What Raph and Oliuer.
AM. Honest fellow *Sam* welcome yfaith, what tricks hast thou brought from London.
                                           Furnisht with things from London.
SA. You see I am hangd after the truest fashion, three hats, and two glasses, . . .
                                                      (Q1, A2r–v)

Firm conclusions are made more difficult by apparent confusion in the text, in which the stage direction 'Sam calls within' is printed in roman as part of Oliver's speech and there is no entry direction for Sam. It is likely that after crying 'where are you there?' from within the tiring-house, whether visible or invisible to the audience, Sam enters the stage and, probably remaining by his entry door, continues to speak to the unseen 'Boy' until he finally perceives Ralph and Oliver. He would then come forward and join his fellow servingmen. This view could be supported by the fact that although Sam delivers two speeches continuously, a separate speech prefix (*Sam.*) is used for the second speech beginning with 'Boy look you walk my horse with discretion.' It is also possible that while Ralph is saying '*Sam's* come, her's Tarry, come, yfaith now my nose itches for news', Sam enters the stage. In this case, the stage direction 'Sam calls within' might indicate that he calls towards within, directing the speech to the addressee offstage. Considering the uncertainties of the text, however, it would not be prudent to rely too much on this example. There is another possible example in Fletcher's *Love's Pilgrimage*, but this will be saved until the next chapter, because it involves the use of the upper playing level.

Admittedly, in none of the three examples examined above is it absolutely beyond doubt that the character referred to as '*within*' is already onstage rather than offstage, even if only just onstage, and that the stage direction is used in the special sense of directing the speech towards an offstage character within the tiring-house. On the face of it, Fletcher, who was particularly keen on writing situations involving communication with offstage characters, is the one dramatist most likely to have done so. He may well have occasionally used the stage direction '*within*' in the sense of 'towards within', and if that were the case, it is entirely conceivable that some of his colleagues consciously or unconsciously followed him. The fact that, despite examining hundreds of early modern play texts, I have not yet come across an irrefutable example of this practice does not require us to rule it out entirely. Instead, not for the first time, we have to accept the frustrating consequences of the fact that very few playhouse documents such as theatrical plots and actors' parts survive; the corresponding stage direction in the actor's part for La-writ, for example, might have provided information as to how the stage direction '*Enter Monsieur la Writ within*' was treated in the theatre.

ECHO SCENES AND PRISON SCENES

Echo scenes would logically seem to require offstage speeches. Webster's *The Duchess of Malfi*, performed by the King's Men, at Blackfriars and at the rebuilt Globe, provides an example, in which the Duchess's voice repeats the last words of Antonio's speeches. Although the scene's initial direction reads '*Antonio, Delio, Eccho, (from the Dutchesse Graue.)*' (Q1, M3v), echoes from the grave are to be heard later. This is because the Q1 text, printed from a copy prepared by Ralph Crane, employs the 'massed entry' technique, meaning that all the characters who are to take part in a scene, no matter when, are listed together at the beginning. The dialogue between Antonio and Delio suggests that the location is the ruins of an ancient abbey. The grave could have been represented by either the stage trap or the central opening in the tiring-house façade. As John Russell Brown observes, Antonio's words, 'and on the sudden, a cleare light / Presented me a face folded in sorrow' (M4r) may indicate that the Duchess was visible.[45] Discussing the staging of this echo scene, Brown argues that Webster was influenced by another King's Men play, *The Second Maiden's Tragedy*, which provides two consecutive tomb scenes.[46] At the beginning of the first of the two, the Tyrant and his soldiers make an immediate re-entrance by the door opposite the one through which they have exited, and the tomb is 'discovered':

Enter the Tirant agen at a farder dore, which opened, bringes hym to the Toombe wher the Lady lies buried; The Toombe here discouered ritchly set forthe; (MS, TLN 1725–7)

It is most likely that the central discovery space between the flanking doors would represent the tomb of Govianus's Lady in the two consecutive tomb scenes. In the second tomb scene, the Lady's ghost first speaks to Govianus from '*With in*': 'I am not here' (TLN 1923). Then her ghost comes forth from the tomb:

On a sodayne in a kinde of Noyse like a Wynde, the dores clattering, the Toombstone flies open, and a great light appears in the midst of the Toombe; His Lady as went owt, standing iust before hym all in white, Stuck with Iewells and a great crucifex on her brest. (TLN 1926–31)

In this example, '*With in*' evidently refers to the central discovery space. Although it is not certain that Webster's echo scene requires such a special lighting effect as is required in *The Second Maiden's Tragedy*, I think it very likely that the Duchess's voice was heard from the discovery area covered by hangings: the Duchess's ghost could have shown herself through a gap between them. Brown thinks that this scene requires a special lighting effect, and that it would have had to be cut for performance at the Globe.[47] Even if any light was required, as R. B. Graves says, 'a torch held by the Duchess's ghost would have done as well at the Globe as at Blackfriars'.[48]

The surviving manuscript of Heywood's *The Captives*, a Cockpit play, also provides an echo scene. Two shipwrecked women, Palestra and Scribonia, find themselves near a monastery and decide to beg for charity from religious men. Before going to its 'backe gate' (TLN 748) with Palestra, Scribonia implores, 'som sweete echo / speake ffrom these walls. and answer' to our wants' (TLN 751–2). The stage direction for their move reads 'They go in' (TLN 755). The fact that their dialogue continues without interruption indicates that, should they actually leave the stage, they would have to make an immediate re-entrance, probably from the opposite door. Their re-entrance after making an offstage crossing would suggest that they have reached the back of the monastery. Alternatively, rather than leaving the stage, they might merely walk towards the door or the doorway that could represent the 'backe gate'. After making whatever move is indicated by the stage direction, the two women then sing a mournful song, designed to arouse the compassion of the monks within. The song is written in couplet form, and after each couplet there is a one-line reply sung by an invisible character representing the echo. The first speech prefix for the echo specifically indicates that the voice of the echo in the scene comes from *within*: 'Answer wthin' (TLN 758). The echo's words are scarcely encouraging for the two women, and a short while later Friar

John enters, and his first words make it clear that he was the voice of the echo: 'what singinge beggers weare these at the gate, / ... / I thinke I answerd them in such a key / as I beeleeve scarce pleasd them' (TLN 788, 791–2). Since the central opening of the tiring-house façade could appropriately have represented the back gate of the monastery, and especially if the women used both flanking doorways in order to come to the back gate, it is most likely that they delivered the song in front of the central opening, with Friar John's voice answering them from behind it. Even if the women used one of the flanking doors as the back gate, and even though Friar John was later to enter from that door, he might have played the echo behind the central hangings so as to ensure better audibility.

Dekker's *Old Fortunatus* begins with an echo scene. The stage direction '*within*' is attached to the first speech prefix for the echo: 'Eccho within' (Q1, A3r).[49] When the play was acted at the enlarged Rose by the new Admiral's Men formed in 1594, either before or after the court performance on 27 December 1599,[50] the actor playing the echo would have occupied the central space behind the stage hangings, since he has twelve speeches. Presumably, the same means of presentation would have been adopted in other echo scenes, such as the one in Lodge's *The Wounds of Civil War*, acted by the pre-1594 Admiral's Men, though the stage direction '*within*' does not in fact occur but only the words of the echo are given (Q1, E3v-E4r). It should be noted that there is one example where the echo comes from under the stage. In Act 1, scene 2 of Jonson's *Cynthia's Revels*, acted at Blackfriars by the Children of the Chapel, the character named Echo first repeats the words of Mercury, who is onstage, and then rises from under the stage: '*Ascendit*' (Q1, B3r). An open trap-door, which served as the 'Fountaine' (B3r), must have been adequate to achieve the desired acoustical effect. The stage direction '*within*' is not used in this scene, either.

Some prison scenes involve offstage speeches. *Measure for Measure*, a Globe play, provides such a scene.

Enter Abhorson.
ABH. Sirrah, bring *Barnardine* hether.
CLO. Mr *Barnardine*, you must rise and be hang'd, Mr *Barnardine*.
ABH. What hoa *Barnardine*.
Barnardine within.
BAR. A pox o'your throats: who makes that noyse there? What are you?
CLO. Your friends Sir, the Hangman: You must be so good Sir to rise, and be put to death.

BAR.	Away you Rogue, away, I am sleepie.
...	
AB.	Go in to him, and fetch him out.
CLO.	He is comming Sir, he is comming: I heare his Straw russle.
	Enter Barnardine.
ABH.	Is the Axe vpon the blocke, sirrah?
CLO.	Verie readie Sir.
BAR.	How now *Abhorson*? What's the newes with you?

(F1, TLN 2096–106, 2111–18; 4.3.19–29, 34–40)

It is most unlikely that the door from which Abhorson has just entered would serve as the entrance to Barnadine's cell. Although the use of the opposite door is certainly possible, the central opening would more fittingly represent the entrance to a place of confinement. Suppose therefore that Pompey (the Clown) and Abhorson summon Barnadine from the central opening. Barnardine would answer their calls behind it, and shortly make his entrance through the doorway. The Clown's speech 'I heare his Straw russle', coming just before Barnardine's entry, may well suggest that he can hear but not see him at this moment. The stage direction '*Barnardine within*', therefore, probably indicates that the prisoner should remain unseen within the tiring-house. It is, however, also possible that either the Clown or Abhorson reveals Barnardine *within* at or around the moment indicated by the stage direction, by opening the curtain while calling his name: 'Mr *Barnardine*, you must rise and be hang'd, Mr *Barnardine*'; 'What hoa *Barnardine*.'

Sir Clyomon and Sir Clamydes, an old-fashioned Elizabethan play, has a prison scene containing references to doors and a window. The title-page of the 1599 Quarto claims that 'it hath bene sundry times Acted by her Maiesties Players' (Q1, A2r), but it may well have been an old play which the Queen's Men revived.[51] They were primarily a travelling company but they spent a considerable amount of time playing in London, at city inns like the Bell and the Bull and at purpose-built playhouses in the suburbs – the Theatre, the Curtain and the Rose – as well as at court.[52] At the beginning of the prison scene in *Clyomon and Clamydes* Subtle Shift enters to rescue his master, Clamydes, who has been kept in a prison. As he approaches the prison, he hears Clamydes's voice. Clamydes, who is directed to be '*in prison*' (D3r), speaks a 24-line soliloquy and also four one-line speeches to Shift. In order to locate Clamydes, Shift asks him to 'Looke out at the windowe' (D3v). When Shift says to him 'So the doores are open, now come and follow after me' (D3v), the stage direction for Clamydes's action reads '*Enter out*' (D3v). In this direction '*out*' is used either in the sense of 'on to the stage' or as a shortened form of 'out of the prison'. In performance in the provinces, some structure representing the prison would very possibly have been set up on the stage.[53] In a purpose-built playhouse, however, it is more likely that Clamydes would have occupied the curtained space. He has many lines to speak from the prison, which would have been appropriately represented by the central area. A gap between the hangings could well have served as the window of the prison door.[54]

A prison scene in Marston's *Antonio's Revenge*, a Paul's Children play, provides a stage direction reference to a 'grate'. In Act 2, scene 3, Antonio, who is alone onstage, hears several people sighing with grief, but he cannot see them. Then Mellida, who is confined in a dungeon, begins to speak: 'O here, here is a vent to passe my sighes. / I haue surcharg'd the dungeon with my plaints. / Prison, and heart will burst, if void of vent' (Q1, D3v). After they have exchanged words, '*Antonio kisseth Mellida's hand: then Mellida goes from the grate*' (D4v). This scene clearly requires some kind of vent, if not a real grating. What is not certain is whether the stage trap represented it, or whether one of the doors in the *frons scenae* included a grating. Instead, perhaps, a gap between the curtains covering the central discovery area could have been used.[55] In the next scene, having a conversation with his mother, Antonio mentions Mellida's confinement 'Vnder the hatches of obscuring earth' (E1v). In Act 5, scene 2, Balurdo's prison certainly lies below the stage trap, since he speaks several lines '*from vnder the Stage*' (I2v) before climbing out. These facts, however, do not automatically support the argument that, in Act 2, Mellida's dungeon also lies below the stage trap. Some editors do indeed place her beneath the stage, but others locate her within the tiring-house.[56] It is noteworthy that some plays, all performed at indoor theatres, contain scenes that appear to require the use of stage doors with grates or grilles. In a scene in Sharpham's *Cupid's Whirligig*, performed at Whitefriars by the Children of the King's Revels, when knocks are heard from offstage, an onstage character (Lady Troublesome) '*lookes through the doore*' (Q1, H4r) and describes the man standing behind the door. Shortly after in the same scene, when more knocks are heard, '*She lookes at the dore againe*' (H4v) and modifies her previous description of the man waiting offstage. Similarly, in Davenant's *The Wits*, performed by the King's Men at Blackfriars, an onstage character (Pert) finds out who is knocking offstage: '*knocking within*, Pert *lookes at doore*' (Q1, E3r).[57] In Act 2 of *Antonio's Revenge*, if a stage door that included a grating were available at St Paul's playhouse, Antonio would probably kiss Mellida's hand through the grating. Such a door would not only have made her partially visible, it would also have made her fully audible.[58]

Eastward Ho, performed by the Children of the Queen's Revels at Blackfriars, has two prison scenes in its final act. In the Q1 text, the opening stage direction of the earlier prison scene lists three characters' names without using the word '*enter*': '*Holdfast. Bramble. Security*' (H4v). This scene begins, however, with only Holdfast (the prison keeper) and Bramble (a visitor to the prison), who would enter together from a stage door. Then Holdfast calls Security (a prisoner) to come and see Bramble. Security would appear either by the opposite door or through the central opening, but he might not join Bramble on the stage, since, when Quicksilver enters later in the scene, he says to Bramble, 'Good *Sir*, goe in and talke with him. The Light dos him harme . . .' (I1r). Security's words, 'My Case, M. *Bramble*, is stone and walles, and yron grates . . .' (I1r), may possibly suggest that he is standing behind a door including a grating.[59] It is also possible that he is showing himself through a gap between half-open hangings. In the later prison scene, towards the finale of the play, Security makes an offstage cry 'Maister *Touchstone?* Maister *Touchstone?*' (I4r) as from his cell ('*A shoute in the Prison*' (I4r)), and then, following Quicksilver's example, sings a song of lament so that he may also win Touchstone's sympathy. He would probably use the same place as in the previous prison scene.

Although some prison scenes contain references to prison doors and grates, these scenes do not necessarily require the use of a door including a grating. It appears that the central opening would as often as not have served as the entrance to a prison cell and that the curtains covering it could have been employed usefully in both aural and visual terms.

'*MALUOLIO WITHIN*'

Regarding the Globe staging of Malvolio's imprisonment, David Carnegie suggests the use of hangings. He says:

> The implications of such a staging are twofold. First, fabric muffles the voice less than a solid wooden door, so any problems of audibility are diminished. Second, and more important, the question of visibility becomes a matter of the actor's discretion. Malvolio can remain unseen, the curtain as still and opaque as a tiring-house door; alternatively, he can use a gap in the curtains for the familiar comic practice of 'peeping'. In other words, the use of hangings can fulfill the demands of both the Folio stage direction '*Maluolio within*' and, at the same time, minimize any problems of audibility and visibility.[60]

I agree with him about the use of the curtained space. We can perhaps refine the speculation a little further. It is at least possible that the imprisoned

Malvolio could have been visible throughout. At the scene's opening, Maria makes Feste disguise himself with a gown and false beard so that he can make Malvolio believe that he is Sir Topas the curate. The Fool baits Malvolio by making use of his complaint about the darkness in which he is confined. Maria then says to him, 'Thou mightst haue done this without thy berd and gowne, he sees thee not' (TLN 2049–50; 4.2.64–5). But, even if Malvolio does not see the Fool, he may still be visible to the Fool and to the audience. A gap between the curtains could have been used. It is even possible that Feste reveals Malvolio *within* by opening the curtains, after or while addressing him in the supposed clergyman's voice, 'What hoa, I say, Peace in this prison' (TLN 2003; 4.2.18) – that is, at or around the very moment indicated by the F1 stage direction '*Maluolio within*' (TLN 2005; 4.2.19). The audience would understand readily enough from his own words that Malvolio's prison is very dark.

Suppose, then, Feste opens the stage curtains, revealing Malvolio *within*, after or while saying 'What hoa, I say, Peace in this prison.' After his interrogation of Malvolio in his guise of Sir Topas, he would briefly close the curtains after or while saying to Malvolio, 'Fare thee well: remaine thou still in darkenesse, . . . Fare thee well' (TLN 2042–5; 4.2.57–60), rejecting his imploring cry 'Sir *Topas*, sir *Topas*' (TLN 2046; 4.2.61). Then the Fool probably takes off his beard and gown. After singing in his own voice, and ignoring Malvolio's repeated addresses to him, he responds to the voice of the unseen Malvolio by saying 'Who calles, ha?' (TLN 2064; 4.2.79). While pretending that he has just recognised the offstage voice as the steward's ('M. *Maluolio?*' he asks in feigned surprise (TLN 2069; 4.2.84)), he would disclose Malvolio again. This time, he has to change his voice as he switches roles between himself and Sir Topas. As well as disguising his voice, he might well turn his face away from Malvolio, in order to ensure that he is not recognised. The steward repeatedly insists on his sanity. When he says 'By this hand I am [as well in my wittes, as any man in Illyria]' (TLN 2094; 4.2.109 [TLN 2091–2; 4.2.106–7]), it is likely that the gesture of his hand would be visible to the audience. The Fool would finally close the curtains before singing the scene-closing song (TLN 2104; 4.2.119). The repeated opening and closing of the curtains could symbolise Malvolio's shifts of mood between despair and the hope of being delivered from the dark prison. It remains the case, of course, that the whole scene could be played with Malvolio remaining unseen.[61] It is certainly true that *Twelfth Night*, 4.2 is Feste's big scene rather than Malvolio's: the scene's focus is on the Fool's skilful performance. What I have suggested above is, however, a possible interpretation of the stage direction '*Maluolio within*', which is consistent with the varied stage practice that I have described earlier.

Twelfth Night, as we know, was performed at the Middle Temple on 2 February 1602, and this raises the further intriguing question as to how it was staged there. It is questionable whether the two doorways of the great hall screen were used for actors' entrances and exits. The great distance between the screen and the high table, at which distinguished members of the audience must have been seated, might have made the actors avoid using the area in front of the screen as the main acting area.[62] Even if the space behind the screen served as a tiring-house, we cannot be sure whether it was used for Malvolio's prison. Given these uncertainties, the only thing we can say with confidence is that Shakespearean actors were versatile, and they would have done whatever was practical or possible at the time and in the venue they were using. However, when the Lord Chamberlain's–King's Men and other playing companies performed at their own playhouses, the performances would have taken place in accordance with the principles underlying the diverse practice set out in this chapter. These principles we may summarise as follows: the places behind the three openings in the tiring-house wall often served as *within*; the central space behind the stage hangings was the best position for actors who had much to say from offstage; and the actor who is referred to as *within* the tiring-house was not necessarily out of sight of the audience.

The need to take into account the possibility that the stage doors were open even in scenes where characters are positioned *within* leads inevitably to the question of whether the stage doors were usually open or closed during the performance. Before proceeding to this question, however, it is necessary first to look at those examples where '*within*' is accompanied by '*above*' or its equivalent, which we have set aside until now. The existence of these variants suggests that there is more to learn about the usage of '*within*' and '*above*' and about the use of the upper level of the tiring-house.

CHAPTER 3

'Music within' *and* 'Music above'

Shakespeare and his contemporaries used music, both on and offstage, for different kinds of dramatic effect. A well-known example involving offstage music is *King Richard II*, Act 5, scene 5, where the imprisoned king is murdered. At the beginning of the scene Richard, alone in his prison cell, meditates on the human condition, concluding bleakly, 'But whatere I be, / Nor I, nor any man, that but man is, / With nothing shall be pleasde, till he be easde, / With being nothing' (Q1, I4r; 5.5.38–41). At this point he hears music played offstage:

               Musicke do I heare,   *the musicke plaies*
Ha ha keepe time, how sowre sweete Musicke is
When time is broke, and no proportion kept.
So is it in the musike of mens liues:
And here haue I the daintinesse of eare
To checke time broke in a disordered string:
But for the concord of my state and time,
Had not an eare to heare my true time broke,
I wasted time, and now doth time waste me:

                                                     (I4r; 5.5.41–9)

The stage direction specifies neither the kind of music nor its location, though the reference to 'string' would imply a stringed instrument such as a lute. M. M. Mahood suggests that the groom who enters shortly after ('*Enter a groome of the stable*' (I4v; 5.5.66)) may also be the musician,[1] but Charles R. Forker questions 'whether a lowly groom would possess or could play a lute, normally an instrument of the aristocracy'.[2] The point is, however, not the identity of the musician but the effect of the music on Richard himself. The music, traditionally a symbol of personal, social and celestial harmony, prompts a series of further reflections. The lutenist's 'disordered string' becomes an emblem of the gross disharmony of his fall: once an anointed king, now a prisoner.[3] It reminds him too, more piercingly, of his own responsibility for what has happened: 'I wasted time, and now doth time waste me.' The digression on time that follows concludes with the inescapable fact that Bullingbrook has triumphed over him, a recognition so intolerable that he instantly projects his exasperation on to the offstage music: 'This music maddes me, let it sound no more' (I4v; 5.5.61). And yet in a typical shift of mood he expresses a final lachrymose gratitude to the unseen musician: 'For tis a signe of loue: and loue to Richard, / Is a strange brooch in this al-hating world' (I4v; 5.5.65–6). It is not clear whether the music halts instantly at Richard's command, though it has presumably stopped by the time of the groom's entrance five lines later. In the 1590s when this play was first staged, the public playhouses appear not to have had a special music room. To judge from what we have learned in the previous chapter, the music would probably be delivered from the discovery space covered by hangings, although there is no reason why it should not be heard from another location within the tiring-house.

The existence of a 'music room' is mentioned in some early modern play texts. For example, a stage direction in Middleton's *A Chaste Maid in Cheapside*, first performed at the Swan about 1613, and first printed in 1630, calls for '*a sad Song in the Musicke-Roome*' (Q1, K2v). The term 'music room' is sometimes linked with '*above*' in stage directions. *The Parson's Wedding*, written by a Caroline courtier, Thomas Killigrew, offers '*Enter Mistress* Pleasant, *Widow* Wild *her Aunt, and* Secret *her Woman, above in the Musick Room* . . .' (F1, K2v). The following two pairs of stage directions are also worth mentioning:

Pythia *speaks in the Musick-room behind the Curtains.*
Pythia *above, behinde the Curtains.* (*The Thracian Wonder* Q1, D1v)[4]

Callumney *above.*
Enter Callumney *in the Musique Room.* (Jordan, *Money is an Ass* Q1, E2v, E3r)

In each pair, the first direction, printed in the left margin of the quarto earlier than the second, appears to have been an annotation by a bookkeeper, and the second direction, printed at the actual moment of the action, in the central position on its own line of the text, must have been written by the author. These and other stage directions suggest that certain theatres had a special music room over the stage, that it was equipped with curtains, and that the area occasionally served as an acting space. Jasper Mayne, in *Jonsonus Virbius*, praises Ben Jonson for his realism by saying 'Thou laidst no sieges to the *Musique-Roome*' (Q1, E4r). Since sieges are laid to castles whose defenders appear above on the 'walls', Mayne in effect suggests that the music room and the upper playing area are the same place.[5]

54 'Music within' *and* 'Music above'

As for music-room curtains, *The Thracian Wonder* offers a further hint. After speaking *'above, behinde the Curtains'*, the goddess Pythia then *'Throws down a paper'* (Q1, D1v) to the priest below, most probably through a gap between the curtains. The music-room curtains would have been at the front edge of the gallery, as can be seen in the frontispiece to Kirkman's *The Wits, or Sport upon Sport* (see Figure 5).[6] Perhaps, in any commercial theatre, whether it had a music room above or not, there may have been a set of hangings at the back of the upper performance area, which could have

Figure 5. The Frontispiece to Francis Kirkman's *The Wits, or Sport upon Sport* (1662). Note the upper curtained area, presumably a music-room.

concealed the interior of the tiring-house upper floor. However, the design of the upper playing level, especially the placement of the curtains may well have been changeable and we should also keep in mind that St Paul's playhouse appears to have had two music rooms, as mentioned in Chapter 1.

In the Swan sketch, made around 1596, the gallery over the stage, containing people looking like spectators, does not appear to be functioning as a music room. But during the period between de Witt's visit to London and the first performance of *A Chaste Maid*, there was a major change in public playhouses such as the Swan and the Globe concerning the use of music. The adoption of *entr'acte* music is generally thought to have changed the use of the upper performance area in public theatres, and evidence of act divisions in early modern play texts does indeed suggest that after around 1607 adult companies gradually began to follow the practice of private theatres in performing plays with intervals between the acts, and that act-intervals were normal by 1616.[7] Discussions of the existence of music rooms in the Globe and other public playhouses often involve an interpretation of the occurrences of '*Music within*' and '*Music above*' directions, and in this chapter I will explore what these directions might indicate, while also reconsidering the use of the upper level in both public and private theatres.

THE RECEIVED THEORY

In his 1960 article, 'Was There a Music-room in Shakespeare's Globe?', Richard Hosley concluded that the Globe playhouse did not have a music room before 1609. He argued that it was not there until after the King's Men had acquired the indoor theatre of Blackfriars and so adopted *entr'acte* music to Globe performances under the influence of the Blackfriars.[8] This theory has been widely accepted, and the fact that the company's plays after 1608 show act divisions must be related to the adoption of *entr'acte* music.

In early public-theatre plays, as Hosley observes, offstage music is invariably noted as '*within*' and never as '*above*'. Some examples are:

Song, to the Musique wthin. (Munday, *John a Kent and John a Cumber* MS, TLN 1149)

They kneele, and solemn musicke the while within, . . . (Heywood, *2 Edward IV* Q1, T2r)

Here some strange solemn musicke like belles is heard within. (*A Warning for Fair Women* Q1, D1r)

On the other hand, early private-theatre plays contain some '*music above*' directions. The following are from pre-1609 plays performed at Blackfriars by the Children of the Queen's Revels/ the Revels/ the Blackfriars:

A short song to a soft Musique aboue. (Marston, *The Wonder of Women, or Sophonisba* Q1, F1v)
Musique and a Song, aboue, . . . (Chapman, *The Conspiracy and Tragedy of Byron* Q1, K4r)

Similar directions appear in late King's Men plays.

Musicke aboue and a song. (Massinger, *The Roman Actor* Q1, D4r)
She dies. still Musicke aboue. (Davenant, *The Cruel Brother* Q1, I1v)
Musicke aboue, a song of pleasure. (Massinger, *The Picture* Q1, H1v)

Unfortunately, no '*music above*' directions can be found in King's Men plays between 1609 and 1613, when the first Globe burned down. However, it may well be that the acquisition of the Blackfriars and its consort musicians led to the reconstruction of the Globe's stage balcony to install a music room there around 1609 and other adult companies gradually followed suit.[9] Hosley's conclusion seems therefore, on the face of it, entirely acceptable.

It is nevertheless over-simple, and we need to re-examine the theory for at least two reasons. First, plays written for the King's Men after 1609 still contain a fair number of '*music within*' directions. In contrast, the references to '*music above*' are relatively few, even if we allow that the location of music is rarely specified in early modern play texts. The '*music above*' directions that we have are rather special cases.[10] As for the above-cited example from *The Cruel Brother*, the departed woman's brother comments on the music as follows: 'Hearke! / As she ascends, the Spheares doe welcome her, / With their owne Musicke' (Q1, I1v). In this case, despite the existence of a music room above in the Blackfriars theatre, the writer of the stage direction – most probably the author himself – nevertheless wanted to specify the location of the heavenly music as *above*.[11] Second, and more important, '*within*' and '*above*' are somewhat slippery terms. We have become used to thinking that '*within*' refers to the stage level of the inside of the tiring-house, and that '*above*' refers to the playing area over the stage. However, the distinction between the two terms was not so clear-cut in early modern theatrical terminology.

'*ABOVE WITHIN*'

In some stage directions '*within*' is used to indicate the use of the upper level, as in the following example:

Enter Talbot and Burgonie without: within, Pucell, Charles, Bastard, and Reignier on the Walls. (*1 Henry VI* F1, TLN 1471–2; 3.2.40)

The terms '*without*' and '*within*' refer here at least as much to the fictional world of the play as to the physical structure of the playhouse. That is to say, the performance area over the stage represents the city walls, with the result that the characters, led by la Pucelle, are all 'within' the city, whereas the English forces remain 'without'. Since the theatrical sense of '*within*' seems present in the stage direction, it appears logical to regard the upper playing area, which serves as the '*Walls*', as '*within*'. This may, however, be an exceptional case. As Alan C. Dessen and Leslie Thomson point out, examples of '*without*' as the opposite of '*within*' are rare: '*without*' usually means '*within*' except when it occurs in the same stage direction as '*within*'.[12] The F1 text of *Richard II* contains what appears, on the face of it, to be a similar stage direction: '*Parle without, and answere within: then a Flourish. Enter on the Walls, Richard, Carlile, Aumerle, Scroop, Salisbury*' (TLN 1646–8; 3.3.61).[13] But in this instance, the contrast of the '*Parle without*' and the '*answere within*' refers, respectively, to what is visible to the audience and what is concealed. The term '*within*' here does not refer to the '*Walls*' represented by the performance area over the stage, although it may refer to the space behind the upper playing area. It is likely that the parley from the main stage was answered from the upper floor of the tiring-house, especially if the trumpeters of the fanfare were to make an entrance on to the upper performance area to announce the royal entry there.[14]

Munday's *Fedele and Fortunio* offers an example where '*within*' seems to be a compressed way of referring to a more complex state of affairs:

Fedele and Pedante speake out at a windowe within. (Q1, G2v)

Although the 1585 Quarto appears to contain additions and alterations made for the court performance mentioned in its title-page ('*Translated out of Italian, and set* downe according as it hath beene presented before the Queenes moste excellent Maiestie' (Q1, A1r)), the play was probably first performed at a commercial playhouse.[15] In any event, this stage direction may well reflect the contemporary usage of theatrical terms, because Munday had himself been an actor,[16] and Luigi Pasqualigo's *Il Fedele*

(Venice, 1576), upon which Munday's play is based, contains no such stage direction. The direction does not necessarily call for the two characters' entrance. Although Fedele might make his appearance on the upper gallery representing the 'windowe', Pedante would remain unseen, positioned somewhat away from it. Pedante's speech, 'I am so fast wrapt in the vpper sheete. / That I can not get out' (G3r) indicates that he is, in fictional terms, in bed. Probably, what 'within' refers to in this example is both the upper playing area itself and the upper floor of the tiring-house, that is, the space behind the playing place.

In at least one case, *'within'* is clearly differentiated from *'window'*:

Goes from the Window, and calls within. (Davenant, *The Distresses* F1, 4E4v)

What *'within'* refers to in this stage direction is evidently the upper floor of the tiring-house, out of sight of the audience. It is unlikely that the character, Claramante, would call from the main stage level, because it would take her a certain length of time to make an offstage descent, and also because she is to reappear on the upper playing area only seven lines after ('*Enter* Claramante *above*' (4E4v)). A similar instance can be seen in *Romeo and Juliet*, 2.2, where Juliet occupies the upper playing space representing the window of her bedchamber. In this case the word *'window'* does not occur in stage directions, but it does figure in the much-quoted opening line of the dialogue between Romeo and Juliet: 'But soft, what light through yonder window breaks?' (Q2, D1v; 2.2.2). When the Nurse calls Juliet three times from *'within'*/*'Within'* (as the F1 text adds the direction at TLN 938, 952, 954; 2.2.136, 149, 151), even if the Nurse was actually on the upper level of the tiring-house, she would have remained out of sight, positioned away from the performance area.

Consider also the following passage from Fletcher's *Love's Pilgrimage*:

GENT.	Ho Generall,
	Look out, Antonio is in distresse.
	Enter Rodorigo above.
THEO.	Antonio?
LEOC.	Antonio! 'tis he.
ROD. *within*.	Ho, [Gunner][17] make a shot into the Town,
	Ile part you: bring away Antonio *a shot.*
	Into my Cabben. *Exit Attendents and Townsmen.*
GENT.	I will do that office.
	I fear It is the last, that I shall do him.
	Exit Soldiers and Gentlemen with Marckantonio.
	(F1, 8C1v)

When Rodorigo shouts 'Ho, Gunner . . .', he is certainly on the upper level. What is not certain is whether, in this instance, '*within*' is used in the same sense as '*above*' ('in sight of the audience on the upper gallery'). It is just possible that '*within*' and '*above*' refer to different parts of the upper level, and that Rodorigo withdraws a few steps from the performance area and becomes temporarily out of sight of the audience while he gives an order to the unseen gunner. After the shot is heard, he returns to the playing area to give another instruction to the gentleman below: 'Ile part you: bring away Antonio / Into my Cabben.' But it would seem awkward to have him make an exit and then return immediately. What is more likely is that he would only turn his face towards the inside to give the order to the gunner. In which case, '*within*' may be used in the same sense as '*above*' or, perhaps, in the sense of 'towards within'.

Another Fletcherian play provides a further instance:

> *Enter Tavern Boyes &c.*
> BOY. Score a gallon of Sack, and a pinte of Olives to the Vnicorne.
> *Above within.* Why drawer?
> BOY. A non, a non.
>
> (*The Captain* F1, 2H3v)

In this case, where an offstage voice is directed to call an onstage tavern boy, '*within*' is undoubtedly used to refer to the space out of sight of the audience on the upper level. When *The Captain* was first performed sometime between 1609 and 1612, whether at the Globe or at the Blackfriars, the upper playing area of the playhouse would have been equipped with curtains. The voice calling a tavern boy might therefore have been heard from the curtained area on the upper gallery, though it is equally likely that the voice came from the space behind the upper gallery. Later in the same scene, another two offstage voices are also directed to call an onstage tavern boy: '*Within.* Drawer' (2H3v); '*Within cry drawer*' (2H3v). It may be that these calls were also intended to be heard from *above within*, but this is by no means certain.

Brome's *The Novella*, performed at Blackfriars by the King's Men, contains a similar example. In Act 4, scene 1, the gallery over the stage represents the window of Flavia's chamber, she and her maid Astutta being present. Astutta says to Flavia, 'Your Father's coming up' (O1, L3v). Flavia's father, Guadagni, then calls from '*Within*', 'Where are you *Flavia*?' (L3v), followed shortly by his entry '*above*' (L4r). The stage direction '*Within*' here clearly refers to the upper floor of the tiring-house. A short time later in the same scene, when the upper playing space becomes empty, and when the action transfers to the main stage level, Guadagni's voice is heard from '*Within*' calling Nanulo (L4v) before he enters with him. What the direction '*Within*' refers to this time is undoubtedly the stage level of the tiring-house. It is noteworthy that both the upper floor and the main stage level of the tiring-house are equally treated as '*Within*' in the same scene.

The occurrences of such phrases as '*Above within*' and 'at a windowe within' confirm that '*within*' could refer to the upper level of the tiring-house. When the use of the upper playing area is involved, the space behind could well be treated as '*within*'. We might then reasonably ask whether '*within*', on its own, can sometimes refer specifically to the upper level, even when it is neither accompanied by nor used in relation to '*above*', '*at a window*' or the like. Some play texts offer suggestive examples in this respect. Middleton and Rowley's *The Changeling* has two scenes in which madmen shout from '*Within*'/'*within*' (Q1, C2v, E1r, E2r). The 1653 Quarto, which was published a long time after the play was first acted at the Cockpit playhouse in Drury Lane, is likely to have been printed from a transcript of a playbook.[18] These and other hospital scenes are usually ascribed to Rowley.[19] The earlier scene has nothing to indicate for certain that the madmen call out from the upper level, but in the later scene it seems very probable that they would have shouted from the upper level of the tiring-house. In the later scene, when a madman's voice is heard from '*within*', 'Bounce, bounce, he falls, he falls', Isabella, who is on the main stage, says to another onstage character, Lollio, 'Heark you, your scholars in the upper room are out of order' (E1r). He exits after replying to her, '. . . I'le go up, & play left handed *Orlando* amongst the madmen' (E1r). These and other speeches suggest that the madmen's ward, unlike the one for idiots, lies upstairs. A short time later in the same scene, another madman's cry is heard from '*within*', 'Catch there, catch the last couple in hell' (E2r), and Lollio exits again. This time he actually appears on the gallery over the stage ('*Enter Lol. above*' (E2r)), and scarcely has he exited from there than madmen also appear there in a grotesque manner ('*Mad-men above*, some as birds, others as beasts' (E2r)).

Look also at Fletcher's *The Night Walker*, Act 4. In the middle of its first scene, Lurcher, in his guise as a constable, knocks at the door of Justice Algripe's house and a servant answers from '*Within*': 'Whose there?' (Q1, G4r). Here, the servant is most probably placed behind the stage door. Although he tells Lurcher that his master is not available, Lurcher insists that he meet the Justice. Then the Justice's voice is heard from '*Within*': 'Who's that?' (G4v). Since Lurcher cries to him, 'Please your worship, come downe, Ile make you happy' (G4v), '*Within*' refers this time to the upper level of the tiring-house. The Justice might appear on the balcony in order to exchange speeches with Lurcher, although there is no stage direction indicating his entrance there. A further example can be seen in Beaumont's *The Knight of the Burning Pestle*, performed by the Children of the Revels. Towards the end of Act 3, Mistress Merry-thought and Michael return to their house, but Old Merry-thought refuses them admittance. Q1's stage directions indicate that he delivers speeches and songs from '*within*' (G3r, G3v, G4r). The songs' words, '*Go from my window*' (G3v) and '*Come aloft Boyes, aloft*' (G4v)[20] seem to confirm that he is on the upper level.[21] Old Merry-thought is referred to as speaking and singing from *within* throughout the episode, but in this instance his presence on the gallery would have been preferable to his remaining unseen.

Admittedly, the use of '*within*' to refer to the tiring-house upper level is by no means common: the above-cited examples are special cases.[22] But although special, they constituted acceptable practice to early modern playwrights, players and theatre personnel. In conclusion, '*within*' could refer to both the upper and lower levels within the tiring-house. It was probably because the upper performance area was continuous with the inside of the tiring-house that the playing space, even when in full sight of the audience, not covered by curtains, might have occasionally counted as '*within*'.

'*UNSEEN ABOVE*'

Since '*within*' could sometimes be equivalent to '*above*', it is at least possible that '*above*', the most common term for the upper performance area, could occasionally be '*within*'. Are there instances where '*above*' refers to the upper floor of the tiring-house, behind the gallery over the stage? When, for example, '*above*' refers to a sound or noise, it may well indicate the use of an unseen space, as in '*Trampling above*' (Fletcher, *The Chances* F1, 3B4v). However, what '*above*' refers to in this stage direction might be the curtained music room rather than the space behind, whether the play (written c.1617) was staged at the Globe or at the Blackfriars.

A more suggestive example can be seen in a late Caroline play, *The Court Beggar*, written by Brome and performed by Beeston's Boys at the Cockpit. In Act 3 Lady Strangelove calls out: 'Helpe, helpe, here helpe – ha –' (O1, Q5r). She is directed to make this cry '*Vnseen Above*'. She then cries again, 'Help, help, a rape, a rape, murder, help!' (Q5r), and then cries for the third time, 'Is there helpe, helpe, helpe?' (Q5r). Although the location of the second cry is not specified, and although the third cry is merely directed to be delivered from '*Above*', it is clear that the lady should remain out of sight throughout. Referring to the third cry, an onstage character says, 'O tis my Lady in the Madmans chamber' (Q5r), and when the doctor treating the madman subsequently cries, 'Help here, help the Lady; help the Lady', he is specifically directed to make an appearance on the upper level: '*Doctor looks out above*' (Q5r). Then the madman, Ferdinand, shouts from '*Above unseen*': 'Away *Medusa*. Hence, thou hast transformd me. Stone, stone, I am all stone. Bring morter and make a bul-wark of me' (Q5r). He speaks two more speeches, probably from the same place, although it is not specifically indicated. This example suggests that even when the presence of characters is concerned, '*above*' refers sometimes to a place where they can remain unseen. In this scene, either the tiring-house upstairs or the upper performance area, covered by the music-room curtains, would have served as such a place. Which is actually referred to in this scene depends largely on whether the doctor was intended to enter on to the upper playing area or whether he was merely expected to show himself between the music-room curtains. If the doctor made an entrance on to the gallery, Lady Strangelove and Ferdinand would have used the space behind it. If, instead, the doctor merely peeped between the music-room curtains, the lady and the madman could have shouted from behind the curtains.

Consider another example from Fletcher's *Monsieur Thomas*. In this example '*above*' is not accompanied by '*unseen*' or the like but is used on its own. In Act 3, scene 3, Thomas comes at night to the lodge where Mary stays alone with her attendants. Despite Mary's earlier refusal of his advances, he stands under her window, accompanied by his servant Launcelot and a fiddler, and their noisy song soon causes Mary and her maid to appear on the balcony. Mary asks the Maid to get rid of him, which she does by initially pretending to be her mistress and inviting him to climb up and join her. As he reaches the balcony, his ascent is brought to a halt by the sudden appearance of a fellow-conspirator, Madge, wearing a devil's mask. She then tries to kiss him, and, in some dismay, he falls to the ground.

MAID   *Come up to my window love, come, come, come,*
Come to my window my deere,
The winde, nor the raine, shall trouble thee againe,
But thou shalt be lodged here.
THOM.   And art thou strong enough?
LAN.   Vp, up, I warrant ye.
MARY   What do'st thou meane to doe?

MAID	Good Mistresse peace,	
	I'le warrant ye wee'l coole him: *Madge,*	*Madge above.*
MADGE	I am ready.	
THO.	*The love of Greece and it tickled him so,*	
	That he devised a way to goe.	
	Now sing the Duke of Northumberland.	
FIDLER	*And climbing to promotion,*	
	He fell down suddenly.	*Madge with a divels*
		vizard roring, offers to kisse him, and he fals down.
MAID	Farewell sir.	

(Q1, H1v)

When Madge answers the Maid's call, saying 'I am ready', she would not be visible to the audience, so her sudden appearance a few lines later makes all the greater impact, simultaneously terrifying for Thomas but comic for the audience as he tumbles backwards. The first stage direction for her reads merely '*Madge above*' and does not include '*Enter*', but this is not to say that an actor was normally meant to be unseen in those cases when the simple instruction '*above*' is used rather than the more explicit '*enter above*'; earlier in the same scene, for example, Mary's maid is given the direction '*Maid above*' (H1r) and it is obvious from the context that she should actually appear. What the stage direction '*Madge above*' indicates is almost certainly that she first of all positions herself out of sight behind the upper playing area and then comes forward at the critical moment to accost her intended victim.

A Shakespearean play offers a problematic scene involving '*above*'. In *Julius Caesar*, 5.3, after sending Titinius off to the field, Cassius orders Pindarus to mount a hill and observe Titinius from there. Pindarus would begin to move immediately after Cassius has said 'Go *Pindarus*, get higher on that hill, / ... / And tell me what thou not'st about the Field' (TLN 2500–2; 5.3.20–2) and he should get *above* before Cassius cries 'Sirra, what newes?' (TLN 2505; 5.3.25) or at least before he himself shouts 'O my Lord' (TLN 2506; 5.3.26) from '*Aboue*' (TLN 2506; 5.3.26). Pindarus is therefore allowed only two and a half lines, or perhaps three lines at most, to ascend to the upper level. His report from *above* causes Cassius to order him to 'come downe' (TLN 2514; 5.3.33) and he then returns to Cassius in only two lines: '*Enter Pindarus*' (TLN 2517; 5.3.36). The editors of some recent editions of the play suggest the possibility that Pindarus made his moves only on the stage, in sight of the audience: Arthur Humphreys and Marvin Spevack assume the onstage presence of some structure representing the 'hill';[23] David Daniell suggests that Pindarus 'may simply stand upstage'.[24] It is certainly true that Pindarus is given no exit direction when he is ordered to mount the hill. Since, however, he is directed to '*Enter*' again a short time later in the same scene, he was most probably meant to exit, ascend the offstage stairs to the upper level, speak from there, descend to the main stage level and then re-enter the stage. Even if the actor began to move from near his exit door, whether he could have appeared on the stage balcony in the space of two and a half or so lines is questionable.[25] As Bernard Beckerman has concluded, 'we must suppose that either Cassius spoke very slowly or Pindarus moved very quickly'.[26] We can perhaps refine the view a little further. '*Aboue*' is only attached to the speech prefix '*Pind.*' and Pindarus is not specifically directed to enter above. It is therefore possible that he might not appear on the playing area; he could deliver his speeches from the tiring-house upstairs, unseen by Cassius and the audience. In which case, the distance he had to move offstage would have been somewhat shorter than is usually assumed. I do not think that this completely solves the above-mentioned 'two to three lines' problem, but it is a possible form of staging consistent with what is indicated in the only surviving text.

Fletcher and Massinger's *The Double Marriage*, acted at Blackfriars, contains a stage direction referring to the 'top'. It occurs in the following passage:

BOTS.	...	
	Ho, in the hold.	*Enter a Boy.*
BOY.	Here, here.	
BOTES.	To th' main top boy.	
	And thou kenst a ship that dares defie us,	
	Here's Gold.	
BOY.	I am gon.	*Exit Boy.*
BOTS.	Come sirs, a queint Levet.	*Trump. a levet.*
	To waken our brave Generall. Then to our labour.	
	Enter Duke of Sesse above and his daughter Martia like an Amazon.	
SESS.	I thank you loving mates; I thank you all.	
...		
BOTS.	Call up the Master, and all the Mates.	
	Enter below the Master and Saylers.	
...		
MAST.	We have liv'd all with you,	*Boy a top.*
	And will die with you Generall.	
SESS.	I thank you Gentlemen.	
BOY *above*.	A Sayle, a Sayle.	
MAST.	A cheerfull sound.	
BOY.	A Sayle.	
...		

BOY.	Of Naples Naples, I think of Naples, Master,	
	Me thinks I see the Armes.	
MAST.	Up, up another,	
	And give more certain signes.	*Exit Saylor.*

...

SAYL. *above.*	Ho.	
SESS.	Of whence now?	
SAYL.	Of Naples, Naples, Naples.	
	I see her top flag how she quarters Naples.	
	I heare her Trumpets.	
SESS.	Down, she's welcome to us.	*Exit Mast. Bots. Gun. Sayl.*
		(F1, 5D1v–5D2r)

As the dialogue suggests, the main stage serves as the main deck of a ship at sea, and the upper playing space represents the quarterdeck. Despite the speech prefixes '*Boy above*' and '*Sayl. above*', neither the boy nor the sailor would join the Duke and his daughter on the upper playing area. They have been sent to the maintop, and not to the quarterdeck. It has been suggested that the 'top' is a term for the level above the upper playing space.[27] I am however somewhat sceptical about a special place for the 'top'. It is not certain that there was a third level in the Blackfriars tiring-house.[28] It seems to me more plausible that in the passage cited above, the direction '*Boy a top*' works in fictional terms, meaning 'Boy on the maintop of the ship', while the speech prefixes '*Boy above*' and '*Sayl. above*' work in theatrical terms, meaning 'Boy/Sailor on the upper floor'. Neither the boy nor the sailor is given an entry direction, and so I think it likely that in the two speech prefixes '*above*' refers to the space behind the performance area, where they remain unseen. If the boy and the sailor delivered their speeches from there, they could well give the impression of shouting from the maintop of the ship.

It may safely be concluded from these examples that in English Renaissance terminology, '*above*' could refer not only to the upper playing area itself but also to the space behind; '*within*' could also be '*above*', and vice versa.

POST-1609 '*MUSIC WITHIN*' DIRECTIONS

Plays written for the King's Men after their acquisition of the Blackfriars still contain a fair number of '*music within*' directions. Some of these may indicate the use of the upper level. We have seen that some Fletcher plays contain references to the presence of characters on the upper level as '*within*'. As for offstage music, *The Chances* provides an interesting example. When in Act 2, scene 2, '*Lute sounds within*' (F1, 3A4r), the offstage music is described in the dialogue as being performed 'Above in my Masters chamber' (3A4r). Another stage direction indicates that a song is then heard from the same place: '*Sing within a little*' (3A4r). What '*within*' refers to in these two stage directions may well be the curtained music room above the stage.

Fletcher and Massinger's *The Little French Lawyer* provides 'A Horrid noise of Musique within' (F1, K4r). This stage direction occurs at the very beginning of Act 5. At the end of the previous act, Lamira and Anabell, who had been captured, were led off to be confined in a vault. The dialogue of Act 5 opens with Lamira's words spoken to Anabell: 'O Cousen how I shake, all this long night. / What frights and noises we have heard' (K4r). The interval between Acts 4 and 5 was evidently intended to be filled with unpleasant music. If the stage direction refers to the act-interval music, the 'Horrid noise of Musique within' might very well be delivered from the music room above, with the musicians being in full sight of the audience. The music-room curtains would have been opened at the end of Act 4 and closed again just before the beginning of the dialogue of Act 5. In the new scene, the ladies are still distressed by continual sounds of music: '*A strange Musick. Sackbut & Troup musick*' (K4r)[29]; '*Lowder*' (K4r); '*New sound within*' (K4r). These were probably delivered from the curtained music room. The first two are heard very early in the scene, and although there are about forty lines between the second and the third, there is no important reason why the musicians would have come downstairs for delivering the '*New sound within*'.[30]

Other Fletcher plays offer '*Musick above*' (*The Woman's Prize* F1, 5O1v) and '*Trumpets small above*' (*Four Plays in One* F1, 8F3v).[31] In each case the musicians should be unseen, and in both stage directions, therefore, '*above*' probably refers to the curtained music room over the stage. Clearly, one should not assume that Fletcher and his colleagues consistently used '*music within*' and '*music above*' in the same way, referring to the curtained music room over the stage. It seems, however, certain that they did not always differentiate between '*music within*' and '*music above*'.

The Hecate material in the witch scenes of *Macbeth* (F1, TLN 1429–69, 1566–72, 1672–80; 3.5, 4.1.39–43, 4.1.125–32) is generally regarded as a later addition, most probably by Middleton, perhaps after Shakespeare's retirement in or about 1613. Although the F1 *Macbeth* may be a version prepared for a court performance, the text appears to reflect the normal practice of the Globe/Blackfriars stage as well.[32] The end of Hecate's long speech in 3.5 is interrupted by offstage music and song:

HEC.   ...
                                              Musicke, and a Song.
  Hearke, I am call'd my little Spirit see
  Sits in a Foggy cloud, and stayes for me.
                          Sing within. Come away, come away, &c.
                                        (TLN 1464–7; 3.5.33–5)

The direction to sing is repeated two lines later. The second direction seems an amplification of the first. Here, '*within*' probably refers to the music room above, whether the F1 *Macbeth* was acted at the Blackfriars or at the Globe. Perhaps, as Hecate's words suggest, while other spirits are singing 'Come away, come away . . .' above in the music room, a spirit descends from the heavens and he and Hecate make a flying departure, although there is no stage direction to this effect.

This interpretation has a further support from Middleton's *The Witch*, performed by the King's Men at Blackfriars. It survives in a manuscript transcribed by Ralph Crane. Act 3, scene 3 of the play contains the full words of a song beginning with '*Come away: come away: / Heccat: Heccat, Come away*' (TLN 1331–2). The song is written in the form of a dialogue, with voices offstage calling on Hecate to join them in their aerial exercises, followed by Hecate's onstage replies to them, which in turn are followed by those offstage callings. What is interesting about it is that the location of the voices is specified first as '*in ye aire*' (TLN 1332, 1337, 1341) and then as '*aboue*' (TLN 1345, 1371) in marginal stage directions. It is very likely that the direction '*Sing within*' in *Macbeth*, 3.5 refers to the same location as the direction '*in ye aire*' in *The Witch*, 3.3: on the upper level, probably out of sight of the audience, that is to say, in the curtained music room over the stage. As for *The Witch*'s change of direction from '*in ye aire*' to '*aboue*', it may indicate that the singers should show themselves at this moment, though it is equally possible that '*in ye aire*' and '*aboue*' are used in the same meaning.[33]

EARLY PUBLIC-THEATRE PLAYS

Although public playhouses may not have developed a special music room at a time when music was occasional and ad hoc, it may be worth considering the possibility that in early public theatres the upper level sometimes served as a temporary music room. In Richard Hosley's view, 'the only adaptation necessary would have been to fit up the window of the chosen box with hangings in order to comply with the custom of concealing musicians during the action of a play'.[34] But is it really the case that, as

Hosley says, no early public-theatre play requires a curtain above (at the front edge of the gallery)?[35]

Take, for example, *Titus Andronicus*, an early Shakespearean play, whose first known performance took place on 23 January 1594, probably at the Rose.[36] In Act 5, scene 2, where Tamora and her two sons visit the mad Titus, Tamora tells the sons to 'Knocke at his studie' (Q1, I3r; 5.2.5) and they obey her: '*They knocke and Titus opens his studie doore*' (I3r; 5.2.8). Since Tamora repeatedly says to Titus, 'Come downe and welcome me' (I3r; 5.2.33) / 'come downe and welcome mee' (I3v; 5.2.43), clearly he was intended to appear on the upper level, not in the discovery space to which the word '*studie*' would usually have referred. How the study door was achieved remains something of a question. One possibility is that Titus occupied a curtained section of the gallery above the stage, and opened the curtain, although if so, Tamora's sons could not have knocked at it.[37] The B-text of *Doctor Faustus*, which appears to reflect the additions made by William Bird and Samuel Rowley in 1602, has 'Enter Benuolio aboue at a window, in his nightcap: buttoning' (QB, E2v). Just before his entrance above, one of the onstage characters, Frederick, says, 'See, see his window's ope, we'l call to him' (E2v). A curtain concealing the upper performance area might have been intended to be drawn so as to indicate that Benvolio had just arisen from bed. However, it is equally possible that the audience was expected to imagine a casement window. In either event, it is true to say that the use of an upper curtain was by no means foreign to staging in early public theatres.

It is largely agreed that in early public theatres some part of the space above the stage was retained for the use of privileged spectators. But it is also certain that some part of the upper gallery was available for acting space. In Hosley's view, 'the gallery over the stage in the public playhouse of Shakespeare's time functioned primarily and constantly as a Lords' room, and only secondarily, occasionally, and then for relatively short periods as a raised production-area; and that during such periods it exercised both functions simultaneously'.[38] Even if any part of the upper gallery of public playhouses had not been available for a music room until around 1609, the space behind may occasionally have been occupied by musicians. Marston's *The Malcontent* was acted *c*.1603–04 at both private and public playhouses, first at the Blackfriars by the Chapel/Queen's Revels Children and later at the Globe by the King's Men. The Induction to the Globe version, which was specially written by Webster when the play was transferred from the Blackfriars, contains the phrase 'the not received custome of musicke in our Theater' (QC, A4r). This phrase is usually interpreted as a reference to *entr'acte* music, although another interpretation may be possible.³⁹ In both the original and adapted versions, Act 1 begins with offstage music: '*The vilest out of tune Musicke being heard*' (QA, B1r; QC, B1r). The origin of the music is identified by an onstage character, Bilioso, as 'the Malcontent *Maleuoles* chamber' (QA, B1r; QC, B1r), and when Malevole appears '*Out of his Chamber*' / '*Out of his chamber*' (QA, B1r/ QC, B1r), Pietro, who is also onstage, requires him to 'Come downe' (QA, B1r; QC, B1r). It is most likely that in the Blackfriars performance, Malevole's chamber was represented by the music room above. In the Globe performance, on the other hand, the origin of the music would probably have been the upper floor of the tiring-house.

Some pre-1609 Shakespearean plays include scenes where music may be heard from the upper level. In the second scene of the Induction to *The Taming of the Shrew*, the upper playing area is occupied by Sly, the Lord and his servants. When the Lord says to the drunkard, 'Wilt thou haue Musicke? Harke Apollo plaies, / And twentie caged Nightingales do sing' (F1, TLN 187–8; Induction.2.35–6), he may be referring to the presence of musicians on the gallery. If, however, there was not ample space above for the musicians, as well as for the actors, the '*Musick*' (TLN 187; Induction.2.35) may have been performed behind the gallery, on the upper floor of the tiring-house. It is, admittedly, equally possible that the musicians supplied the music from the main stage.

Consider the use of music in *The Merchant of Venice*. The Folio text of the play, which was printed from a copy of Q1, introduces musical effects in the Belmont casket-choosing scenes: '*Flo. Cornets*' (F1, TLN 517; 2.1.0); '*Cornets*' (TLN 565; 2.1.46); '*Flo. Cornets*' (TLN 1055; 2.8.0 [misplaced]⁴⁰); '*Flor. Cornets*' (TLN 1116; 2.9.3); '*Here Musicke*' (TLN 1406; 3.2.62). These instructions must have originated in the theatre. The specification of cornets indicates later staging for the indoor theatre at Blackfriars.⁴¹ Although the Q1 text does not contain these musical directions, nevertheless even in the first performances of the play at the Theatre a trumpet fanfare might well have been sounded for Morocco's arrivals and departures in 2.1 and 2.7 and Arragon's arrival and departure in 2.9, and there would probably have been a musical accompaniment to the '*Song the whilst Bassanio comments on the caskets to himselfe*' (Q1, E4r; 3.2.62). The curtained discovery space was required for the caskets and would therefore not be available for the use of the musicians and the singers. In the Morocco and Arragon scenes, the musicians might have positioned themselves unobtrusively around the stage door from which these suitors made their entrances and exits, while in the more dramatically significant Bassanio scene, the musicians and the singers might have taken a prominent position on the stage itself. We cannot be sure, and it is also possible that in these scenes the musicians and singers simply occupied the upper level. In the play's last scene the sound of music serves its traditional role as expressive of the achieved harmony. Having heard the news of Portia's approach, Lorenzo asks the messenger Stephano to go in the house and 'bring your musique [i.e., musicians] foorth into the ayre' (Q1, I2v; 5.1.53). In the meantime, he makes Jessica sit with him to enjoy the music together: 'How sweet the moone-light sleepes vpon this banke, / heere will we sit, and let the sounds of musique / creepe in our eares' (I2v; 5.1.54–6). He then calls to the musicians: 'Come hoe, and wake *Diana* with a himne, / with sweetest tutches pearce your mistres eare, / and draw her home with musique' (I2v; 5.1.66–8). The stage direction for the musicians merely reads '*play Musique*' (I2v; 5.1.68). The dialogue does not necessarily require their entrance on to the stage, and they might well have appeared on the stage balcony, transforming it into a window of the house, and played the music there, enhancing the blessedness of Portia's house in a final distant contrast to that of Shylock whose windows are closed against music (as he tells Jessica, 'stop my houses eares, I meane my casements, / let not the sound of shallow fopprie enter / my sober house' (D1r; 2.5.34–6)).

In *1 Henry IV*, 3.1, before Lady Mortimer sings a Welsh song for her husband, Glendower summons supernatural musicians and music is heard from offstage: '*The musicke playes*' (Q1, F3v; 3.1.228). The music may well have been performed on the upper floor of the tiring-house, if the performance takes even half-seriously Glendower's boast about the musicians being aerial spirits from far away: 'those musitions that shal play to you, / Hang in the aire a thousand leagues from hence, / And straight they shalbe here' (F3r; 3.1.223–5). However, Hotspur's response to the music, though sarcastic, may possibly suggest that it came from below the stage: 'Now I perceiue the diuell vnderstands Welsh' (F3v; 3.1.229).[42] When in *Pericles*, the titular character has regained his peace of mind, he hears 'the Musicke of the Spheres' (Q1, I1v; 5.1.229). Although there is no stage direction for the music, and although no other onstage characters can hear it, the 'Most heauenly Musicke' (I1v; 5.1.233) would have been shared by the audience.[43] I think it probable that when the play was performed at the Globe, most likely during the first six months of 1608, the celestial music came from the upper floor of the tiring-house, since that would have been the most symbolically appropriate location for such music.

In this context, consider *Richard II*, 5.5 again. Even in the early performances of the play the music might have come from the tiring-house upstairs.

In that case Richard's miserable state of imprisonment in the dungeon would have been spatially emphasised by the musician's use of the upper level.

An interesting example of music played not '*above*' but '*below*' occurs in *Antony and Cleopatra*, Act 4, scene 3. The stage direction reads '*Musicke of the Hoboyes is vnder the Stage*' (F1, TLN 2477; 4.3.12).⁴⁴ A soldier first describes it as 'Musicke i'th'Ayre' (TLN 2486; 4.3.13), and then another soldier identifies it (more accurately, at a literal level) as 'Vnder the earth' (TLN 2487; 4.3.13). Even if the music had been performed within the tiring-house, the audience would have willingly accepted it as music 'Vnder the earth'. But the Globe musicians used the space below the stage so as to achieve the required sound effect. This example suggests that Shakespeare and his company colleagues attached great importance to spatial meaning of the areas above, behind and below the stage. It is therefore extremely difficult to believe that they would have confined the location of offstage music to the stage level even before they had begun using the Blackfriars as well as the Globe.

Our analysis of the early modern usage of '*within*' and '*above*' does not necessarily support Hosley's theory. Certainly as far as the acoustics are concerned, the upper level seems the better place for musicians, a view confirmed by Hugh Richmond's reflections on the music room at the new Globe Theatre:

Experience in the restored Globe confirms the likelihood of the placing of musicians at the level of the gallery above the tiring house at the back of the Elizabethan stage. The acoustics have proved generally satisfactory, and the musicians' visibility is limited and therefore undistracting.⁴⁵

Until more secure evidence is found, it seems better to keep in mind the possibility that in public theatres as well, the upper level was available for musicians throughout, both before and after around 1609.

CHAPTER 4

Were the doors open or closed?

The stages of most London professional playhouses of the early modern period almost certainly had three doorways: a broad central opening and two flanking doorways. Although we cannot be certain, it is very likely that the central opening was fitted with double doors and the two flanking doorways had single doors. The central space, however, appears to have been normally covered by curtains or hangings of some kind, which could be drawn open as required, and so any double doors may well have been fastened against the tiring-house wall during the play's performance. It is reasonable to assume that the flanking doors opened out on to the stage rather than into the tiring-house, the main reason for this assumption being that de Witt's Swan sketch, which is the only extant contemporary picture of the stage façade of a London public theatre, shows the stage doors opening outwards. However, as mentioned in Chapter 1, this drawing seems untrustworthy in many ways, and clearly some improvements were made to the stage doors during this period. For example, as Gabriel Egan argues, a speech in *The Duchess of Malfi*, written in 1613–14, implies that the second Globe's stage doors may have had 'strange geometricall hinges' (Q1, K2v) so that they could open 'both ways' (K2v), outwards and inwards. Webster's reference to the strangeness of the hinges, Egan thinks, suggests that they were a new invention introduced in the newly rebuilt playhouse.[1]

Most entrances and exits were made through the flanking doors, and the central opening was used for special events, such as 'discoveries', eavesdropping and ceremonial entrances and exits. In certain grave scenes and prison scenes, as we saw in Chapter 2, the central space would have served as the tomb or the prison cell, and the flanking doorways would have been left for entrances and exits. The flow of the action was greatly dependent on the smoothness of entrances and exits through the flanking doors. It is therefore important to investigate how these doors were handled during the performance. Scenes in which a character opens, closes or knocks at a door are relatively few. How were the stage doors usually handled in most scenes that do not involve any such action? Were they kept open or shut throughout the scenes? If open, was it usual for an entering actor to become visible to the audience before crossing the threshold of his entry door and, therefore, while being still within the tiring-house? If shut, did an entering or exiting actor have to open and close the door himself? Or were stage attendants standing by the doors in order to open and close them?

Some scholars argue that, if closed, the heavy wooden doors would make it impossible for actors offstage to hear their entrance cues. They believe that the doors were therefore kept open and that backstage activities were concealed by curtains hanging in the doorways.[2] However, as mentioned in Chapter 2, some stage directions imply that stage doors including grates or grilles may have been available, at least at certain indoor playhouses. If fitted with grates or grilles, even closed doors would not have prevented onstage and offstage characters from being fully audible to each other. The question of audibility might, therefore, not be a vital factor in the larger question of how the stage doors were handled. It is possible that quite different ways of handling stage doors were adopted at different playhouses and at different times, but in my view there would have been throughout this period broad agreement about how they functioned. In this chapter, I examine a range of early modern play texts to see what kinds of evidence or information they provide about the use of stage doors in the theatres of Shakespeare's time.

DEFINING FICTIONAL AND NON-FICTIONAL DOORS

One might hope to find stage directions which indicate that the opening or closing of a stage door took place not as a dramatic event but for purely practical reasons. Act 5 of *The Little French Lawyer* begins with the opening of a door:

A Horrid noise of Musique within. *Enter one and opens the Chamber doore, in which Lamira and Anabell were shut, they in all feare.* (F1, K4r)

According to Dessen and Thomson's *Dictionary of Stage Directions*, the term *chamber* 'is often linked to the discovery space or a stage door'.[3] As the stage direction itself clarifies, '*the Chamber*' is the same place as the 'vault' in which Lamira and Anabell were confined at the end of the previous act (K3v). On the early modern stage, a place of confinement was often represented by either the stage trap or the discovery space, so '*the Chamber*' here likely refers to the central discovery space. This stage direction may therefore suggest that the central door has been closed. It may however be that the hangings covering the centre served as '*the Chamber doore*'.⁴ It is also possible that a flanking door might have served as the 'vault' and '*the Chamber doore*'. What is interesting about this example is that an unnamed person enters and opens '*the Chamber doore*'. Perhaps '*one*' refers to one of the gentlemen who have confined the ladies in the 'vault'.⁵ He neither speaks, nor is addressed nor is referred to in the dialogue. His arrival signifies virtually nothing in the world of the play. His task is only to open the door. He would exit immediately after having done the task. The dramatic situation of the scene requires the person to open the door so that the imprisoned ladies can emerge and begin the scene. It would be helpful if we had other examples that without question involve the use of flanking doors, but, regrettably, early modern play texts, so far as they have been examined up to now, do not provide any such stage direction.

In this situation it is useful to examine scenes where the opening or closing of a stage door takes place as an event belonging to the narrative fiction. In such scenes, the actor is obviously intended to use the door as a fictional door, that is, a door of a particular room or building or place in the dramatic world. Scenes where stage doors are used as fictional doors are relatively few. In most scenes, either their physical presence is given no fictional significance or their signification in fictional terms is ambiguous. Compare the following two Shakespearean examples. In *Macbeth*, 2.3, Macbeth leads Macduff to a stage door, and says to him 'This is the Doore' (F1, TLN 797; 2.3.51), identifying it as the door leading to Duncan's bedchamber. Macduff exits through the door to wake Duncan and re-enters soon from the same door, crying 'O horror, horror, horror' (TLN 816; 2.3.64). The player acting Macduff, when he exits and when he returns, uses the stage door as a door belonging to the world of the play. On the other hand, when, at the end of *King Lear*, 3.1, usually known as a 'heath scene', Kent says to the Gentleman, 'when we haue found the King, in which your pain / That way, Ile this: He that first lights on him, / Holla the other' (F1, TLN 1651–3; 3.1.53–5), he refers to the flanking doorways as 'That way' and 'this'. When the actors exit through them, they, of course, do not use the doors as fictional doors. Consider further another Shakespearean example. When in *Hamlet*, 4.7 the Queen enters with the sad news of Ophelia's death, does she use the stage door as a door into wherever the King and Laertes have been contriving their treacherous plot against Hamlet? If she does, the following comment on the Q2 version by June Schlueter and James P. Lusardi makes sense: 'Since she is intruding on a very private conversation, she may despite her heavy news knock at the door before she enters.'⁶ However, this scene is not precisely localised, and it is by no means certain that the door was intended to represent a fictional door. In Q2, Gertrude's entrance is preceded by the King's speech 'but stay, what noyse?' (M1r; 4.7.162); in F1, the King's corresponding words read 'how sweet Queene' (TLN 3153); and in Q1, her arrival is first heralded by Laertes's announcement 'Here comes the Queene' (H3v) and then received with the King's greeting 'How now Gertred, why looke you heauily?' (H3v). In none of these substantive texts does the dialogue contain any reference to a door.

In order to evaluate the use of stage doors as fictional doors, I have identified a number of scenes where a character opens, closes or knocks at a door. Analysing these scenes in theatrical terms will show if there are any practical requirements for their staging. While examining cases where stage doors represent fictional doors, I will also consider how the doors might have been disposed where they do not serve as fictional doors and also where their significance in fictional terms is ambiguous. Most scenes in which actors use stage doors as fictional doors can be divided into the following types:

1. scenes where an onstage character seeks an interview with an offstage character; the location is usually outside a house
2. scenes where an offstage character seeks admission; the location is mostly inside a house

After examining examples of scenes to see how the doors would have been handled in each situation, I shall also deal with other miscellaneous scenes. As scenes of each of the two major kinds are similar in pattern of entrances and exits, I will take a limited number of typical examples so as to avoid unnecessary repetition.

SCENES WHERE AN ONSTAGE CHARACTER SEEKS AN INTERVIEW WITH AN OFFSTAGE CHARACTER

Jonson's *Every Man in His Humour*, performed by the Lord Chamberlain's Men, offers three scenes of this type (1.3, 3.5 and 5.1). Act 5, scene 1 is a representative example.

Enter Lorenzo *senior.*
LO.SE. Oh heare it is, I am glad I haue found it now,
      Ho? who is within heare?   *Enter* Tib.
TIB. I am within sir, whats your pleasure?
LO.SE. To know who is within besides your selfe.
. . .
LO.SE. Go to, your honestie flies too lightly from you:
      Theres no way but fetch the constable.

TIB.	The constable, the man is mad I think.		*Claps to the doore.*
	Enter Pizo, *and* Biancha.		
PIZO.	Ho, who keepes house here?		
...			
BIA.	Knocke *Pizo* pray thee.		
PI.	Ho good wife.		
TIB.	Why whats the matter with you.		*Enter* Tib.
BIA.	Why woman, grieues it you to ope your doore?		
	Belike you get something to keepe it shut.		

(Q1, K2v)

At the beginning of the scene, Lorenzo Senior would enter from one flanking door and go to the opposite door, which he designates as the door of the house he has been trying to find, that is, Cob's house.[7] The door is most probably closed at this moment, since at the end of 3.5, Cob told his wife, Tib, to keep the door of his house closed: 'Keepe close thy doore, I aske no more' (H3v). Although the text does not specifically direct Lorenzo Senior to knock, he might well tap on the door at the same time as he directs his words inside. Tib opens the door in answer to his call, and although she is directed to 'enter', she might only show herself at the door, because she is offended by Lorenzo Senior's rude attitude, and very quickly shuts the door again.[8] The words that Tib speaks while making her brief 'entrance' are significant in both fictional and theatrical terms, because they imply that she actually remains inside the house as represented by the tiring-house: 'I am within sir'. (How such an entrance would have worked in the theatre depends greatly on which way the door opened. If outwards, as suggested in the Swan sketch, the door would have obstructed most spectators' view of her, unless she had opened the door fully against the tiring-house wall. If inwards, her cautious half entrance, in which the door would have been only partly opened, could have been appreciated by those spectators in front of the stage.) Then Bianca and Pizo enter from the opposite door, and approach the door that Tib has just closed. Responding to Pizo's knock, she opens it again, and this time she would come out of the door. Thorello arrives shortly after, presumably through the opposite door. As soon as he appears, Bianca recognises him and probably goes to him.[9] Then Giuliano enters from the same door as Thorello, asks Bianca about his cloak and exits almost immediately the same way. When, as a result of all this activity, the focus of the attention has been somewhat diverted from Cob's house, Cob returns home by the door opposite to the one representing his house. Thorello says to him, 'oh I am abusd, /And in thy house, was neuer man so wrongd' (K3v). His words make Cob furious with his wife, and he beats her, saying 'Doe you here? did I not charge you keepe your dores shut here, and do you let them lie open for all commers' (K3v). Finally, on Lorenzo Senior's suggestion, all the onstage characters leave for the magistrate's house. They would exit by the door opposite to the one representing Cob's house. This opposite door remains unlocalised throughout the scene. It is only vaguely imagined to lead to the places from which Lorenzo Senior, Bianca and Pizo, Thorello, Giuliano and Cob have come, and also to the places for which Giuliano and all the other characters involved in this scene leave. In short, throughout the scene it remains no more than a neutral stage door, having no specific fictional significance.

Early modern plays provide many '*Enter and knock*' directions including the following:

Enter Mountsorrell *and knocks at* Serouns *doore*. (Marlowe, *The Massacre at Paris* O1, B2r)

Enter Lelio with his sword drawn, hee knockes at his doore. (*A Knack to Know an Honest Man* Q1, A4v)

Enter Pogio running in, and knocking at Cynanches doore. (Chapman, *The Gentleman Usher* Q1, E4v)

These and similar directions usually occur at the beginnings of scenes. In each case, the actor would enter by one door, cross the stage and knock at the opposite door. The door by which he enters is not even referred to in the stage direction. On the other hand, the door at which he knocks is specifically localised. The localised door would have been closed, although, even if it had been open, the actor could have knocked at it.

In this connection, a passage in Fletcher's *Love's Pilgrimage*, already considered in Chapter 2, is worth citing here once again. It occurs at the beginning of Act 2, scene 1.

    Enter Alphonso and a Servant.
ALPH. Knock at the door.
SER. 'Tis open Sir.
ALPH. That's all one
   Knock when I bid you.
SER. Will not your worship enter.

ALPH. Will not you learn more manners Sir, and do that
   Your Master bids ye; knock ye knave, or ile knock
   Such a round peal about your pate: I enter
   Under his roofe, or come to say god save ye
   To him, the Son of whose base dealings has undone me.
   Knock lowder, lowder yet:

(F1, 8A4r)

As in other door-knocking scenes, Alphonso and his servant would enter from one of the flanking doors and cross the stage to the other, which represents the entrance to Leonardo's house. In this particular case, however, the localised door is already open. As the dialogue indicates, Alphonso expresses his antipathy towards Leonardo by not entering through the open doorway and making his servant knock at it. This special example seems to confirm, as one would expect, that when a character is directed to knock at a door, the door would normally be closed. The wilful failure of a servant even to understand his master's order that he should open the door or get the door opened is a source of humour in certain door-knocking scenes, as in the opening exchange of *The Taming of the Shrew*, 1.2: 'Petr. . . . I trow this is his house: / Heere sirra *Grumio*, Knocke I say'; '*Gru*. Knocke sir? whom should I knocke? Is there any man ha's rebus'd your worship?' (F1, TLN 569–72; 1.2.4–7).

A prominent feature common to scenes of type 1 is that one door is specifically designated as the entrance door of a house, while the other remains no more than a stage door. The situation implies that the localised door is closed. Unless the playing company had the practice of keeping the stage doors closed through the performance, either a stage keeper, or perhaps the actor who is to stand behind the door, might have had to make sure that it was closed before the start of the scene. In contrast, the other door is required to remain as neutral as possible. Presumably, keeping this door open throughout the scene would have achieved the desired effect.[10]

SCENES WHERE AN OFFSTAGE CHARACTER SEEKS ADMISSION

Act 1 of Jonson's *Volpone*, a Globe play, takes place in Volpone's chamber, and the action is continuous through the act.[11] Volpone's opening soliloquy begins with his morning prayer to the treasure he has amassed: 'Good morning to the day; and, next, my gold: / Open the shrine, that I may see my *saint*' (F1, 2P3v). Most probably the discovery space was intended to serve as the 'shrine': all the entrances and exits in Act 1 would have been made through the flanking doors. After saying his prayer of adoration to the gold, Volpone makes Mosca fetch Nano, Androgyno and Castrone. While Volpone is enjoying their singing, a knocking is heard from offstage: '*One knocks without*' (2P5v).¹² The door behind which the visitor is waiting for his entrance should be kept closed. Since Volpone orders Mosca to find out who is knocking – 'Who's that? . . . looke MOSCA' (2P5v) – the door may have included a grille. Mosca, however, replies to his master without moving to the door: ''Tis signior VOLTORE, the Aduocate, / I know him, by his knock' (2P5v). Dismissed by Volpone, the entertainers would exit by the opposite door, because it is important that they do not meet Voltore, who is waiting 'Without i' th' gallerie' (2P5v). After applying ointment to make himself look like a dying man, Volpone finally tells Mosca to call Voltore in. When Mosca has ushered him in, the door would be closed again. Voltore gives Volpone a piece of plate, and Volpone promises him a reward. Shortly after, another knocking is heard: '*Another knocks*' (2Q1r). Mosca makes Voltore leave and then calls in the next visitor, Corbaccio. Corbaccio gives a bag of money to Volpone, and Mosca advises that he go home immediately and make a will in which Volpone is designated as his heir. After Corbaccio has left, the third visitor, Corvino, arrives: '*Another knocks*' (2Q3r). He brings a pearl and a diamond as his gift for Volpone. After Corvino's departure, '*Another knocks*' (2Q4r). Mosca exits and returns with a message from Lady Would-be. For all these entrances and exits, Mosca and the three visitors to Volpone would use the same door, which represents a door of Volpone's chamber, imagined to lead to the street via the 'gallery'. It would be kept closed throughout Act 1. The opposite door, through which Nano, Androgyno and Castrone withdraw, would signify another door out of Volpone's chamber. This second door would probably be used when Mosca fetches the entertainers earlier, and when Volpone and Mosca exit at the end of Act 1. Although it is not so precisely localised as the other stage door, it too might well be kept closed throughout the act.¹³

In *Romeo and Juliet*, 3.3, where the Nurse visits Friar Lawrence's cell, she repeatedly seeks admittance from offstage: '*Enter Nurse, and knocke*' (Q2, G4v; 3.3.70); '*They knocke*' (G4v; 3.3.73); '*Slud knock*' (G4v; 3.3.75); '*Knocke*' (G4v; 3.3.77). Unlike most other '*Enter and knock*' directions, '*Enter Nurse, and knocke*' indicates that the entering Nurse stands behind the door and knocks at it.¹⁴ '*They knocke*' and '*Slud knock*' may possibly suggest that a stage attendant produced the required sound effect by beating on something with an iron bar or the like. Whether the Nurse actually raps on the door or not, it should be kept closed until the Friar opens it. As for the timing of the Nurse's entrance, another entry direction for the Nurse, '*Enter Nurse*' (G4v; 3.3.78), is printed eight lines later, just before her and the Friar's speeches: '*Nur:* Let me come in, and you shal know my errant: / I come from Lady *Iuliet*'; '*Fri.* Welcome then' (G4v; 3.3.79–80) – two lines too early, if the direction indicates her actual entrance. But it may merely mean that she is to speak. It is also possible that the Friar opens the door partway, making her partially visible at the moment indicated by the entry direction, though for her to be even partly visible the door would have had to open inwards. Probably this scene begins with both stage doors closed. Although in the Q2 text, which is agreed to have mostly been set from Shakespeare's draft, the scene-opening direction reads '*Enter Frier and* Romeo' (G3v; 3.3.0), the subsequent dialogue suggests the possibility that the Friar enters alone by one stage door and calls Romeo out from the other: '*Fri. Romeo* come forth, come forth thou fearefull man'; '*Ro.* Father what newes? what is the Princes doome?' (G3v; 3.3.1, 4). Q1, which is now more generally regarded as an acting version of the play, gives the Friar and Romeo separate entries: '*Enter Frier*' (F4r; 3.3.0); '*Enter Romeo*' (F4r; 3.3.3).[15] At the beginning of the scene, the Friar would enter by opening his entry door, but he would close it immediately in order to protect the young man who is hiding in his cell. This door, which would represent the entrance door of the Friar's cell, is to be knocked on by the Nurse later. The other door, when Romeo enters by it, might well signify an internal door, leading to another room in the Friar's cell. When the knocks are heard from offstage, the Friar says to Romeo, 'stand vp. / Run to my studie' (Q2, G4v; 3.3.75–6). There is no indication whether the door should be closed or open after Romeo has entered by it. Admittedly, it is also possible that the scene begins with both doors open, and that the Friar and Romeo enter from the same door, whether together or one after the other. In that case, the Friar would make certain that at least the door to be used by the Nurse is closed.

King Richard II, 5.3 also contains offstage knockings, though it is not certain that the scene begins with the doors closed. While the newly crowned King Henry is talking with other lords, Aumerle arrives suddenly and requests him to dismiss them, so that he can confess his treachery and seek pardon. The lords may close their exit door behind them, but even if they leave it open, it must be closed when Henry permits Aumerle to lock the door: 'Then giue me leaue that [I] May turne the key, / That no man enter till my tale be done' (Q1, I2r; 5.3.36–7). As soon as Aumerle locks the door, York raps on it: '*The Duke of Yorke knokes at the doore and crieth*' (I2r; 5.3.38). He calls out, 'Open the dore, secure foole, hardie King, / Shall I for loue speake treason to thy face, / Open the dore, or I will breake it open' (I2r; 5.3.43–5). The door is opened for York, but it must be closed again immediately, because the Duchess of York is to shout behind it shortly after: 'What ho, my Liege, for Gods sake let me in' (I2v; 5.3.74); 'Speake with me, pitie me, open the doore' (I2v; 5.3.77). As for the other door, the text provides no indication of how it should be disposed during the scene. It might have represented another door of the room, but the signification would have been vague, since it is neither used nor mentioned.

In scenes of type 2, one stage door is clearly intended to serve as the entrance door of the place represented by the stage. The opposite door might signify another door out of the place, although its fictional significance is often less precise and less important. Since the character who is seeking admittance uses no more than one door, there would be no problem even if the other door is left open throughout the scene. In these scenes, however, the onstage characters' frequent concern is preserving their security, which usually means avoiding contact with offstage characters. Keeping both stage doors shut could well reinforce the tense atmosphere created in such scenes.[16]

Scenes of both types contain moments that raise the question of which way the stage doors opened. For instance, an entering character may show himself/herself by opening the door only partway or halfway, as Tib might well do in *Every Man In*, 5.1; and an onstage character may open the door partway to see who is seeking admittance offstage, as Friar Lawrence possibly does in *Romeo and Juliet*, 3.3. Both examples suggest that the stage doors in certain playhouses could have opened inwards rather than outwards. We should, however, be wary of concluding too much from the relatively small number of such examples.

SHUTTING A DOOR

The opening and closing of doors, of course, occurs in many other scenes that do not belong to either of the above-mentioned two types. It is worth dealing with some examples in which a character shuts a door in the middle of the scene. *Romeo and Juliet*, 4.1, where Friar Lawrence gives Juliet the sleeping potion, takes place at the Friar's cell. The scene begins with the Friar and Paris, and when Juliet enters, the Friar says to him, 'Looke sir, here comes the Lady toward my Cell' (Q2, I2v; 4.1.17). These words, which precede the direction '*Enter* Iuliet' (I2v; 4.1.17), may suggest that the Friar sees Juliet through an open door before she actually enters the stage representing his cell. It is, however, equally possible that Shakespearean players treated the central and marginal areas of the stage differently, and that, in this case, the Friar refers to the central part as his cell.[17] In any event, even if the door by which Juliet enters has been left open, it might not indicate that the entrance door of the Friar's cell is kept open, because, when entering by it, she does not necessarily use the stage door as a fictional door. Courteously dismissed by the Friar, Paris leaves, followed by Juliet's words to the Friar: 'O shut the doore, and when thou hast done so, / Come weepe with me, past hope, past care, past help' (I2v; 4.1.44–5). Probably, Paris did not close the door behind him, but even if he had closed the door, the phrase 'shut the door' could have equally well meant 'lock the door'.[18] The dialogue provides the Friar with a cue to make certain at all events that the door is shut, so we can assume that he did so. It is almost certain that the Friar was intended to shut the door. When closed, the door begins to represent the door of the Friar's cell, transforming the whole stage into an enclosed space fit for the confidential conversation between the Friar and Juliet. At the end of the scene, after saying good-bye to each other, they might well exit by opposing doors. One of them, presumably Juliet, would have to open her exit door, but she would not have to close it. The door, being left open, regains normal neutrality before the beginning of the next scene.

A similar transformation can be seen in an outdoor scene. *Twelfth Night*, 3.1 begins with the meeting of Viola (in man's attire) and the Clown. From their conversation, it is gradually made clear that they are imagined to be outside Olivia's house: '*Vio.* . . . Is thy Lady within?' (F1, TLN 1259–60; 3.1.48); '*Clo.* . . . My Lady is within sir. I will conster to them whence you come' (TLN 1267–8; 3.1.55–7). Feste's departure might therefore localise his exit door as a door of the house, if only vaguely. After his exit, Sir Toby comes to Viola with Sir Andrew and invites her to enter the house: 'Will you incounter the house, my Neece is desirous you should enter, if your trade be to her' (TLN 1286–7; 3.1.74–5). But then Olivia herself arrives with her gentlewoman (probably Maria). These four characters would enter from the door by which Feste has made his exit. Olivia dismisses Sir Toby, Sir Andrew and the gentlewoman, saying 'Let the Garden doore be shut, and leaue mee to my hearing' (TLN 1304–5; 3.1.92–3). Possibly the three exiting characters use 'the Garden doore' for their departure. It is, however, more likely that one of them, most probably the gentlewoman, was intended to shut 'the Garden doore' before exiting with the others through the other door, that is, the one by which the three characters had entered. It is not certain whether only 'the Garden doore' should be shut, or whether the other door should be also shut. (This would depend greatly upon whether the other door was localised as a fictional door. If it was meant to represent a door of Olivia's house, it would have been shut.) What is important is that 'the Garden doore' has been no more than a stage door until it is closed. The stage, after the closing of at least one of its doors, becomes a private space appropriate for the intimate conversation between Olivia and Viola/Cesario. One might ask why the scene's locale is not announced until the middle of the scene. Is it because some garden property was intended to be brought on before the beginning of the scene? These questions will be saved until the next chapter. When Olivia and Viola eventually make their scene-closing exit, probably by different doors, they would leave them open.

Act 4, scene 2 of *Troilus and Cressida* offers an interesting passage. I quote from the F1 text:

CRES.	... Harke, ther's one vp?	
PAND. *within*.	What's all the doores open here?	
TROY.	It is your Vnckle.	*Enter Pandarus.*
CRES.	A pestilence on him: now will he be mocking: I shall haue such a life.	
PAN.	How now, how now? how goe maiden-heads? Heare you Maide: wher's my cozin *Cressid*?	
	(F1, TLN 2278–84; 4.2.18–24)[19]	

Pandarus may well already be visible while he is still *within* the tiring-house, because, as he says there, the stage doors are clearly open. One might wonder why Shakespeare requires him to say 'What's all the doores open here?' On one level, Pandarus's comment may be taken metaphorically as a reference to Cressida's unchastity, particularly if he places a heavy lewd emphasis on 'all'. On another level, the comment may suggest that Pandarus literally closes the stage doors as he enters, transforming them into fictional doors. Thus, shortly afterwards, knockings are to be heard from offstage: '*One knocks*' (TLN 2293; 4.2.33); '*Knocke*' (TLN 2300; 4.2.40).

In all these scenes the stage door represents a fictional door only temporarily. When it is being opened or shut, it becomes briefly, for the purpose of the play, what it is in reality. Furthermore, when kept closed, it could continue to represent a fictional door. But if left open, particularly for any length of time, it ceases to function in this way and becomes a neutral fixture.

MAKING AN ENTRANCE BY OPENING THE DOOR

Several plays by Middleton, Fletcher and Shakespeare provide good examples of situations where a stage door is quickly localised as a specific fictional door when an entering character opens it, but then it reverts again to a neutral passage for exit or entrance. For an instant it becomes the door of a burial chamber, a castle or a house, but then it returns to its primary function as a means of ingress and egress.

The surviving playbook of Middleton's *The Second Maiden's Tragedy* has the following stage direction:

Enter the Tirant agen at a farder dore, which opened, bringes hym to the Toombe wher the Lady lies buried; The Toombe here discouered ritchly set forthe; (MS, TLN 1725–7)

This direction occurs at the beginning of a scene. At the end of the previous scene, the Tyrant received the 'keyes of the *Cathedrall*' (TLN 1702) and exited, followed by soldiers. His immediate re-entrance from the opposite door indicates that he has arrived at the burial chamber in the cathedral.[20] When it is opened by the entering Tyrant, the door instantly becomes that of the burial chamber. (If it had already been open, it would not necessarily have signified the door of the burial chamber.) There is no need for the door to have been kept closed throughout the previous scene. It could be closed after the end of the scene only to be opened again immediately at the beginning of the new scene. Since in this tomb-breaking scene, the stage door is not treated as the door of the burial chamber afterwards, it would be left open and regain its normal neutrality very soon. When, at the end of the scene, the Tyrant and his soldiers exit with the Lady's dead body (TLN 1870, 1876), it might not matter whether they use the same door that they have used for their entry. Although this and its succeeding scene take place in the same burial chamber, the scene-ending exits of the Tyrant and his soldiers and the entrance of Govianus and his page at the beginning of the next scene (TLN 1877–8) would have been made through opposing doors. This is because the use of the same door by the exiting characters and the entering characters would create the undesirable impression that the two groups have passed each other off-stage, unless a fairly long pause comes between the exits and the entrance. The use of stage doors by the exiting characters and the entering characters at the scene break would not have been governed by the logic in the fictional world but would have been determined by the necessity for a smooth scene change.[21]

Fletcher's *The Island Princess* offers another example. Although the earliest recorded performance of the play took place at court on 26 December 1621,[22] the 1647 Folio text appears to reflect the normal practice of the Blackfriars/Globe stage.

                    Enter Captaine and Citizens.
CAP.   Up souldiers, up, and deale like men.
CIT.   More water, more water, all is consum'd else.
CAP.   All's gone, unlesse you undertake it straight, your
        Wealth too, that must preserve, & pay your labor bravely.
        Up, up, away.   *Ex. Cap. and Cit. Then,*
      Enter Armusia and his company breaking open a doore.
AR.   So, thou art open, keep the way cleare
        Behinde still. Now for the place.
SOLD. 'Tis here sir.
AR.   Sure this is it.
        Force ope the doore – A miserable creature!
        Yet by this manly face   *The King discover'd.*
                                                       (F1, 3N3v)

In this sequence of scenes, while the Governor is employing all the troops to extinguish a sudden great fire, Armusia and his followers break into the castle to rescue the King from imprisonment. The captain and the citizens would have entered by one flanking door, crossed the stage and exited by the other. This hasty move, which is understood to take place in a street, need not have involved the opening and closing of the doors. Suppose therefore that the flanking doors were kept open. Since Armusia and his followers are directed to break open a door, the door should have been closed for this to take place. The central opening would not have been available for their entrance; it would have been saved for the discovery of the King. It is just possible that the trapdoor was intended to serve as the prison door as in another prison scene that occurs earlier in the play: '*King appeares loden with chaines, his head, arms only above*' (3N2r). But in this regard it is worth quoting Leslie Thomson's observation about the use of the stage direction '*discover*': 'To my knowledge, *discover* is never used in relation to the opening of a trapdoor in the stage.'[23] It is, therefore, most likely that Armusia and his company would have entered by the door that the captain and the citizens had used for their entrance. If this were the case, one of the actors, probably the actor playing Armusia, would have closed the door, unperceived by the audience, while the captain and citizens were still crossing the stage. At the start of the new scene, the door, being opened, would have signified a fictional door, instantly transforming the stage space into the inside of the castle.

The first known performance of *The Comedy of Errors* took place at Gray's Inn on 28 December 1594.[24] When Shakespeare wrote this play, he was possibly expecting a performance there, although we cannot be sure whether the Gray's Inn performance was the play's première. The Folio text contains a series of stage directions that might suggest the use of a classical-style set representing houses, with which educated gentlemen of the Inns of Court were familiar. One of these directions reads '*Enter Antipholus Ephes. Dromio from the Courtizans*' (F1, TLN 995; 4.1.13). Around this stage direction there is no speech that specifically refers to the Courtesan's house: the only reference is the Officer's words, 'See where he comes' (TLN 996; 4.1.14). Assuming that this play was performed on the bare stage of a public playhouse, and regardless of whether the performance was the first or a revival, how could the entry door have signified a fictional door? Presumably the door would have been closed beforehand, most probably just before the scene's beginning, and Antipholus of Ephesus and Dromio of Ephesus would have entered by opening the door. Since, at the end of Act 3, scene 1, Antipholus of Ephesus mentioned his intention to visit the Courtesan's house, the door could well have signified the door of the Porpentine: 'Bring it I pray you to the *Porpentine*, / . . . / Since mine owne doores refuse to entertaine me, / Ile knocke else-where, to see if they'll disdaine me' (TLN 777, 781–2; 3.1.116, 120–1). It would have been left open, and its significance in fictional terms would end very quickly. Later in the same scene, this door might have been used by Dromio of Syracuse when he enters '*from the Bay*' (TLN 1073; 4.1.84). It would certainly have been used at the end of the scene either by Antipholus of Ephesus or by Dromio of Syracuse, when they make their exits separately, one going to a prison and the other to the Phoenix: '*Ant*. . . . To *Adriana* Villaine hie thee straight: / . . . hie thee slaue, be gone, / On Officer to prison, till it come' (TLN 1091, 1096–7; 4.1.102, 107–8). Since the action does not really involve the Courtesan's house, the actors playing Antipholus of Ephesus and Dromio of Ephesus at a public playhouse might not have bothered to use their entry door as the door of the Porpentine.

THE DOOR OF A HOUSE

Leaving aside classic and academic plays, some more professional plays provide stage directions written in the form '*Enter from the house*' or the like. For example, Greene's *James IV* has '*After a solemne seruice, enter from the widdowes house a seruice, musical songs of marriages, or a maske, or what prettie triumph you list, to them, Ateukin and Gnato*' (Q1, H4v).[25] This entrance occurs at the beginning of a scene, and so, in order to suggest that the characters (i.e., servingmen carrying dishes, musicians, singers and maskers) have come out of the named house, some device would have been used. The stage door would need to be opened. A similar point can be made about another scene-opening entry from an anonymous play: '*Enter* Bario *and the Doctor from* Balias *house*' (*The Wit of a Woman* Q1, C1v). Heywood's *The Silver Age* contains '*Thunder and lightning. All the seruants run out of the house affrighted, the two Captains and* Blepharo, Amphitrio *and* Socia *amazedly awake*' (Q1, F1v). Earlier in the scene Jupiter, disguised as Amphitrio, led the Captains and Blepharo into Amphitrio's house, shutting out Amphitrio and his man Socia: '*Iup.* Gentlemen, / My house is free to you; onely debar'd / These Counterfets: These gates that them exclude, / Stand open to you' (E4v). Since the stage door has clearly been shut, it needs to be opened for all the servants and others to run out of the house. In the Trinity Manuscript of *A Game at Chess*, a copy transcribed by Middleton himself, the opening stage direction of Act 1, scene 1 reads 'Enter from the Black-house, the Bl. Queens pawne, from the whitehouse the white Qs: pawne' (TLN 99–101). This is the only stage direction in the whole manuscript that mentions the two houses as places, as opposed to groups. During the Induction that precedes Act 1, Error says to Loyola 'behold there's the full Number of the Game, / Kings, and theire pawnes, Queenes, Bishops, Knights & dukes' (TLN 71–2). At this point, the Black and White Houses would make their separate entrances from the two flanking doorways,[26] and at the end of the Induction, when Loyola and Error retire into the central discovery space, from which they have appeared,[27] the two groups would exit through the doorways from which they have entered, thus establishing the location of their respective houses. At the end of the Induction the doors could well have been closed, so that they might be opened again at the start of the play for the entrance of the Black and White Queens' Pawns. The simultaneous opening of the doors of the two houses would contribute to the audience's awareness of the formal beginning of the game of chess that makes up the play.[28]

A variant form which uses '*as*' can be seen in *How a Man May Choose a Good Wife from a Bad*, possibly by Heywood: '*Enter as out of the house, M. Arthur, Mistris Arthur, old Arthur, old Lusam, yong Lusam, Pipkin, and the rest*' (Q1, B4r).[29] This direction is preceded by a speech from another character Anselme (a suitor to Mistress Arthur), already on stage with his advisor Fuller, which identifies the stage door as the door of Master Arthur's house, 'Here dwels the sacred mistris of my hart, / Before her doore Ile frame a friuolous walke / And spying her, with her deuise some talke' (B4r). Obviously, the first entering character, Master Arthur was intended to open the stage door; the subsequent dialogue suggests that he has left the dinner table angrily and rushed out of his house, chased by his wife, father and father-in-law and others. It may be safely concluded that what the stage direction '*Enter [as] out of the house*' indicates is the entering character's opening the stage door.

A stage door, located in the tiring-house façade, could easily serve as the door of a house. Beginning a scene with opening the entry door was therefore probably a common device by which the actor suggested the locale or situation of the new scene, giving the impression that the character has just come out of the house represented by the tiring-house façade. Although the opening direction of *The Taming of the Shrew* reads merely '*Enter Begger and Hostess, Christophero Sly*' (F1, TLN 2; Induction.1.0), the play would very likely have begun with the opening of the stage door, suggesting that the hostess has pushed Sly out of her alehouse. In *The Taming of a Shrew*, which is generally thought to be a derivative version of Shakespeare's *The Shrew*,[30] the opening direction clearly indicates that the entry door was used as a fictional door: '*Enter a Tapster, beating out of his doores Slie Droonken*' (Q1, A2r). The opening stage direction of *Julius Caesar*, 2.1 reads '*Enter Brutus in his Orchard*' (F1, TLN 615), and here too the ensuing dialogue with his servant Lucius suggests that Brutus has just come out of his house. Rather than just walking through an already open stage door, he might well have opened it, as if entering the orchard from his house. (How the stage direction's location of the scene in an orchard would have functioned in the theatre is a question we shall deal with in the next chapter.) As a final example, at the beginning of *Pericles*, 4.5, it would make sense if the two gentlemen entered by opening their entry door. Clearly they have just come out of the brothel ('such a place as this' (Q1, G3v; 4.5.2–3)), because in their brief amazed exchange it is all they talk about, and the implication of their words is that they are standing outside it.

The Merchant of Venice, 2.5 is the only scene in the play where the narrative requires the opening and closing of a stage door, but Shakespeare makes clear how this procedure is also illustrative of character. The scene, which takes place in front of Shylock's house, begins with the entrance of Shylock and Launcelot: '*Enter Iewe and his man that was*[,] *the Clowne*' (Q1, C4v). One of these entering characters, probably Launcelot, would open the door, thereby establishing the stage door as the street door of Shylock's house. His greatest concern at this moment is to secure the house during his absence. He calls out to his daughter who is within, and although Jessica is directed to enter ('Enter *Iessica*' (D1r; 2.5.9)), she might well only make her appearance either on or behind the threshold of the door, an incomplete entrance that would hint at the confined nature of her existence. Shylock gives her his keys, and finally leaves by the opposing doorway, after ordering her to go back in and lock the doors and windows: 'Well *Iessica* goe in, / perhaps I will returne immediatlie, / do as I bid you, shut dores after you' (D1v; 2.5.51–3). Shylock's exit door would have remained open throughout the scene, unlike the door into his house which Jessica would have shut behind her. Shylock's repeated references in this scene to his house and its doors and windows do more than establish unequivocally that the tiring-house façade represents his house; they make clear the extent of his identification with it. The closed door is a visual reinforcement of Shylock's structural role in the comedy. In emphasising the need to lock away within his house all his possessions, including his own daughter, Shylock underscores something of his essential nature: mean, suspicious, secretive, inward-looking and closed against all the larger, generous currents of life.

INDOOR SCENES

Since the opening of a door could be so significant, it is reasonable to infer that in scenes located in open spaces, both doors were usually kept open, lest the opening of them for actors' entrances and exits might create the wrong impression. In indoor scenes, on the other hand, the opening of doors would not disrupt the reality of the fictional world and in fact would be wholly consistent with it. Commenting on the stage doors in the Swan sketch, Peter Thomson offers the idea that the reason why they are shut may be because an indoor scene is in progress.[31] However, scenes of early modern plays are rarely precisely localised by the dialogue, and it is sometimes almost impossible to decide whether the scene takes place indoors or outdoors. Take, for example, *Romeo and Juliet*, 2.6, where Juliet meets Romeo at Friar Lawrence's cell. It is by no means clear whether the dialogue takes place inside or outside the cell. Furthermore, Shakespearean and contemporary plays provide not a few examples where the location changes from outside the house to inside without a clearing of the stage.[32] It is worth questioning if it is likely that in indoor scenes actors' entrances and exits would generally involve their opening and closing the doors. In *Epicoene*, performed by the Children of the Whitefriars,[33] Jonson concentrates on indoor scenes. I will examine those taking place in Clerimont's and

Morose's houses to see whether the actors may always have been intended to use stage doors as fictional doors.

As Clerimont's play-opening entrance suggests, the scene is located in his house throughout Act 1: '*He comes out making himselfe ready*' (F1, 2Y1v). He has three visitors in this act, but none of them knocks offstage before his entrance. Truewit's appearance is abrupt. Dauphine's arrival is merely preceded by Clerimont's words, 'See, who comes here' (2Y3v). Only La Foole's visit is formally announced by Clerimont's page: 'The gentleman is here below, that ownes that name' (2Y5r). The speeches spoken around the arrivals of the visitors give the impression that at least the stage door used by the visitors is kept open throughout the act. The door is given no significance in fictional terms. As the page's above-mentioned speech suggests, the characters are understood by the audience to be upstairs, and neither stage door is intended to represent the entrance door of the house.[34]

Regarding the scenes located in Morose's house, on his first appearance in Act 2, scene 1, he expresses his strong concern with the entrance door of his house.

You haue taken the ring, off from the street dore, as I bad you? . . . And, you haue fastened on a thicke quilt, or flock-bed, on the out-side of the dore; that if they knocke with their daggers, or with bricke-bats, they can make no noise? . . . And haue you giuen him a key, to come in without knocking? . . . And, is the lock oild, and the hinges, to day? (2Y6r)

Since the street door is likely imagined to be offstage, neither stage door need be kept closed. However, the fact that both stage doors are kept shut might significantly contribute to the audience's consciousness of the enclosed space in which Morose tries to confine himself. In any event, towards the end of the scene, the sound of a horn is heard from offstage, and at the beginning of 2.2 Truewit enters, feigning to be a messenger from the court. After tormenting Morose by impudently speaking of the miseries of marriage, Truewit finally leaves. Then Morose says to his servant, 'Come, ha' me to my chamber: but first shut the dore. O, shut the dore, shut the dore' (2Z1v), possibly referring to the stage door by which Truewit has just exited. Before the servant closes the door, Cutbeard enters by it, and Morose asks him to take him in to his bed, presumably by the opposite door. When, at the beginning of 2.5, Morose says to his servant, 'Is the dore shut?' (2Z4v), he is probably asking whether the street door of his house is locked. Even though the door is imagined to be offstage, the stage doors might have been closed so as to re-establish Morose's closed world after the intervening scenes. He finds Epicoene a perfect lady, and orders Cutbeard to prepare for his marriage with her. This time he is not disturbed by anybody, and exits, fully satisfied.

The location of the 3.4–3.7 sequence is also inside Morose's house. As soon as Morose marries Epicoene, she reveals her talkativeness. Truewit's sudden entrance without seeking admission upsets Morose. He cries 'Barre my dores! barre my dores' (3A4r), but then his newly-married wife says 'Let 'hem stand open. . . . Shal I haue a *barricado* made against my friends, to be barr'd of any pleasure they can bring in to me with honorable visitation' (3A4r–v). Many more visitors arrive thereafter. Daw ushers in Haughty, Centaure, Mavis and Trusty. Clerimont brings in musicians, and makes them play '*Musique of all sorts*' (3A6v). La Foole leads in servers of a wedding-dinner: '*La-Foole passes ouer sewing the meate*' (3A6v). Finally, Otter comes in and invites onstage characters to join him in carousing, after which they make a noisy exit. Morose's confined space has been smashed to pieces. It therefore seems probable that the stage doors were intended to be kept open throughout the 3.4–3.7 sequence. It would not have much mattered whether the actors, entering or exiting, used the open stage doors as the doors of the room represented by the stage. Acts 4 and 5 are also located in Morose's house, but the situation is the same as in the 3.4–3.7 sequence.

Apart from the above-mentioned possible scene (2.2), the play contains no more than two scenes in which stage doors are referred to as fictional doors. In Act 4, scene 5, Truewit presents a 'tragi-comedy' of Daw and La Foole. He requests Dauphine and Clerimont to participate in the performance.

Doe you obserue this gallerie? or rather lobby, indeed? Here are a couple of studies, at each end one: here will I act such a *tragi-comoedy* betweene the *Guelphes*, and the *Ghibellines*, DAW and LA-FOOLE – which of 'hem comes out first, will I seize on: (you two shall be the *chorus* behind the arras, and whip out betweene the *acts*, and speake.) (3B6v–3C1r)

It appears that they are imagined to be in a gallery or lobby. As Truewit describes the tiring-house façade, the flanking doors represent the doors of studies and the central opening, which is covered with an arras, serves as a hiding place.[35] At the beginning of Act 5, scene 3, while instructing Dauphine to fetch Morose, Truewit refers to the three doorways for the second time: 'Thou shalt keepe one dore, and I another, and then CLERIMONT in the midst, that he may haue no meanes of escape from their cauilling, when they grow hot once' (3D1v). It is a curious fact that this play, in which indoor scenes predominate, should contain so few scenes where actors use stage doors as fictional doors.

To judge from the use of stage doors in *Epicoene*, it is unlikely that in indoor scenes characters' entrances and exits would generally involve their opening and closing the doors. In some indoor scenes the stage doors should or could be kept closed; in other indoor scenes the doors might have been kept open. Even where a visitor's entrance takes place, unless the stage door represents the entrance door of the house, it might well be kept open. On the other hand, even if the scene does not involve the street door of the house, the fact that the stage doors are closed might contribute to the establishment of the atmosphere or situation of the scene. In short, the evidence from *Epicoene* indicates that there was no general rule governing the use of stage doors in indoor scenes, and other plays shed no additional light on the matter.

POSITIONS BEHIND STAGE DOORS

Stage doors were most likely kept open in those scenes where they were not intended to represent fictional doors. We should therefore consider whether it follows that, like the central opening, the flanking doorways were also covered by hangings. Tim Fitzpatrick is confident that this was indeed the case and adduces four pieces of evidence in support of his view.[36] The first is a scene in Sharpham's *Cupid's Whirligig*, which, as he sees it, clearly requires two sets of hangings:

> Wages gets Lady and Nan to hide behind hangings to await the arrival of the Knight ([Q1,] G4v). The Knight enters and is engaged in dialogue by Wages, who sees the Lady entering, as he had directed her, from behind the hangings. Wages then gets the Knight to hide himself to overhear the Lady, and he can hardly do this in the space she is entering from. That he too is to be concealed by hangings rather than another means is indicated by the symmetry of language in the scene – his action mirrors hers – and by her complaint about 'a man behinde the hangings to evise-drop' (H2r).[37]

Despite the text's occasional use of verbal symmetry, nothing in it requires a corresponding symmetry of action, and so two sets of hangings are not at all essential for the staging of this scene; while the Lady and Nan are coming forward from the central hangings, the Knight could hurry unobserved behind the same hangings. In his second example, he refers to a scene in Davenant's *The Wits*, where Lucy comes to Lady Ample's house, having been cast out by her aunt because of the amorous attentions of Young Pallatine. Early in the scene a knock is heard from offstage ('*Knocking within*' (Q1, C3r)) and the door is opened for Lucy's entrance in response to Lady Ample's command. There is every likelihood that, as Fitzpatrick concludes, it would not be closed again; the immediately ensuing action does not involve its further use as the street door of Lady Ample's house, and as a result of being left open, the doorway would resume its customary neutrality. Towards the end of the scene, as Lucy is about to exit following Lady Ample, '*Young Pallatine beckens Lucy from between the Hangings*' (C4v). Fitzpatrick argues that, since Young Pallatine has followed Lucy, he should appear in the same doorway that she used for her entrance, and he uses this possibility to reinforce his claim that the doorway was curtained. But if the stage door's fictional significance had ended shortly after it was opened to allow Lucy to enter, about 120 lines earlier, it would not automatically revert to its previous function. The simpler interpretation of this stage direction is that it refers not to hangings in the flanking doorways but to those in front of the central discovery space, which would enable Young Pallatine to make a stronger, more dramatic entrance than would be achieved by his entry through one of the doors. For his third example, Fitzpatrick offers visual evidence. He sees the illustration on the title-page of Jonson's 1616 *Works* as reflecting a contemporary tiring-house façade and as therefore constituting visual evidence for doorway hangings. But John H. Astington observes that the Jonson title-page is classical in format and imagery, with no reason to link it to the contemporary English stage. The crucial point about it, he says, is that it was made by an engraver, William Hole, who would have used graphic sources, and not first-hand sketches of the Globe or any other playhouse. The 'Theatrum' at the top, for example, is a reversed copy of a 1558 Italian engraving of the theatre of Marcellus (Antonio Lafreri, *Speculum Romanae Magnificentiae* (Rome, 1548–68)). And, as he points out, architectural frames with flanking figures are a compositional commonplace in title-pages and the recesses in Jonson's illustration are conventional niches, not doorways.[38] Finally, Fitzpatrick cites Henry Peacham's description of Richard Tarlton making himself partly visible to the audience:

As *Tarlton* when his head was onely seene,
The Tire-house doore and Tapistrie betweene,
Set all the mulltitude in such a laughter,
They could not hold for scarse an houre after,
. . .

(*Thalia's Banquet* O1 (1620), C8r; Epigram 94)

Even if Peacham is recalling performances at purpose-built public playhouses in London – Tarlton played at court, at city inns and in the provinces as well[39] – it is far from certain that he is referring to a flanking door rather than a central doorway. (As mentioned above, the central opening may well have been equipped with doors as well as hangings.) Making an appearance from the central discovery space would have appealed to a comedian of Tarlton's extrovert nature far more than making it from either of the two flanking doors; and in addition, given that initially only his head was to be visible, an appearance from a flanking door would have made it more difficult to gain the instant attention of the whole theatre audience. Although the example from *Cupid's Whirligig* is suggestive, I do not think the case has been conclusively made that the flanking doorways were covered with hangings, and in order to pursue the matter a little further, I think we should now examine some more scenes in which players take up positions close to the stage doors.

In Act 2, scene 3 of Jonson's *The Alchemist*, which was apparently written to be performed at Blackfriars, Dol makes a brief appearance, supposedly as a distracted gentlewoman, in order to attract Mammon's interest. In this and other indoor scenes of the play, which are all located inside Lovewit's house, one door represents the door of Lovewit's house and is mainly used by the various gulls who visit the house, and when not in use it should be kept closed. The other door is mostly used by Subtle, the alchemist and his confederates. The conspirators often change costumes offstage between their exits and re-entrances, and the space behind this door serves literally as their 'tiring-room'. Most probably, this door was also intended to be kept closed throughout the indoor scenes. In 2.3, the stage direction for Dol reads '*Dol is seene*' (F1, 3G2r), implying that she does not really enter the stage.[40] Subtle, pretending to be upset by her unexpected appearance, immediately makes her withdraw, by saying 'God's precious – What doe you meane? Goe in, good lady, / Let me intreat you' (3G2r). Although she could possibly make herself visible between the hangings covering the central opening, it seems more likely that she was intended to show her offstage presence by opening the door of her and her confederates' 'tiring-room'.[41] Presumably, she would not have been fully visible to most members of the audience, even if she had opened the door fully. Her partial visibility might, however, have greatly contributed to the audience's appreciation of Dol's and Subtle's artfulness in letting Mammon have a glimpse of her so as to whet his appetite.

The opening scene of *3 Henry VI* supplies another example. The play begins with the violent entry of York and his followers: '*Alarum. Enter Plantagenet Edward, Richard, Norfolke, Mountague, Warwicke, and Souldiers*' (F1, TLN 2–4; 1.1.0). The soldiers probably leave the stage shortly after: York's words, 'And Souldiers stay and lodge by me this Night' (TLN 37; 1.1.32) can serve as a cue for their move.[42] Then King Henry makes a royal entry with his friends: '*Flourish. Enter King Henry, Clifford, Northumberland, Westmerland, Exeter, and the rest*' (TLN 56–7; 1.1.49). As editors note, the phrase '*and the rest*' here probably means 'and soldiers'.[43] Henry finds York seated in the chair of state, and orders him to descend and kneel for mercy at his feet. York, however, calls the King's grandfather, Henry IV, a usurper, and insists on his legal title.

PLANT.   *Henry* of Lancaster, resigne thy Crowne:
        What mutter you, or what conspire you Lords?
WARW.   Doe right vnto this Princely Duke of Yorke,
        Or I will fill the House with armed men,
        And ouer the Chayre of State, where now he sits,
        Write vp his Title with vsurping blood.
                He stampes with his foot, and the Souldiers shew themselues.
                           (TLN 183–90; 1.1.164–9)

What the stage direction '*the Souldiers shew themselues*' indicates is that the soldiers make their own presence known through a doorway or doorways. In this example, where the royal chair must have occupied centre stage, it is unlikely that the soldiers would have used the central opening. They were probably intended to stand either just behind or on the threshold of one or both of the doors. This would have allowed the company to stage the scene with fewer hirelings, and in practice they could have done with as few as two or three.[44] When Warwick threatens Henry by saying 'Or I will fill the House with armed men', the entrance on to the stage of such a small number of soldiers would have been thought somewhat ridiculous, especially if the King was guarded by at least the same number of soldiers. But even a small band of soldiers, glimpsed by the audience crowded together in the doorway, could have represented unseen troops. This device would have functioned successfully as a form of visual synecdoche, quite apart from the practical advantage of saving the time that would have been required for the actual entrance and exit of a large number of actors.

Interestingly, in the Octavo text of the play, when Warwick threatens the King by mentioning 'armed men' (A5r), the soldiers are given an entry direction: 'Enter Souldiers' (A5r). Furthermore, after York's words to Henry, 'Confirme the crowne to me and to mine heires / And thou shalt raigne in quiet whilst thou liu'st' (A5r; 1.1.172–3) come these Octavo-only lines, which would serve as an exit cue for the soldiers:

KING. Conuey the souldiers hence, and then I will.
WAR. Captaine conduct them into *Tuthill* fieldes.

(A5r)

In this version it seems on the face of it that all the available players were intended to make an actual entrance; in which case they would perhaps have had to make up in the fierceness of their demeanour what they lacked in numbers. However, the Octavo staging might in practice have been identical to the F1 staging, because in the Shakespearean theatre, as argued in Chapter 2, peeping through a doorway could be counted as an entry.

Hamlet offers a parallel case. When in 4.5 Laertes bursts in on Claudius, the stage directions in the Q2 and F1 texts read as follows: '*Enter Laertes with others*' (Q2, L1r; 4.5.111); '*Enter Laertes*' (F1, TLN 2851). In these versions, whether Laertes's followers are mentioned in the entry direction or not, the dialogue, virtually the same in both texts, suggests that they do not really enter the stage. I quote from Q2:

> *Enter Laertes with others.*
> KING. The doores are broke.
> LAER. Where is this King? sirs stand you all without.
> ALL. No lets come in.
> LAER. I pray you giue me leaue.
> ALL. We will, we will.
> LAER. I thanke you, keepe the doore, ô thou vile King,
> Giue me my father.
>
> (L1r; 4.5.111–17)

In both versions the followers are meant to show themselves through the doorway from which Laertes has entered. In view of the narrowness of the opening, a few actors would have sufficed to represent a much larger crowd. For the corresponding action the Q1 text provides the stage direction '*enter Leartes*' (H1r). In this version, however, the followers may be entirely unseen, because their presence is indicated only by '*A noyse within*' (H1r) and the entering Laertes's order for them to 'Stay there vntill I come' (H1r).

We have seen that plays written or co-written by Fletcher contain a fair number of stage directions indicating the use of positions behind stage doors. Some of these are also related to the need to give the impression of a crowd. *Cupid's Revenge*, for example, has '*Enter Leucippus and Ismenus: the people within stoppes*' (Q1, I4v), which has already been discussed in Chapter 2. A few actors visible in the doorway would have represented the people. *The Little French Lawyer* provides '*Enter La-writ, and a Gentleman at the dore*' (F1, I3r). This entry direction clearly indicates that the second character remains '*at the dore*', that is, either on or just behind the threshold of the door by which the first character has entered. What is interesting about this example is that La-writ and the Gentleman speak as if some more gentlemen had come with them:

LA-WRIT. I'll meet you at the Ordinary, sweet Gentlemen,
And if there be a wench or two—
GENT. We'll have 'em.
. . .
GENT. We'll see what may be done, sir,

(I3r)

La-writ gives instructions to 'Gentlemen' and the Gentleman replies to him as their representative, using the plural form of the first person pronoun. By standing '*at the dore*', the actor playing the Gentleman could make the audience believe that there were some others behind him.

Certain entry directions that seem at first glance to have been placed too early may indicate the use of positions behind stage doors. An entry is sometimes marked before the entering character's call from offstage, as can be seen in the following example:

Enter Isabella.
ISAB. What hoa? Peace heere; Grace, and good companie.
PRO. Who's there? Come in, the wish deserues a welcome.
. . .
ISA. My businesse is a word or two with *Claudio*.
(*Measure for Measure* F1, TLN 1248–52, 1255; 3.1.43–5, 48)

Modern editors usually reposition Isabella's entry so as to make it come immediately before her second speech, and attach '*within*' to the first speech prefix '*Isab.*'[45] However, Isabella is not directed to knock at the door. Although this scene takes place in a prison, the stage doors might well be kept open. She could show herself while delivering her first speech either just behind or on the threshold of the door.[46]

Where an onstage character invites an offstage character to come in, the timing of the invited character's entry sometimes appears too early. *All's Well That Ends Well*, 2.1 offers such an example:

LAF. Nay, Ile fit you,
And not be all day neither.

KING. Thus he his speciall nothing euer prologues.
LAF. Nay, come your waies.
        Enter Hellen.
KING. This haste hath wings indeed.
LAF. Nay, come your waies . . .
                                     (F1, TLN 695–701; 2.1.90–4)

Lafew would begin to move immediately after saying 'Nay, Ile fit you, / And not be all day neither.' He would have been standing either centre- or front-stage, since he has been conversing with the King, the central character of the scene, for as many as thirty lines (TLN 662–96; 2.1.61–91). It is, therefore, unlikely that he would exit and return with Helen while the King is speaking only one line: 'Thus he his speciall nothing euer prologues.' It seems more reasonable to conclude that Lafew walks a few paces towards the door, which has been open, and beckons Helen to enter, while saying 'Nay, come your waies.' She would make her appearance through the doorway at the moment indicated by the entry direction. Since, however, Lafew has to repeat the same words to encourage her to come forward, she might be standing hesitantly on or immediately behind the threshold for a few lines.

The occurrences of these kinds of early entry direction, as well as the inconsistent and flexible use of the theatrical terms '*enter*' and '*within*', seem to reflect an awareness by Shakespeare and his colleagues of the visibility of positions behind stage doors. I therefore take the view that the flanking doorways were not covered by hangings either in front of or immediately behind the threshold of the doors. Even if curtains were used to conceal backstage operations, they would have been placed at a certain distance from the threshold, and not immediately behind it. (There might also have been another curtain at the back of the discovery area.) For all we know, it may have been quite common for an actor waiting for his entrance to be visible some lines before his actual entrance. Unless he speaks from offstage, or is addressed or referred to by an onstage character, the audience might not have cared about the fact that he was wholly or partially visible prior to his entry on to the stage.

CONCLUSIONS

We have examined scenes where actors use stage doors as fictional doors either consistently throughout the scenes, or only temporarily or momentarily, together with others in which actors, entering or exiting, do not appear to use the stage doors as fictional doors. We have also considered

Conclusions

scenes in which an actor shows himself through a doorway, and as a result we can better appreciate the subtle variations of theatrical craft involved in marking a character's entrance. The situations and devices found in these scenes recur throughout Elizabethan, Jacobean and Caroline plays including those written by Marlowe, Shakespeare, Heywood, Jonson, Chapman, Fletcher, Middleton and Shirley. No situation or device is peculiar to any particular playwright, playing company, playhouse or period. Certainly, the use of stage doors in London professional theatres does not appear to have varied over the decades. The information provided by early modern play texts seems to support the following conclusions:

1. When it is shut, the door would signify a fictional door. On the other hand, being left open, the door's presence could be neutral. Unless it is specifically identified as a door by the dialogue, the physical presence of an open door would have no significance in fictional terms.
2. Thus, the stage doors were shut only in those scenes where they serve as fictional doors. In most scenes, including many indoor scenes, they were kept open throughout the scenes.
3. In certain indoor scenes, however, even when the doors were not specifically localised, they might have been shut for the establishment of the atmosphere or situation of the scenes.
4. Unlike the central opening, the flanking doorways were free from curtaining. Early modern playwrights and players were often eager to extend the stage space, using the visibility of positions behind the stage doors.

These might serve as an assumption on which to discuss characters' entrances and exits and their presence within the tiring-house.

CHAPTER 5

'Enter Brutus in his Orchard'

The early modern theatre employed no scenery or set and so the stage structure always remained visible to the audience. There were early modern ways of signalling the locales of scenes. For example, the arrival of an actor dressed in a prisoner's costume and bound in shackles could rapidly establish the stage as a prison cell. What the stage direction '*Enter in prison*' indicates is such a manner of entering, as noted in the introductory chapter. An entering character could bring in the scene's locale with him, as it were, by wearing a suitable costume and carrying an appropriate property. And, as we saw in the previous chapter, if an entering character crosses the stage and knocks at the door opposite to his entry door, the audience would recognise that the stage is serving as the street in front of the house represented by the tiring-house façade. In this way a character could transform the stage space into a specific place by making an entrance in a particular manner. But not all questions of locale are so easily resolved, and Shakespeare's *Julius Caesar* offers a particularly problematic entry stage direction.

Julius Caesar, Act 2, scene 1 is a very long scene, lasting over 330 lines, in which Brutus is continuously onstage. It consists of four main elements: Brutus's reflective soliloquy; the visit of Cassius and other conspirators; Portia's pleading with Brutus to know the cause of his grief; and Ligarius's visit. In the 1623 Folio text, which is the sole authority for the play, the scene's opening stage direction reads '*Enter Brutus in his Orchard*' (F1, TLN 615; 2.1.0). The F1 text is fairly generally agreed to have been printed either from a theatre playbook, itself a scribal copy based on authorial papers, or from a transcript of the playbook.[1] The stage direction '*Enter Brutus in his Orchard*' probably derives from Shakespeare's manuscript. The dialogue does not contain any specific reference to the scene's locale. This stage direction, therefore, raises the following questions. How important was its locale? How could the Globe audience recognise that Brutus is in his garden? Was a property tree or any other appropriate property intended to be brought on unobtrusively before the beginning of the scene? Could the way in which Brutus entered suggest in some way the scene's locale? Alternatively, does the stage direction relate merely to the dramatic fiction and not to theatrical effect? In other words, did Shakespeare not expect either the actor (most probably, Richard Burbage) or stage keepers to do anything specific to establish the locale? In that event one has to wonder what Shakespeare, as a practical man of the theatre, had in mind when he wrote this stage direction.

Garden scenes are fairly common in early modern English plays, and this is the larger context that we must consider. Shakespeare's plays, including those in which he collaborated with others, contain at least nineteen scenes located in gardens.[2] A study of Shakespearean and non-Shakespearean garden scenes will reveal the kinds of event that usually take place in gardens, the way the locale is generally communicated to the audience, the usage of garden properties and the significance of the stage direction '*Enter in a garden*' and variants. By examining this evidence, I will try to answer the questions raised by the stage direction '*Enter Brutus in his Orchard*'.

THE SHAKESPEAREAN GARDEN

It is useful to bear in mind how Shakespeare and his contemporaries would have imagined a garden. About the actual gardens of Shakespeare's day we can learn some basic matters from contemporary books and essays on gardens and gardening, such as Thomas Hill's *The Gardener's Labyrinth* (1577). *The Riverside Shakespeare* reproduces two woodcuts from this gardening book, and the comment by a *Riverside* editor on one of the woodcuts (see Figure 6) is worth quoting here:

> The design pictured above is generally characteristic. Such a garden was walled for privacy, with a single door ... and in addition to the central flower beds and grass plots, geometrically laid out and surrounded by gravel walks, it contained fruit trees trained to grow flat against the inside of the walls.[3]

It appears that walls, a door and walks were essential elements of the structure of a garden. Contemporary maps are also useful. For example, Ralph Agas's *Civitas Londinum* (*c.*1561, published 1633) shows numerous enclosed and walled gardens.[4] From these it is clear that the most prominent feature of the gardens of Shakespeare's day was that they were strictly enclosed. *Richard II*, Act 3, scene 4, in which King Richard's misrule and fall are told in gardening metaphors, offers a speech including references to a garden as an area enclosed with a fence or a wall:

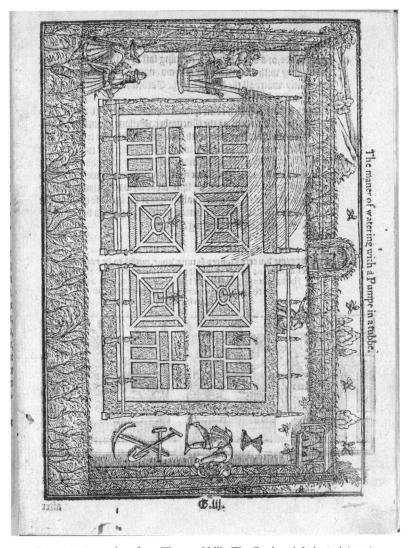

Figure 6. A woodcut from Thomas Hill's *The Gardener's Labyrinth* (1577).

MAN. Why should we in the compas of a pale,
Keepe law and forme, and due proportion,
Shewing as in a modle our firme estate,
When our sea-walled garden the whole land
Is full of weedes ...

(Q1, G3r; 3.4.40–4)

Events taking place in gardens 103

Equally important as the features of actual gardens are the traditional associations of the garden which had been mediated to Shakespeare and his contemporaries through a variety of literary and cultural traditions. In medieval literature, the garden was the place for lovers, as Nan Fairbrother notes:

All that palm beaches and Mediterranean moonlight are for modern popular romancers, their tiny enclosed gardens were for the Middle Ages. The hero first sees his lady among the flowers, which are no fairer than her face; it is in the garden they meet and promise to love forever; and if either of them is shut up by disapproving parents or jealous husband, the window of their tower is sure to overlook a garden where birds sing and flowers blow and it is always summer.[5]

On the other hand, gardens were also frequently associated with beneficial solitude and the love of God. Fairbrother comments further on the enclosed monastic gardens of the Dark Ages: 'The four walls of the cloister garden symbolized contempt for oneself and the world, love of one's neighbour and of God.'[6] Behind the association between gardens and both erotic and divine love are the gardens of the Bible. The allegorical tradition of 'the enclosed garden' (*hortus conclusus*), which flourished in literature and art throughout the Middle Ages and the Renaissance, is based upon the figure in the Song of Songs: 'My sister my spouse *is as* a garden inclosed, as a spring shut vp, *and* a fountaine sealed vp' (4.12).[7] The figure of 'the enclosed garden', an image of the splendour of Solomon's kingdom and of his Bride, was interpreted as a reference to the supernatural quality of the Virgin Mary's chastity.[8] The original enclosed garden was the prelapsarian Garden of Eden, but of course its ambiguous status is that it was also the site of the Fall of Man, and it embodies therefore both human perfection and human weakness and error. Drawing on both elements, Terry Comito, in *The Idea of the Garden in the Renaissance*, refers to meditation, poetry, contemplation and love as the sorts of activity that traditionally find their proper place in gardens, and he argues that what is shared by monks, poets, philosophers and lovers is a nostalgia for Paradise.[9] We shall see that many Shakespearean and non-Shakespearean garden scenes and references to gardens reflect in varying ways these traditional views of the garden.

EVENTS TAKING PLACE IN GARDENS

In some cases the dramatist follows his source for the scene's place-setting; in some cases he invents the locale; and in others he does not seem to be concerned about the locality. In precisely localised scenes, the locale must be of some significance, whether it is borrowed from the source or invented by the playwright himself. In practice, events taking place in many garden scenes have one thing in common: they involve or imply privacy. These privacy-related events can be divided into several kinds: romantic encounters; intimate conversations and confidential talks; melancholic meditations; and violation of privacy by eavesdroppers or intruders. I will take representative scenes involving each kind of event, and consider in what ways the garden setting contributes to the functioning of the scene.

Romantic encounters

Probably, Shakespeare's best known garden scene is *Romeo and Juliet*, 2.2, which is usually referred to as the balcony scene. Shakespeare owes the locale to his source, Arthur Brooke's long narrative poem, *The Tragical History of Romeus and Juliet* (1562).[10] No act or scene division is provided in the Q1, Q2 and F1 texts of the play,[11] and what is traditionally designated as 2.1 and 2.2 is actually one continuous scene. At the beginning of 2.1, Romeo's solo entrance is immediately followed by the arrival of Benvolio and Mercutio, whom he avoids by retiring to a marginal position on the stage. The play was probably performed first at the Theatre and then at the Curtain, and there is no evidence for a stage roof, supported by posts, at either venue. Even if, therefore, the actor could not conceal himself behind a stage pillar, the audience would understand that Romeo has disappeared from the view of his friends, as Benvolio's words make clear: 'He ran this way and leapt this Orchard wall' (Q2, D1r; 2.1.5), followed a little later by, 'he hath hid himselfe among these trees' (D1v; 2.1.30).[12] When his friends have finally given up calling him and left the stage, Romeo comes forward. Then he perceives Juliet's appearance on the upper playing level: 'But soft, what light through yonder window breaks? / It is the East, and *Iuliet* is the Sun' (D1v; 2.2.2–3). In this way, the location changes from outside Capulet's orchard to inside during the course of the scene. After hearing Juliet speak to herself for a while, Romeo finally addresses her. She instantly knows who he is, and asks him, 'How camest thou hither, tel me, and wherfore? / The Orchard walls are high and hard to climbe' (D2v; 2.2.62–3). Romeo answers, 'With loues light wings did I orepearch these walls' (D2v; 2.2.66). The repeated references to the walls contribute to the audience's awareness of the privacy of the place. Rosalie L. Colie sees Shakespeare's use of the locale as a brilliant dramatic treatment of the figure of 'the enclosed garden' (*hortus conclusus*): 'The virgin is, and is in, a walled garden: the walls of that garden are to be breached by a true lover, as Romeo leaps into the orchard.'[13] Terry Comito observes that 'Juliet's orchard is like a medieval garden of love in the rigidity with which it attempts to wall out age and the impoverishment of everyday experience' and that in her orchard 'lovers find no more than a precarious refuge, illuminated by their own beauties, from the world's law and the yoke of inauspicious stars'.[14] It may be significant therefore that towards the end of the scene the young lovers' conversation is interrupted again and again by the Nurse's voice calling Juliet: '*Iu.* I heare some noyse within, deare loue adue: / Anon good nurse' (D3v; 2.2.136–7); 'Madam' (D4r; 2.2.149); 'Madam' (D4r; 2.2.151). The Nurse's offstage calls may suggest the unseen presence of 'age' and 'the world's law'.[15]

This scene is succeeded by another outdoor scene – perhaps another garden scene – where Friar Lawrence enters '*alone with a basket*' (D4v; 2.3.0).[16] As he collects plants, he meditates on the ambivalence of things such as plants, herbs and stones. Unlike Juliet's garden, this place contains 'balefull weedes' as well as 'precious iuyced flowers' (D4v; 2.3.8). The Friar knows that 'The earth that's natures mother is her tombe' (D4v; 2.3.9). The sharp contrast between the two scenes emphasises the purity, beauty and, especially, fragility of the young lovers. The Friar's soliloquy serves as a comment on the event in the previous scene, suggesting that the young, unworldly and, therefore, vulnerable hero and heroine have begun to follow their tragic course.

A less clearly romantic garden appears in *The Two Noble Kinsmen*. Towards the end of 2.1, Palamon and Arcite, who are now prisoners, appear on the upper level: '*Enter Palamon, and Arcite, above*' (Q1, D1v; 2.1.46). Although there is another entry for them at the beginning of the next scene ('*Enter Palamon, and Arcite in prison*' (D2r; 2.2.0)), and although this entry direction does not include '*above*' or its equivalent, they would probably remain on the upper level throughout. As Eugene M. Waith suggests, the double entry may be due to the division of labour between Shakespeare and Fletcher.[17] What is striking about this example is the moment at which the stage begins to represent explicitly the garden beneath the window of the kinsmen's prison. When the two prisoners appear on the upper level, this area of the stage would represent the window of their prison, although explicit references to the window do not occur until very late in 2.2: 'this window' (E1v; 2.2.212); 'The windowes' (E2r; 2.2.262); 'kinde window' (E2v; 2.2.274). On the other hand, the main stage is not precisely localised and remains a neutral location until Emilia enters with her waiting woman. Although the Quarto text prints the line 'This garden has a world of pleasures in't' (D3v; 2.2.118) as the last line of Arcite's speech, it should probably be the first line of Emilia's speech, as modern editors usually treat it.[18] The arrival of the young noble lady and her reference to the garden create a romantic atmosphere, which has not been there until then. She is assumed to be gathering flowers, since, later in the scene, while leaving the stage, she says to the waiting woman, 'lets walk in, keep these flowers' (D4v; 2.2.148). Perhaps she enters with some flowers, already gathered, in her hand, rather than empty-handed.[19] When she refers to flowers – 'What Flowre is this?' (D3v; 2.2.119); 'such flowers' (D4r; 2.2.127); 'these' (D4r; 2.2.128); 'This' (D4r; 2.2.129) – she might make gestures of either pointing to or picking imaginary flowers, or she could show one or two of the flowers she has in her hand. Emilia talks with her waiting woman about flowers such as narcissus and rose, commenting on the boy Narcissus and maiden chastity. Palamon and Arcite love her at first sight, and the devoted friends become deadly foes because of their rivalry for her love. Although the author(s) may have been merely following their main source, 'The Knight's Tale' in Chaucer's *Canterbury Tales*, in locating the scene in the garden beneath the window of the kinsmen's prison,[20] the garden, as we have seen already, is the symbolically appropriate location for the manifestation of romantic love.

Similarly, May's comedy, *The Heir* contains a scene taking place in a garden beneath a window. This scene also involves the encounter of young lovers whose fathers are enemies to each other. In an earlier preliminary scene, Clerimont talks to Philocles about Leucothoe, the daughter of Philocles's father's enemy, and offers to show her to him: 'My lodging's the next doore to this Lords house, / And my backe Window lookes into his Garden, / There euery morning faire *Leucothoe*, / (For so I heare her nam'd) walking alone' (Q1, B3v). The garden scene begins at the upper level with the two men, closely followed by the arrival of the lady and her waiting woman below.

        Enter Philocles, Clerimont at the window.
CLER.   See *Philocles*, yonders that happy shade,
        That often vailes the faire *Lucothoe*,
        . . .
        Yonder she comes, and thats her waiting woman.
              Leucothoe and Psecas in the garden.
        Now gaze thy fill, speake man how likest thou her.
LEU.   *Psecas*.
PSECAS.   Madam.
LEU.   What flower was that
        That thou wert telling such a story of
        Last night to me.
PSE.   Tis [called] *Narcissus* Madam.

                                                            (C2r)

The stage direction for the entrance of Leucothoe and Psecas includes the phrase '*in the garden*'. It apparently functions in the same way as the entry direction for Philocles and Clerimont: just as the phrase '*at the window*' refers to the upper playing space, so the phrase '*in the garden*' seems to refer only to the main stage. Later we shall consider if the direction '*Leucothoe and Psecas in the garden*' could have indicated anything other than the women's entrance on to the main stage. The conversation between Leucothoe and Psecas about the myth of Narcissus, which is similar to the dialogue between Emilia and her waiting woman in *The Two Noble Kinsmen*, 2.2, would create a romantic mood. Philocles falls in love with her at first sight, and immediately begins to write a letter to her. In the meantime, in the garden below, Leucothoe confidentially reveals to her waiting woman that she has loved Philocles since she saw him riding on a street from a window of her house. Philocles throws his letter down to her, and she kisses it after reading it. This scene also reinforces the traditional view of a garden as a place of privacy and secrecy in which passionate emotions can at last be expressed, or to put it another way, in which they can 'flower'.

Intimate talks and confidential conversations

The private space of gardens is a site for intimate talks and secret meetings. *Twelfth Night*, 3.1 begins with a witty exchange between Viola (in her guise as Orsino's manservant Cesario) and Feste: '*Vio*. Saue thee Friend and thy Musick: dost thou liue by thy Tabor?'; '*Clo*. No sir, I liue by the Church' (F1, TLN 1214–16; 3.1.1–3). From their dialogue, it is gradually made clear that they are imagined to be outside Olivia's house. After Feste's exit, Sir Toby and Sir Andrew come to Viola with Olivia's message for her, and then Olivia arrives with her gentlewoman (probably Maria). Olivia dismisses Sir Toby, Sir Andrew and the gentlewoman, saying 'Let the Garden doore be shut, and leaue mee to my hearing' (TLN 1304–5; 3.1.92–3). The three characters would exit, closing at least one of the stage doors. The stage, now identified as a garden, instantly becomes a private space fit for the intimate conversation between Olivia and Viola/Cesario. Olivia's first words to Cesario are 'Giue me your hand sir' (TLN 1305; 3.1.93–4). Despite his apparent indifference to Olivia's increasingly passionate demeanour, Olivia finally confesses her love for him: '*Cesario*, by the Roses of the Spring, / By maid-hood, honor, truth, and euery thing, / I loue thee so, that maugre all thy pride, / Nor wit, nor reason, can my passion hide' (TLN 1364–7; 3.1.149–52). Clearly, the garden setting adds to the romantic mood of the second half of the scene.[21]

A similar effect is created in the opening scene of *Cymbeline*, which is, in the F1 text, divided into two separate scenes: '*Actus Primus. Scoena Prima*' (TLN 1) and '*Scena Secunda*' (TLN 82). In '*Scoena Prima*', two anonymous gentlemen provide the audience with basic information about the situation of the play. This choric part is not precisely localised. They leave the stage, as the Queen, Imogen and Posthumus enter to begin '*Scena Secunda*'. The Queen soon exits, leaving Imogen and Posthumus alone. Her exit speech reads 'Ile fetch a turne about the Garden, pittying / The pangs of barr'd Affections, though the King / Hath charg'd you should not speake together' (TLN 97–9; 1.1.81–3). Thus, I think, she localises the scene as the royal garden, thereby providing it with a romantic mood, although, as Martin Butler says, the reference to the garden might also be taken to imply that the scene is laid in 'a room giving on to a garden'.[22] Imogen weeps, lamenting that Posthumus is being forced from her, while he in turn comforts her, promising to 'remaine / The loyall'st husband, that did ere plight troth' (TLN 112–13; 1.1.95–6). Then the Queen returns and tells them to be brief lest the King should come, but, as indicated in her aside, she exits in order to achieve precisely this aim: 'yet Ile moue him / To walke this way' (TLN 122–3; 1.1.103–4). The occurrence of the verb 'walk' in this speech might well be related to the garden setting. (At the end of the scene, the Queen, leaving the stage, invites Imogen to walk with her: 'Pray walke a-while' (TLN 220; 1.1.176).) While Imogen and Posthumus are exchanging tokens of their love, Cymbeline arrives and orders Posthumus to depart immediately. As will also be apparent later, not only private conversations between lovers but also violations of privacy are common events in garden scenes. It is certainly true that Shakespeare continued the two parts designated as '*Scoena Prima*' and '*Scena Secunda*' by making the exiting gentlemen announce the arrival of the new characters: 'Heere comes the Gentleman, / The Queene, and the Princesse' (TLN 80–1; 1.1.68–9). But, in the matter of location, he differentiated this choric dialogue from the intimate conversation between Imogen and Posthumus.

In *Troilus and Cressida*, the lovers meet for the first time in a garden. At the beginning of 3.2, Troilus asks Pandarus in somewhat grandiloquent terms to take him to Cressida: 'O be thou my Charon. / And giue me swift transportance to these fieldes, / Where I may wallow in the lilly beds / Propos'd for the deseruer' (Q1, F1v; 3.2.10–13). To which Pandarus replies, 'Walke heere ith'Orchard, Ile bring her straight' (F1v; 3.2.16–17). If, as T. W. Baldwin suggests, 'lilly beds' are derived from the Bible's Song of Songs (2.16, 4.5, 6.1–2, 7.2), rather than from Virgil's *Aeneid* (6.637–59),[23] 'th'Orchard' carries overtones of the Song of Songs and, perhaps more distantly, of the postlapsarian Garden of Eden, in keeping with the erotic rather than romantic atmosphere of the scene. Pandarus fetches Cressida, who is almost certainly wearing a veil, because Pandarus says to her, 'Come draw this curtaine, and lets see your picture' (F2r; 3.2.46–7). Her veil reflects her maidenly modesty. It might also be partly related to the garden setting, if wearing a veil was a standard form of protection for the female complexion outdoors. However, early modern English plays, so far as they have been examined up to now, provide no other garden scene where some special kind of headgear or attire might be related to the locale, except for those involving entrances of gardeners.[24] The fact that Cressida is ushered in to Troilus with her face covered by a veil emphasises both the ritualistic and the secretive nature of the lovers' meeting, both aspects reinforced by the enclosed garden setting.[25] The couple's vows of fidelity, made later in the scene, are destined not to be fulfilled, as the play's original audience would have well understood, and this fact transforms the traditional associations of the garden setting from the romantic and erotic to the sourly disenchanted.

The use of a garden for secret purposes is illustrated also in a political scene. When, at the very end of the conjuration scene in *2 Henry VI*, the exiting York orders his servant to invite Salisbury and Warwick to 'suppe with [him] to morrow Night' (F1, TLN 713; 1.4.80), the audience would probably expect to see York entertain the two lords in his house. At the beginning of 2.2, York enters with Salisbury and Warwick.

> *Enter Yorke, Salisbury, and Warwick.*
> YORKE. Now my good Lords of Salisbury & Warwick,
> Our simple Supper ended, giue me leaue,
> In this close Walke, to satisfie my selfe,
> In crauing your opinion of my Title,
> Which is infallible, to Englands Crowne.
> (TLN 959–64; 2.2.0–5)

From York's scene-opening speech, it is first made clear that the supper has already ended. His reference to 'this close Walke' identifies the stage as an enclosed, quiet place at night-time; it also suggests that he has taken Salisbury and Warwick to the garden so that they may talk without being overheard. The stage doors might be closed throughout this scene in order to reinforce the sense of enclosure and secrecy. York, despite having just bluntly told them that his claim is 'infallible', nevertheless now seeks to persuade them of its truth. His attempt would seem to be successful and the two lords kneel to him in fealty.

WARW.	...
	Then Father *Salisbury*, kneele we together,
	And in this priuate Plot be we the first,
	That shall salute our rightfull Soueraigne
	With honor of his Birth-right to the Crowne.
BOTH.	Long liue our Soueraigne *Richard*, Englands King.
	(TLN 1023–8; 2.2.59–63)

When, however, the plotting politician and his guests are becoming partners, the associations of what Warwick calls 'this priuate Plot' are enlarged to encompass not merely secrecy but also the well-established realities of politics. The audience notes the presence both of formal ritual, as the two lords kneel in submission to their future king, and of rather more earthy calculation of political advantage by everyone present. York's final words to his new supporter ends the scene on a suitably astringent note: '*Richard* shall liue to make the Earle of Warwick / The greatest man in England, but the King' (TLN 1048–9; 2.2.81–2).

Melancholic meditations

Not a few garden scenes either begin with or contain fairly long soliloquies. Not surprisingly, most of these are melancholic soliloquies spoken by lovers. It is noteworthy that when in Chapman's *The Widow's Tears* Tharsalio is told that the widow Countess has 'Retir'd into her Orchard' (Q1, E1r), he comments on her behaviour as follows: 'A pregnant badge of loue, shee's melancholy' (E1r). *Twelfth Night* opens with the lovesick Orsino listening to melancholic music. Although the location of the scene is not precisely defined, his description of a musical phrase might suggest a garden setting: 'O, it came ore my eare, like the sweet sound / That breathes vpon a banke of Violets; / Stealing, and giuing Odour' (F1, TLN 9–11; 1.1.5–7). If, on the other hand, he is imagined to be in a room in his palace, his scene-concluding exit with his attendants would suggest that he is leaving for the garden of his palace (as opposed to another part of the garden) in order to spend more time meditating on love: 'Away before me, to sweet beds of Flowres, / Loue-thoughts lye rich, when canopy'd with bowres' (TLN 46–7; 1.1.39–40).

The consensus of scholarly discussion of the authorship of *The Reign of King Edward III* is that at least Act 2 was written by Shakespeare.[26] Act 2, scene 1 begins with Lodwick's soliloquy. He speaks about King Edward's attitude towards the Countess, confirming that the King has fallen in love with her. This explanatory soliloquy ends with the announcement of the

King's arrival: 'Here comes his highnes walking all alone' (Q1, B4r; 2.1.24). Lodwick would withdraw to a side position on the stage lest he should disturb the King's privacy. The King soliloquises:

Shee is growne more fairer far since I came [hither],
Her voice more siluer euery word then other,
Her wit more fluent, . . . (B4r; 2.1.25–7)

No verbal reference to the scene's locale is made until later, when the King says to Lodwick, 'Then in the sommer arber sit by me, / Make it our counsel house or cabynet' (B4v; 2.1.61–2). This speech does not necessarily indicate the presence of an arbour on the stage. The King and Lodwick could have used the discovery space as the arbour. Since, however, their confidential conversation lasts for more than 130 lines (B4v-C2v; 2.1.61–193), and since the action does not really require the structure, it seems more likely that the actors would have remained centre- or front-stage, sitting, perhaps on a bench or chairs, in an imaginary arbour.[27] Lodwick's description of the King's approach as a solitary walk might be a hint of the garden setting: 'Here comes his highnes walking all alone'. When the King comes walking alone, even if no arbour or other garden property has been brought on, the audience, knowing the King's love for the Countess, might conclude that he is meditating in the garden of the Countess's castle. His behaviour is that of a typical melancholy lover, and even though the location is only hinted at, the garden setting helps to reinforce the scene's mood and atmosphere.

Suckling's *Brennoralt*, acted by the King's Men at Blackfriars, has a garden scene that begins with a grief-stricken character's emotional soliloquy.

            Enter Iphigene as in a Garden.
IPH: What have I got by changing place,
       But as a wretch which ventures to the warres,
       Seeking the misery with paine abroad,
       He found, but wisely thought,
       And had left at home   weepes,
                                      (Q1, D3v; D3 missigned 'D5')

Iphigene's soliloquy does not contain any reference to the scene's locale, and what the stage direction '*Enter Iphigene as in a Garden*' might have indicated in any practical sense is something we shall consider later. While Iphigene is weeping, Francelia enters and also soliloquises, revealing her love for Iphigene. Then they recognise each other's presence, and their conversation begins. Iphigene first apologises for disturbing her privacy: '*Francelia*, If through the ignorance of places, / I have intruded on your privacies, / Found out forbidden paths, / 'Tis fit you pardon *Madam*. / For 'tis my melancholy, not I offends' (D4r). He then confesses that his melancholy is because of his love for her. At the end of the scene, she invites him to follow her to a more private place: 'My Lord this ayre is common, / The walkes within are pleasanter' (D4v). On the face of it, Francelia's description of the place as 'common' seems to be inconsistent with Iphigene's apology for intruding into her private space, but the primary function of her speech is to make the scene-concluding exit possible, and in theatrical terms the stage surrounded as it was by spectators – let alone gentlemen stool-sitters on it – was certainly 'common' rather than private. The garden setting clearly adds to both the melancholy and the romantic atmosphere of the scene.

Eavesdropping

The privacy of a garden is not always secure. A garden can in practice be a public space, where one is not wholly secluded from unwanted contact with other people; it can offer a hiding-place for an eavesdropper. *Twelfth Night*, 2.5 supplies a lively example where the puritanical steward's private thinking is overheard by his tormentors. Maria's announcement of Malvolio's approach establishes the locale of the scene: 'Get ye all three into the box tree: *Maluolio's* comming downe this walke' (F1, TLN 1031–2; 2.5.15–16). Sir Toby, Sir Andrew and Fabian hide themselves, as Malvolio enters. The reference to the box tree would have made it possible for the eavesdroppers to use a part of the stage as the box tree, either the hangings covering the discovery space or one of the stage posts. Since they make comments on every speech Malvolio speaks, it is somewhat unlikely that they would have hidden behind the stage hangings; a stage post would have served the purpose better. (When the play was performed on 2 February 1602 in the Middle Temple Hall, a property tree might have been needed.) Malvolio would make a slow and meditative entrance. With the eavesdroppers visible to the audience, making comments from behind a stage post, the stage is far from being the private space that Malvolio, lost in a reverie about his supposed married life with Olivia, believes it to be. The dream world is seemingly verified when he finds the letter left for him by the conspirators, even though in reality the moment represents the triumph of the invaders of his private space.

An illicit love affair is disturbed in Webster's *The White Devil*, 1.2. The time of the scene is established as night at the very beginning of the scene, in this exchange between Bracciano and Vittoria: 'BRA. Your best of rest'; 'VIT. Vnto my Lord the Duke, / The best of wellcome, More lights, attend the Duke' (Q1, B2r). The place-setting is not altogether clear at the beginning of the scene. The speech reading 'gentlemen / Let the caroach go on, and tis his pleasure / You put out all your torches and depart' (B2r) appears to suggest that the scene's event is taking place outside the house of Vittoria's husband Camillo, while the following speeches appear to be spoken inside the house: 'Shrowde you within this closet, good my Lord' (B2v); 'How now brother what trauailing to bed to your kind wife?' (B2v). Vittoria's brother Flamineo makes arrangements for a secret meeting between her and Bracciano. In the middle of the scene, while making sure that Camillo will not disturb the meeting, Flamineo speaks an aside to Vittoria: 'sister my Lord attends you in the banquetting house' (B3v). The reference to the banqueting house might have suggested a garden setting to the original audience. It is perhaps worth mentioning that Francis Bacon's celebrated essay 'Of Gardens' includes a reference to a *'Banquetting House'* as an element of the structure of an ideal princely garden (*The Essays or Counsels, Civil and Moral*, 1625 Quarto, 2N1v).[28] Camillo leaves for his chamber, as Bracciano comes to join Vittoria. Then her chamber-maid, Zanche, '*brings out a Carpet[,] Spreads it and layes on it two faire Cushions*' (B4v). This action of spreading a carpet for the lovers to sit on together might well serve as a visual signal for the garden setting. The specific reference to the locale comes later, and it is perhaps at this point that the scene achieves its distinctive atmosphere of illicit sexuality, reminiscent in some ways of the scene in *Troilus and Cressida* discussed earlier. At the same time, however, Cornelia, the mother of Flamineo and Vittoria, makes her entrance, unperceived by Zanche, Flamineo and the lovers. She would either remain by her entrance door or hide herself behind a stage post. She observes the love tryst from there, lamenting her children's shameless immorality, and finally comes forward to curse them: 'O that this faire garden, / Had all poysoned hearbes of *Thessaly*, / At first bene planted, made a nursery / For witch-craft; rather [than] a buriall plot, / For both your Honours' (C1v).

Much Ado About Nothing, 2.3 and 3.1 are both garden scenes, where the gullers of Benedick and Beatrice deliberately make their supposedly confidential conversations overheard by the gulls. At the beginning of 2.3, Benedick's order for his page to fetch a book establishes the locale of the scene: 'In my chamber window lies a booke, bring it hither to me in the orchard' (Q1, C4v; 2.3.3–4). When he shortly perceives the arrival of Don Pedro, Leonardo and Claudio, he withdraws, saying 'I wil hide me in the arbor' (D1r; 2.3.36). After insisting that Balthasar sing a love song, the Prince and his companions begin to talk about Beatrice's sufferings as a result of her hidden unrequited love for Benedick. They are all sympathetic to her. The Prince observes, 'I loue Benedicke wel, and I could wish he would modestly examine himselfe, to see how much he is vnworthy so good a lady' (D3r; 2.3.206–9). After the gullers have exited, Benedick comes forward and declares his intention to marry her in terms that are richly, if unintentionally, comic: 'it seemes her affections haue their full bent: loue me? why it must be requited ... When I saide I woulde die a batcheller, I did not think I should liue til I were married' (D3r–v; 2.3.223–4, 242–4). The succeeding scene (3.1) begins with Hero sending Margaret off to Beatrice. When Beatrice enters and hides herself in 'the pleached bowere' (D3v; 3.1.7), Hero and Ursula start talking about Benedick's desperate love for Beatrice and about her arrogance. After their departure Beatrice comes forward and addresses the absent Benedick: 'Contempt, farewel, and maiden pride, adew, / No glory liues behind the backe of such. / And Benedicke, loue on I will requite thee, / Taming my wild heart to thy louing hand' (E1r; 3.1.109–12). Clearly, the parallelism here increases the comic effect of these lines.

In these two garden scenes, Benedick and Beatrice hide themselves in the 'arbour'/'bower'. This does not necessarily mean that a property arbour/bower was used for the scenes. As in the eavesdropping scene in *Twelfth Night*, a stage post would have worked just as well if not better,[29] but given that *Much Ado* was very possibly first performed at the Curtain, where the absence of stage cover meant there were no convenient posts to hide behind, this option would not have been available. For this reason, it is very likely that the central discovery space would have represented the arbour/bower and that part of the comic effect would have been created by Benedick and Beatrice peeping through half-open hangings. In 5.1, Claudio teases Benedick with an oblique reference to his eavesdropping in 2.3, 'God sawe him when he was hid in the garden' (H3r; 5.1.179–80). This somewhat clumsy allusion to Genesis, 3.8 retrospectively associates the garden of 2.3 and 3.1 with the postlapsarian Garden of Eden, whose erotic shame is, however, here transposed into comedy.[30]

Intrusion

In some cases, the privacy of a garden is violated by an intruder to unhappy effect, for instance, when a lovers' meeting or a solitary meditation is suddenly interrupted. At the beginning of *The Spanish Tragedy*, 2.4, the entering Horatio and Bel-imperia go to 'the bower' (Q1, D2r) in order to spend there 'a pleasant bower' (D2r) 'in safetie' (D2r), while ordering the (unknown to them) treacherous Pedringano to 'watch without the gate' (D2r). The action of this scene requires the use of a property arbour – possibly a trellis-work arch as illustrated on the title-page of the 1615 edition (Q7).[31] It would have been set up in the central discovery space between the flanking doors. For one thing, the property arbour is used again in 4.2, where Horatio's mother Isabella 'cuts downe the Arbour' (Q1, D3r). When such a large property is repeatedly used in the same play, the curtained discovery space would have been the most convenient place for showing and hiding it. More importantly, when, towards the end of the play, Hieronimno 'Shewes his dead sonne' (K4r), presumably by opening the curtain covering the central discovery space, he is likely reconstructing the murder scene by using the same part of the stage.[32] In 2.4, one of the flanking doors, by which Pedringano exits, represents the gate. He might have shut the door when he left the stage. While the lovers are having an intimate conversation in the arbour, Pedringano returns with Lorenzo, Balthazar and Cerberin. If they are obliged to open the door in order to enter, the intrusiveness of their arrival would be emphasised.[33] As stated in stage directions, 'They hang him [Horatio] in the Arbor' (D2v), and then 'They stab him' (D2v). They leave the stage, carrying Bel-imperia, who is crying 'Murder, murder, helpe *Hieronimo* helpe' (D2v). This example shows how the existence of a door, a necessary feature, renders those who are already in the garden vulnerable to attack.

A similar effect can be observed in Smith's *The Hector of Germany*. This play involves the illicit love story of Young Fitzwaters and his father's betrothed, Floramell. Their meeting takes place in the garden of the house belonging to Floramell's father, Lord Clinton. In the previous scene, the lady's page waits for Young Fitzwaters's arrival at 'a backe dore' (Q1, B3v) and unlocks it for him, after telling him that Floramell is 'Walking in the Garden' (B3v). As soon as Young Fitzwaters exits through the 'backe dore' as if going to see her, Old Fitzwaters arrives with his steward. The steward tells him that Clinton has 'promist to meete [him] in the Garden couertly' (B4r). They attack the page, and exit through the 'backe dore'. The garden scene begins with the arrival of the young lovers: '*Enter in the Garden, Floramell the Lord Clyntons Daughter, and Young Fythwaters. They sit on a banke*' (B4r). While they are enjoying their talk together, their fathers steal in and interrupt it.

Olde Fyth-waters and the Lord Clynton come behinde, and ouer-heare them.

FLO. We grow too iealous of our prosperous daies,
Making an euill, where no ill is meant:
Like hallowed ground, loue sanctifies this place,
And will not suffer danger to intrude.
Here we are ringd in earthly Paradise,
And may haue all the heauen to our selues:
Be then Mistrust an exile from my brest,
Where liues no iealousie, dwells present rest.
CLYN. But wee'l disturbe it, & your amorous ioyes.
Y.FYT. Our Fathers present; Sweet, we are betraid.

(B4r–v)

The furious Old Fitzwaters at first makes to kill his son, but, appeased by Clinton, he forbears and orders Young Fitzwaters to leave England immediately. As Floramell's reference to the garden as 'earthly Paradise' suggests, the vulnerability of gardens may well be related to the Garden of Eden's associations of innocence, temptation and betrayal.[34]

The surviving manuscript of a scenario of a play set in Thrace and Macedon (Folger Shakespeare Library MS X.d.206) offers an outline of Acts 1–3. Unfortunately the play text itself does not survive. Even if the lost play was designed for a private performance by amateur players, this extant manuscript is worth examining in the present context for one reason in particular: the author might have been familiar with performances on the London stage.[35] In the scene-by-scene description of events, the author rarely specifies the locales, but Act 3, scene 10 is an exception:

Ascania meditating in ye priuate walkes of her garden Phonops with ye pas key and Philocles enter: cast a hood over her and carry her away. Phonops bidd's him gagge her and bind her: he warrants her and leades her by ye two thumbes. leades her of ye stage and brings her on againe. <vnco> tells her her doome then vncovers her, discovereth himself and palaceth her with ye Sibyll.

The author specifically locates the scene in the private walks of Ascania's garden. Since the key to the garden is used later in the scene, it might begin with the stage doors being closed, supposing that the stage was equipped with doors. Ascania would enter alone and deliver a meditative soliloquy. Two men suddenly invade her private space by opening one of the stage doors. They bind her and carry her off the stage. They would immediately re-enter by the door opposite the one through which they have exited, suggesting the change of location. The author appears to have thought that the location of something as private and inward as a lady's meditation

The use of garden properties 117

should be nowhere but her garden, and so the effect of the violation of her privacy is all the greater.

*

From this observation of a variety of garden scenes, we can make several important inferences. Shakespeare and his contemporaries appear to have had in their minds the traditional idea and image of the garden. A verbal reference to a garden could create a particular atmosphere on the stage, transforming the stage space into a private, quiet, but potentially vulnerable place. The garden setting could also enhance the secret, romantic, meditative or ominous mood of the scene. Even if, however, the dialogue includes no specific reference to the garden setting, the scene's locality might somehow be suggested indirectly by non-verbal means. The structure of the stage was useful for staging garden scenes. If designated, a stage door, the stage balcony, the discovery space and the stage posts could serve variously as the garden door, a window over the garden, an arbour and trees.

THE USE OF GARDEN PROPERTIES

A garden setting could be established in dialogue alone, but, sometimes visual signals are employed to create a garden atmosphere. Werner Habicht argues that since such scenes as gardens and woods are clearly set off against the more neutral scenes that surround them, they would have been marked visually with property trees. He concludes that 'the tree may be said to have been one of the essential properties on the Elizabethan public stage'.[36] Not a few editors, in their editions of Shakespearean plays, suggest the use of property trees for garden scenes.[37] However, we need to consider whether it really was the case that property trees were necessarily introduced in order to establish garden scenes, given that the stage posts and the curtained space were already available for this purpose.

Property trees were certainly used on the early modern stage. The list of properties compiled by Henslowe in 1598 includes three trees: 'j bay tree', 'j tree of gowlden apelles' and 'Tantelous tre'.[38] These are so special that they must have been prepared for the staging of particular plays. As R. A. Foakes notes, the 'tree of gowlden apelles' was needed for *1 Fortunatus*, mentioned in Henslowe's *Diary* as being performed at the Rose from February 1596, assuming that this play was the basis of Dekker's *Old Fortunatus*.[39] *Old Fortunatus* has a stage direction that directs Vice and others to 'bring out a faire tree of Gold with apples on it' (Q1, C3r) and Virtue and other nymphs to 'bring a tree with greene and withered leaues mingled together, and litle fruit on it' (C3r). Greene's *Friar Bacon and Friar Bungay*, acted by the

Queen's Men, also requires a special tree in the magic competition scene, when Friar Bungay shows Vandermast 'the tree leavd with refined gold, / Wheron the fearefull dragon held his seate, / That watcht the garden cald Hesperides, / Subdued and wonne by conquering Hercules' (Q1, E4r). The stage direction reads '*Heere Bungay coniures and the tree appears with the dragon shooting fire*' (E4r). The elaborate property would have been pushed up through the stage trap, when the play was performed at a purpose-built playhouse.[40] In *The Two Noble Kinsmen*, 5.1, where the prayers of Arcite, Palamon and Emilia are presented successively one by one, the section of Emilia's prayer calls for a specially devised rose tree: '*Here the Hynde vanishes under the Altar: and in the place ascends a Rose Tree, having one Rose upon it*' (Q1, L2r; 5.1.162); '*Here is heard a sodaine twang of Instruments, and the Rose fals from the Tree*' (L2r; 5.1.168). Whereupon, Emilia says 'The flowre is falne, the Tree descends' (L2r; 5.1.169). The rose tree would have appeared and disappeared through the stage trap. There are also stage directions that mention more ordinary trees. In a dumb show in *A Warning for Fair Women*, as the stage direction for it reads, 'suddenly riseth vp a great tree betweene them, whereat amazedly they step backe, wherupon *Lust* bringeth an axe to mistres *Sanders*, shewing signes, that she should cut it downe' (Q1, E3v). Here, too, the big tree was meant to appear from the stage trap. In Peele's *The Battle of Alcazar*, there is a '*last dumbe show*' (presented in the Induction to Act 5), where a 'tree' is required: '*Enter Fame like an Angell, and hangs the crownes vpon a tree*' (Q1, E4v). Her entrance is rather more poetically described by the presenter: 'Fame from her stately bowre doth descend, / And on the tree as fruit new ripe to fall / Placeth the crownes of these vnhappie kings' (F1r). On the assumption that no playhouse had a stage roof before the Rose had one constructed in 1592, there would have been no machinery to manage her descent in the play's original venue, but she could still have been lowered, even if a little awkwardly, from the upper playing level.[41] The representation of a tree would have been less of a problem. One of the columns of the tiring-house façade could have been used for this purpose, or alternatively it could either have been carried on before the dumb show or it might have appeared through the stage trap.[42] In each of these examples, the presence or the appearance of the tree or the trees is deeply involved in the spectacle created. The point I want to emphasise here is that none of these examples is from a garden scene.

A few garden scenes certainly utilise a tree and other garden properties such as an arbour and a bank. *1 Henry VI*, 2.4 requires two rose bushes, one with white flowers and the other with red, so that the men who are quarrelling can pluck the flowers to identify their factions. It is Suffolk's speech 'Within the Temple Hall we were too lowd, / The Garden here is more conuenient' (F1, TLN 931–2; 2.4.3–4) that establishes the scene's place-setting. When, however, the property rose bushes were brought on just before the beginning of the scene, they might well serve as a visual signal for the garden setting. In *The Spanish Tragedy*, 2.4, the use of an arbour is essential, because at the end of the scene it is where Horatio is hanged. Its use by Horatio and Bel-imperia for conversing privately would emphasise the garden atmosphere and the lovers' intimacy. In 4.2 of the same play, the arbour is needed again. To revenge herself upon the place where her son was murdered, the mad Isabella 'cuts downe the Arbour' (Q1, K2r) before 'She stabs her selfe' (K2r). The garden scene in *The Hector of Germany* begins with a stage direction mentioning a bank: '*Enter in the Garden, Floramell the Lord Clyntons Daughter, and Young Fythwaters. They sit on a banke*' (Q1, B4r). In this scene, as in others, the use of the named property is not essential, in that the dialogue includes no reference to the bank, and the action does not absolutely require it, but a real bank would certainly be useful to enhance the romantic mood of the scene. The lovers would sit together on it and conduct an intimate conversation until they are suddenly interrupted by their fathers. This example suggests that garden properties might occasionally have been usefully employed, even though not strictly essential.

While the use of a tree or other garden properties might well contribute to the audience's awareness of a garden setting, it does not seem to have been general practice to create a garden atmosphere by means of such properties. Admittedly, there are cases in which a garden setting is established at the very beginning of the scene and the stage continues to represent the garden throughout the scene. But these are by no means the majority. In some examples, the stage remains a neutral location for a long while until a garden atmosphere is finally created, as in *Cymbeline*, 1.1. In other cases, the locale changes to a garden from another place, or vice versa, during the course of the same scene. A remarkable transition occurs in *Romeo and Juliet*, 3.5, where the locale changes from Capulet's orchard with Juliet's chamber window above to the inside of Juliet's chamber. Such a feat would be easily achieved on a bare stage, and in fact would be more convincingly achieved if the stage were free of the property trees whose sole function is to identify the locale as a garden. Clearly, the mere reference to 'yond Pomgranet tree' (Q2, H2v; 3.5.4) at the beginning of the scene would have served the purpose better than the use of a property tree onstage. It is not always the case that a garden scene is clearly distinguished from the scenes surrounding it.

Even for those scenes where the locale remains a garden throughout, the use of a tree or other garden property might not be desirable: its arrival before the beginning of the scene and its removal at the end would tend to disrupt the smoothness of the scene change. One cannot over-emphasise the flexibility of the early modern stage, which could remain neutral and also, when desired, become specific. A verbal reference to a garden could suffice to establish the garden setting. Merely by being named as such by an actor, the discovery space and the stage posts could then serve as an arbour and trees. It does not appear to have been an early modern practice to use a tree or other garden property as a signal for a garden setting. We must conclude that most garden scenes would have been staged without property trees or garden properties of any kind.

'*ENTER IN A GARDEN*'

Stage directions in the form '*Enter in a garden*' do not therefore imply the use of garden properties onstage. What, then, did such directions actually indicate? Examples besides the one in *Julius Caesar* include the following:

Enter Morosa, *and* Oriana *in the garden.* (Shirley, *The Traitor* Q1, D3v)

Leucothoe and Psecas in the garden. (*The Heir* Q1, C2r)

These may be merely 'fictional' directions, referring to the dramatic world. In other words, what they indicate may be no more than the characters' entrance on to the stage representing the garden. There are also examples of the variant, '*Enter as in a garden*':

Enter Iphigene as in a Garden. (*Brennoralt* Q1, D3v; D3 missigned 'D5')

Enter Cornari *and* Claudiana, *as in the Duke Garden.* (Shirley, *The Gentleman of Venice* Q1, C2v; C1-3 missigned 'B1-3')

These can be counted as 'theatrical' directions because of their inclusion of '*as*'. As Alan C. Dessen has cogently argued, even the form without '*as*' may actually have functioned as 'theatrical' directions, indicating some conventional way of entering that could suggest the locale.[43]

Philip Sidney's *An Apology for Poetry* (*c.*1583, published 1595) offers comments on locale in early Elizabethan drama, which include a remark referring to a method of suggesting a garden setting: 'Now ye shall haue three Ladies, walke to gather flowers, & then wee must beleeue the stage to be a Garden' (1595 Q, K1r). This remark, though contemptuous, might have been actually applicable to some garden scenes. As we have already seen, in *The Two Noble Kinsmen*, 2.2, Emilia is assumed to be gathering flowers in a garden, and she might well have entered with flowers in her hand. An anonymous play, *Wily Beguiled* provides a scene which begins as follows:

> *Enter* Lelia *and* Nurse *gathering of Flowers.*
> LELIA. See how the earth (this fragrant spring) is clad,
> And mantled round in sweete Nymph *Floraes* roabes.
> Here growes th'alluring Rose,
> Sweet Marigolds, and the louely Hyacinth:
> Come Nurse, gather:
> A crowne of Roses shall adorne my head,
> Ile pranke my selfe with flowers of the prime,
> And thus Ile spend away my primerose time.
>
> (Q1, B2r)

Although the dialogue contains neither 'garden' nor 'orchard', the references to 'rose', 'marigolds' and 'hyacinth' and the young lady's action of gathering flowers for making a crown would create the effect of a pleasure garden on the stage. The presence of actual property flowers would have been both unnecessary and unlikely in the early modern theatre. The women's gesture of picking imaginary flowers would be sufficient to create the necessary theatrical illusion, especially if they have entered with flowers in their hands. Later in the scene, Sophos, whom Lelia loves, enters alone. He is weeping, because Lelia's father wants to marry her to a wealthy man and will not allow Sophos to meet her. Lelia and Sophos are overjoyed by this unexpected encounter and declare their love for each other. The garden thus becomes, as so often, the setting for a romantic encounter. Similarly, Dekker's *The Shoemaker's Holiday* has a scene that begins with the stage direction '*Enter Rose alone making a Garland*' (Q1, C1r), the action confirmed by Rose's opening soliloquy: 'Here sit thou downe vpon this flowry banke, / And make a garland for thy Lacies head, / these pinkes, these roses, and these violets' (C1r). The 'flowry banke' that she mentions may well be imaginary, since the action does not really require a property bank. This bank, whether real or imaginary, would not have needed to be strewn with flowers. The boy actor would have entered with either some flowers or an unfinished garland in his hand and made a gesture of picking imaginary flowers for the garland. Such a manner of entering could create a garden atmosphere before she refers to the scene's locale as a secluded place: 'Here as a theefe am I imprisoned / (For my deere Lacies sake) within those walles' (C1r).

It is worth considering whether any of the above-mentioned '*Enter (as) in a garden*' stage directions might indicate that the named character enters carrying flowers and makes a gesture of picking more. In the example, '*Leucothoe and Psecas in the garden*' (*The Heir*), Leucothoe is accompanied by her waiting woman, like Lelia in *Wily Beguiled* and Emilia in *The Two Noble Kinsmen*. Like Emilia, she begins the conversation by asking the name of the flower narcissus. Leucothoe might well have entered with flowers in her hand, suggesting that she is gathering flowers. In another example, '*Enter* Cornari *and* Claudiana, *as in the Duke Garden*' (*The Gentleman of Venice*), Cornari says to his wife Claudiana, 'I prethee give me thy opinion / Who deserv'd best of all the gentlemen? / ... tell me / If thou hadst been to give the garland, prethee / Whose head should wear it?' (Q1, C2v-C3r; C1-3 missigned 'B1-3'). His words might suggest that Claudiana is making a garland of flowers, like Lelia in *Wily Beguiled* and Rose in *The Shoemaker's Holiday*, although it is more likely that Cornari uses the word 'garland' as a metaphor for honour. In a further instance, '*Enter* Morosa, *and* Oriana *in the garden*' (*The Traitor*), neither Morosa nor Oriana mentions any flower. Since, however, they are women (mother and daughter), it is possible for them to enter with flowers in their hands. In the final example, '*Enter Iphigene as in a Garden*' (*Brennoralt*), it is clearly unlikely that the man would have been imagined to be gathering flowers. Although the use of flowers is possible in the three cases involving female characters, it is not certain that even there the stage direction '*Enter (as) in a garden*' indicates that the named character enters carrying flowers. Admittedly, entering with flowers in one's hand could have been one way of '*entering (as) in a garden*'. There must however have been another, perhaps more usual, way of indicating the setting that could have been adopted by male as well as female characters.

The surviving playhouse manuscript of *Sir Thomas More*, originally written by Munday (and Chettle?),[44] provides a garden scene. The playbook was certainly prepared for stage production, although it is not known whether the play was actually performed in the early modern period.[45] The garden scene, which appears in the original portion of the play, begins with an entry direction indicating the way in which the characters make the entrance:

>   Enter the Lady Moore, her two daughters, and M^r. Roper, as walking<
> RO.   Madame, what ayles yee for to looke so sad.
> LADY.   Troth Sonne, I knowe not what, I am not sick,
>   and yet I am not well: I would be merie
>   but somewhat lyes so heauie on my hart:
>   I cannot chuse but sigh.
>   (MS, TLN 1282–7)

The dialogue of the scene includes no specific reference to a garden. The scene is, however, most likely located in the garden of More's house, because, a short time later in the same scene, when More arrives there, Roper and Lady More greet him as follows: '*Ro.* your Honor's welcome home' (TLN 1344); '*Lady.* will your Lordship in?' (TLN 1347). Although the stage direction does not include the phrase 'in a garden' or the like, it seems very plausible that the entering actors were intended to appear as if they were walking in a private garden.[46] In order to create this impression, the actors would, for a start, have been suitably attired in house dress. Female characters might have been wearing a special kind of headgear to protect their complexions from the sun. More importantly, the entering actors would have walked as if they were in a garden. Generally speaking, on the Shakespearean stage, an entering actor usually walked the distance between a stage door and the main acting area, i.e., the front part of the stage. In what special manner, then, should Lady More and other entering characters walk on the stage in order to convey to the audience that they are in a garden? Vittorio Gabrieli and Giorgio Melchiori, who locate the scene in the garden of More's house in Chelsea, think that the entering characters pace up and down the stage.[47] A passage from *The Gardener's Labyrinth* helps to suggest what 'walking up and down' might mean in this case.

> The commodities of these Alleis and walkes, serue to good purposes, the one is, that the owner may diligently view the prosperitie of his herbes and flowers, the other for the delight and comfort of his wearied mind, which he may by himselfe, or fellowship of his friendes conceyue, in the delectable sightes, and fragrant smelles of the flowers, by walking vp and downe . . . (1577 Q, C4v)

Some garden scenes contain verbal references to garden paths. In the second gulling scene in *Much Ado About Nothing* (3.1), while waiting for Beatrice's arrival in 'the orchard' (Q1, D3v; 3.1.5), Hero gives detailed instructions to Ursula. The instructions include 'As we do trace this alley vp and downe, / Our talke must onely be of Benedicke' (D4r; 3.1.16–17). At the beginning of *2 Henry VI*, 2.2, the entering York, Salisbury and Warwick were very likely intended to stroll on the 'close Walke' imagined on the stage (F1, TLN 962; 2.2.3). In 4.10 of the same play, the entering Iden would pace along an imaginary path while delivering these lines: 'Lord, who would liue turmoyled in the Court, / And may enioy such quiet walkes as these?' (TLN 2921–2; 4.10.16–17).[48] Shortly after the beginning of *Twelfth Night*, 2.5, Maria places a false love letter on the stage, after announcing Malvolio's approach: '*Maluolio's* comming downe this walke' (F1, TLN 1031–2; 2.5.15–16). The entering Malvolio might well stroll on the imaginary walk, while speaking to himself: ''Tis but Fortune, all is Fortune. *Maria* once told me she did affect me' (TLN 1039–40; 2.5.23–4). He might continue pacing to and fro until he finally finds the letter. In the preceding examples of '*Enter (as) in a garden*' various characters are involved, including a carefree young lady (Leucothoe) and a grief-stricken man (Iphigene). These entering characters might well have walked up and down imaginary paths, whether pensively or cheerfully, with flowers in their hands, as appropriate. When Iphigene first speaks to Francelia in *Brennoralt*, he mentions garden paths: '*Francelia*, If through the ignorance of places, / I have intruded on your privacies, / Found out forbidden paths' (Q1, D4r). There might be exceptional cases. The following stage direction, for example, might suggest that the entering characters go directly to the bank: '*Enter in the Garden, Floramell the Lord Clyntons Daughter, and Young Fythwaters. They sit on a banke*' (*The Hector of Germany* Q1, B4r). It seems, however, certain that a standard way of '*entering (as) in a garden*' was strolling along an imaginary path before and while speaking the first lines of the dialogue or soliloquy.[49]

We have earlier concluded tentatively that, when in *Edward III*, 2.1 the King makes his entrance, 'walking all alone', the audience, who have preliminary knowledge about his love for the Countess, might have understood that he is meditating in the garden of the Countess's castle. Although the stage direction for his entry simply reads '*Enter King Edward*' (B4r; 2.1.24), and includes no phrase such as '*(as) in a garden*', the entering King might well have created the impression of being in a garden by pacing along an imaginary alley. In modern productions of *As You Like It*, as Cynthia Marshall notes, Orlando is often discovered, as the curtain rises, working at some menial chore, nailing ivy, digging with a spade or chopping wood.[50] On the Globe stage, the play began with the entrance of Orlando and Adam: '*Enter Orlando and Adam*' (F1, TLN 2; 1.1.0). Both characters might have walked to and fro during Orlando's pensive opening speech in such a way as to suggest that they were following imaginary paths.[51] The movement could have provided a hint, even if not a very strong one, as to where they were. Shortly after, Oliver has scarcely arrived than he asks Orlando,

'Now Sir, what make you heere?' (TLN 32; 1.1.29) with the implication that Orlando should not be there.[52] The audience is made fully aware of the location ten more lines later when Orlando replies to his brother's contemptuous question, 'Know you where you are sir?' (TLN 43, 1.1.40) with the bitter reply, 'O sir, very well: heere in your Orchard' (TLN 44; 1.1.41).

JULIUS CAESAR, ACT 2, SCENE 1

As frequently observed, a comparison between Thomas North's translation of Plutarch's *Lives of the Noble Grecians and Romans* (1579) and Shakespeare's *Julius Caesar* shows how closely Shakespeare followed his source, and this is especially true of the Portia and the Ligarius episodes.[53] In Plutarch's *Lives*, however, these events are narrated separately and neither takes place in Brutus's orchard. The locale of *Julius Caesar*, 2.1 is Shakespeare's own invention. Let us examine the scene, with our findings about contemporary garden scenes in mind. It begins as follows:

> *Enter Brutus in his Orchard.*
> BRUT. What *Lucius*, hoe?
>   I cannot, by the progresse of the Starres,
>   Giue guesse how neere to day – *Lucius*, I say?
>   I would it were my fault to sleepe so soundly.
>   When *Lucius*, when? awake, I say: what *Lucius*?
>   *Enter Lucius.*
> LUC. Call'd you, my Lord?
> BRUT. Get me a Tapor in my Study, *Lucius*:
>   When it is lighted, come and call me here.
> LUC. I will, my Lord.   *Exit.*
> BRUT. It must be by his death: and for my part,
>   I know no personall cause, to spurne at him,
>   But for the generall.
>   (F1, TLN 615–28; 2.1.0–12)

Judging from the fact that knockings are to be heard offstage later on, this scene might begin with the stage doors closed. (In that case, they would have been closed immediately before the start of the scene, because they were most likely kept open throughout the previous scene, which appears to take place in a street.) Suppose that Brutus enters the stage by opening one of the flanking doors and comes slowly forward as if he were walking along a path in a garden. He suddenly stops and calls Lucius, turning back to face the door by which he has entered: 'What *Lucius*, hoe?' Then he resumes his meditative walk, perhaps towards the other side of the stage, following another imaginary path. While walking in this manner, he looks up at the heavens and speaks the succeeding two lines about 'the progresse of the Starres'. The Shakespearean audience would have instantly understood that he had come out of his house and was walking in his garden before daybreak. He is wearing his clothes unfastened, since later in the same scene, Portia says to him, 'Is *Brutus* sicke? And is it Physicall / To walke vnbraced, and sucke vp the humours / Of the danke Morning?' (TLN 902–4; 2.1.261–3). The manner of wearing his clothes is significant. For one thing, in the previous scene, Cassius was dressed in the same way: '*Cassi*. . . . And thus vnbraced, *Caska*, as you see, / Haue bar'd my Bosome to the Thunder-stone' (TLN 486–7; 1.3.48–9). He made the scene's concluding exit with Caska as if going to Brutus's house, after or while saying 'let vs goe, / For it is after Mid-night, and ere day, / We will awake him, and be sure of him' (TLN 610–12; 1.3.162–4). Brutus's entrance, with his clothes unfastened, would show that he is not only 'awake' in both literal and metaphorical meanings but is also almost ready to be involved in the enterprise conceived by Cassius.[54]

Although the opening part of the scene contains no verbal reference to the door or the wall of the place, the stage, with its doors closed, would serve as an imaginatively enclosed space, a perfect place for Brutus's private contemplation. Brutus ponders on the significance of killing Caesar: 'It must be by his death . . . .' He is suffering a dilemma, torn between 'personall' love for Caesar and the 'generall', public good. It may be that each time Lucius comes to Brutus, he opens the door, and each time he is sent off, he closes the door. One thing that is almost certain is that Lucius would enter and exit through the door by which Brutus himself made his entrance. The dialogue implies that this door leads to Brutus's 'Study'/'Closet' (TLN 623, 652; 2.1.7, 35) and to Lucius's 'Bed' (TLN 655; 2.1.39). Scarcely has Lucius appeared from this door for the third time with the news that 'March is wasted fifteene dayes' (TLN 679; 2.1.59) than a knocking is heard from offstage ('*Knocke within*' (TLN 680; 2.1.59)). Brutus orders him to 'Go to the Gate' (TLN 681; 2.1.60), defining the other flanking door as 'the Gate'. Lucius exits and re-enters by that door and says to Brutus, 'Sir, 'tis your Brother *Cassius* at the Doore, / Who doth desire to see you' (TLN 692–3; 2.1.70–1).[55] The secretive nature of the visit of Cassius and his companions is reflected in the manner in which they are wearing their clothes: Lucius cannot tell the names of Cassius's companions, because 'their Hats are pluckt about their Eares, / And halfe their Faces buried in their Cloakes' (TLN 697–8; 2.1.73–4). The conspirators are admitted,

Cassius apologising for disturbing Brutus so early: 'I thinke we are too bold vpon your Rest' (TLN 713; 2.1.86). But Brutus welcomes him and his companions. After hearing something from Cassius, he addresses all the conspirators.

BRU. Giue me your hands all ouer, one by one.
CAS. And let vs sweare our Resolution.
BRUT. No, not an Oath: . . .
                       Then Countrymen,
What neede we any spurre, but our owne cause
To pricke vs to redresse? What other Bond,
Then secret Romans, that haue spoke the word,
And will not palter? And what other Oath,
Then Honesty to Honesty ingag'd,
That this shall be, or we will fall for it.
                     (TLN 743–5, 753–9; 2.1.112–14, 122–8)

Brutus's speech is the fulcrum of the scene. In explicitly repudiating Cassius's suggestion that they should swear an oath of allegiance, he not only commits himself to the conspirators' cause, he also becomes its leader. It is, furthermore, the fatal moment in which he finally severs the ties of friendship that connect him to Caesar. He and the other conspirators make arrangements for assassinating Caesar. As soon as they depart, probably through the door by which they have entered ('the Gate'/'the Doore'), Portia enters, presumably from the opposite door (i.e., the one by which Brutus entered at the beginning of the scene). She is probably wearing a nightgown, because Brutus tells her to return to bed (TLN 901; 2.1.260). Her costume would greatly contribute to the intimacy of her talk with Brutus. She kneels and by 'the Bond of Marriage' (TLN 922; 2.1.280) pleads to know the cause of his trouble. Their conversation is, however, interrupted by a '*Knocke*' from offstage (TLN 946; 2.1.303). Brutus promises to disclose his secret to her and makes her withdraw, naturally through the door by which she has entered, as Lucius leads in Ligarius, the final member of the conspiracy, from the other door ('the Gate'/'the Doore'). Ligarius addresses Brutus as 'Soule of Rome' (TLN 966; 2.1.321) and asks him what his enterprise is. Brutus replies, 'What it is my *Caius*, / I shall vnfold to thee, as we are going, / To whom it must be done' (TLN 975–7; 2.1.329–31). Fully satisfied with this answer, Ligarius offers to follow Brutus. Finally, Brutus leaves the stage with Ligarius, most plausibly through the door by which Ligarius entered.[56]

What is striking about this long and varied scene is that many of its elements (solitary contemplation, a secret meeting, an intimate conversation and interruptions of privacy) are common features of very many Shakespearean and non-Shakespearean garden scenes. The actors' use of the stage doors is particularly significant. When Brutus leaves the stage by the door designated as 'the Gate' and 'the Doore', and not by the other one that is imagined to lead into his house, his departure would give the impression that, prompted by the conspirators and despite his wife's concern about his health and safety, the man who puts Rome's good before his own welfare leaves his home to face his ruinous fortune. No other place would have been more appropriate than his orchard for the setting of the scene where he makes up his mind to sacrifice his private self for what he takes to be the public good. Although the dialogue contains no specific reference to the locale – and certainly there is nothing to indicate that garden properties would have been brought on – nevertheless even without these hints, the Globe audience, seeing Brutus pacing his imaginary alley, would undoubtedly have imagined a private garden on the bare stage.

CHAPTER 6

What to do with onstage corpses?

In the London commercial theatres of Shakespeare's time the stage projected into the auditorium and there were no curtains between the stage and the audience. Characters could not simply be discovered on stage, as they can in the modern theatre, and the action of the play necessitated first getting them on stage and then getting them off again. Entrances and exits were therefore the most basic elements of early modern theatre, and dramatists and actors, as well as handling them in a routine way, used them to create different effects. We have seen how Brutus would have transformed the Globe stage into 'his orchard' while making his scene-opening entrance of *Julius Caesar*, 2.1 and how significant the scene's concluding departure would have been when he made it with Ligarius through the door opposite the one by which he had 'entered in his orchard'. But this is a relatively simple dramatic effect. A more challenging situation arises when a character dies on the stage. At some point, usually by the end of the scene, his/her body had to be removed from the stage, and this chapter deals with how the early modern theatre handled exits of dead characters.

The dumb show presented prior to the *Gonzago* play in *Hamlet*, Act 3, scene 2 illustrates Shakespeare's careful treatment of onstage corpses. I quote from the Q2 text, which is thought to have been printed from authorial papers:

Enter a King and a Queene, . . . he lyes him downe vpon a bancke of flowers, she seeing him asleepe, leaues him: anon come in an other man, takes off his crowne, kisses it, pours poyson in the sleepers eares, and leaues him: the Queene returnes, finds the King dead, makes passionate action, the poysner with some three or foure come in againe, seeme to condole with her, the dead body is carried away, the poysner wooes the Queene with gifts . . . (H1v; 3.2.135)

Even in the play-within-the-play, Shakespeare did not allow the dead body to stand up and walk off.[1] He thought that the king's body should be borne out by at least three players: certainly it should not be dragged off as unceremoniously as Polonius's body is carried away later in the same play.

In the F1 text, which appears to derive from a transcript of a playhouse manuscript, the number of the bearers is different: '*The Poysoner, with some two or three Mutes comes in againe, seeming to lament with her. The dead body is carried away*' (TLN 1998–2000). In this stage direction the term '*Mutes*' refers to hired players. In actual performances, the king's corpse may therefore have been carried away by no more than two hirelings. Further, as we shall see later, an even more economical form was possible.

The removal of dead bodies from the stage was a theatrical necessity, but it had to be carried out in a way consistent with the reality of the play world. In some cases stage directions specifically indicate the disposal of the dead body by one or more onstage characters, as in the following examples:

Here they beare away his Body. Exeunt. (*3 Henry VI* F1, TLN 2854; 5.2.50)

Exit Hamlet tugging in Polonius. (*Hamlet* F1, TLN 2585; 3.4.217)

Then they lay the body in the Countinghouse. (*Arden of Faversham* Q1, I1v)

In many cases the dialogue contains a cue for onstage characters to carry away the corpse.

> EXTON ... This dead king to the liuing king Ile beare.
> Take hence the rest, and giue them buriall heere.
> (*Richard II* Q1, K1r; 5.5.117–18)

> BOS. ... Come, I'll beare thee hence.
> And execute thy last will; that's deliuer
> Thy body to the reuerend dispose
> Of some good women:... *Exit.*
> (*The Duchess of Malfi* Q1, K4v)

> CAR. Take vp these slaughtered bodies, see them buried ...
> (*'Tis Pity She's a Whore* Q1, K4r)

In other cases the text, slightly disconcertingly, gives no information about the removal of the dead body.[2] It may simply be that, where no specific instruction is provided, one or more onstage characters were usually expected to carry the body offstage at the end of the scene. If so, however, some of these situations pose practical theatrical problems. A consideration of these problems may reveal some staging practices offering ingenious solutions to the question of what to do with an onstage corpse. It may also give us some insight into how the early modern period accommodated the fictional reality of the play world to the physical reality of the playhouse and how actors onstage mediated between the one and the other.

CARRIED OFF BY STAGE ATTENDANTS?

1 Selimus, a Queen's Men play, generally ascribed to Greene, contains many scenes in which a character dies onstage (Scenes 6, 13, 14, 19, 23, 25, 28 and 31). In none of these cases does the text provide any clear information about the removal of the corpse. In some cases either the killer of the victim or other onstage characters would probably carry the body away when they leave the stage. But in other cases it is less easy to see what would take place. Consider Scene 6. Its opening stage direction reads 'Alarum, *Mustaffa* beate *Selimus* in, then *Ottrante* and *Cherseoli* enter at diuerse doores' (Q1, C4r). Although this direction does not mention Mustaffa's immediate exit after beating Selimus off, the fact that Mustaffa is not involved in the subsequent action suggests that he would exit, running after Selimus.[3] Suppose therefore that when Mustaffa and Selimus have left the stage, Ottrante and Cherseoli make a simultaneous entrance from different doors. They exchange vehement words before fighting. The scene's closing direction, 'They fight. He killeth *Cherseoli*, and flieth' (C4v), implies that Ottrante exits, leaving the dead body of Cherseoli. The corpse, however, had to be carried off the stage, since the opening direction of Scene 8 requires the body to be brought on: 'Enter *Bajazet, Mustaffa*, the souldier witth the bodie of *Cherseoli*, and *Ottrante* prisoner' (C4v). It may be that the mute soldier mentioned in Scene 8's opening direction was intended to carry off Cherseoli's body after Ottrante has made his exit at the end of Scene 6, although his involvement in Scene 6 is not specifically indicated. Since an alarum sounds at the beginning of Scene 7 ('Alarum, enter *Selimus*' (C4v)), the soldier could enter and immediately take away Cherseoli's body, before Selimus's arrival, while the battle sound is being heard.

Scene 19 is more problematic. This scene begins with the entrance of three characters: 'Enter *Baiazet, Aga*, in mourning clokes, *Abraham* the Iew with a cup' (G3v). Abraham offers the drink to Bajazet and Aga, but he is made to drink it first. After Bajazet and Aga have followed his example, Abraham reveals that the drink was a poison and dies (G4v). Bajazet curses Abraham and dies (H1r), and Aga also dies (H1r). One of the three corpses is mentioned in the opening stage direction of Scene 21, which reads 'Enter *Selimus, Sinam-bassa*, the courses of *Mustaffa* and *Aga*, with funerall pompe, *Mustaffa*, and the Ianizaries' (H3r). In this direction, 'the courses of *Mustaffa* and *Aga*' is clearly an error for 'the courses of *Bajazet* and *Aga*', because Mustaffa's name is mentioned twice, and in the second reference he is self-evidently alive. Further confirmation is provided by Selimus saying at the start of the scene, 'Why thus must *Selim* blind his subiect eies, / And straine his owne to weep for *Baiazet*' (H3r). Since, therefore, the corpses of Bajazet and Aga should be brought on at the beginning of Scene 21, their dead bodies and also Abraham's corpse had to be removed at the end of Scene 19. But, how and by whom? The absence of any other indication may suggest that the author was simply indifferent to the theatrical problem of how to remove dead bodies from the stage. Nevertheless, there is a practical problem here that has to be solved, and two possibilities are that, regardless of whatever kind of playing place the company was using, either stage attendants would have been expected to carry off dead bodies or, alternatively, corpses would have occasionally been allowed to make exits by themselves.

One difficulty with the first suggestion is that there is no evidence that stage attendants performed the task of carrying corpses offstage. In two of the eighteen surviving manuscript playbooks, one from the Revels Company at the Red Bull and the other from the Lady Elizabeth's Men at the Cockpit, stage keepers are mentioned: '*Guard Tay: Stage k:*' (*The Two Noble Ladies*, TLN 400); '*Tay. Gib: Stage k:*' (*The Two Noble Ladies*, TLN 900); 'Gib: Stage: Taylo'' (*The Captives*, TLN 1492); 'Stagekeepers as a guard' (*The Captives*, TLN 2805). These four annotations are all marked by the same book-keeper.[4] The important thing to stress here is that in these cases the stage keepers make their entrances on to the stage as characters belonging to the world of the play, and not as theatre employees. No extant theatrical plot mentions stage keepers, although the plot of *The Dead Man's Fortune* calls for an entry of the company 'tyre man' as an attendant (TLN 34–5). Even if many more playbooks and theatrical plots survived, that still might not confirm whether a stage servant would have carried off a corpse. Extrapolating from such little evidence as there is suggests that if stage keepers were occasionally expected to remove onstage corpses, they would have performed the task as characters such as soldiers and servants.

ALLOWED TO WALK OFF?

As for the possibility that corpses were occasionally allowed to walk off, there is no stage direction supporting it. Although there is a stage direction reading '*Exit Coarse*' (*Richard III* F1, TLN 423; 1.2.226), what this direction actually indicates is the departure of the funeral procession. (The scene's opening stage direction, which indicates the arrival of the procession, reads '*Enter the Coarse of Henrie the sixt with Halberds to guard it, Lady Anne being the Mourner*' (TLN 173–4; 1.2.0)). A post-Restoration play, *Knavery in All Trades*, provides a valuable passage, in which a character tells a nostalgic anecdote about the legendary hero of the Fortune playhouse in the 1630s, Richard Fowler:

fourth. But did you know *Mat Smith, Elis Worth*, and *Fowler* at the Fortune?
fifth. Yes, and I will tell you by a good token; *Fowler* you know was appointed for the Conquering parts, and it being given out he was to play the Part of a great Captain and mighty Warriour, drew much Company; the Play began, and ended with his Valour; but at the end of the Fourth Act he laid so heavily about him, that some Mutes who stood for Souldiers, fell down as they were dead e're he had toucht their trembling Targets; so he brandisht his Sword & made his *Exit*; ne're minding to bring off his dead men; which they perceiving, crauld into the Tyreing house, at which, *Fowler* grew angry, and told 'em, Dogs you should have laine there till you had been fetcht off; and so they crauld out again, which gave the People such an occasion of Laughter, they cry'd that again that again, that again. (Q1, D4v-E1r)

What can be inferred from the anecdote is that in fighting scenes, actors were usually expected to carry their victims offstage.[5] The anecdote also suggests that usually even the corpse of a mute character would not have been expected to crawl off the stage, let alone to stand up and walk off. The Fortune, by Fowler's time, had already adopted act-intervals. Even at the end of an act, however, the corpses would normally have lain onstage till being carried off.

The situation is different of course when a character is merely assumed by those onstage to be dead but is in fact alive. In Marlowe's *The Jew of Malta*, Barabas's sudden death is announced and his supposedly dead body is brought on: '*Offi*. Dead, my Lord, and here they bring his body' (Q1, I1v). The moment all the other onstage characters depart, the 'dead' Barabas rises with 'What, all alone? well fare, sleepy drinke' (I2r) and immediately plans his revenge on 'this accursed Towne' (I2r). Shakespeare's *1 Henry IV* supplies these correlated stage directions: '*Enter Douglas, he fighteth with Falstalffe, he fals down as if he were dead*' (Q1, K2v; 5.4.76); '*Falstalffe riseth vp*' (K3r; 5.4.110). Similarly, Marston's *Jack Drum's Entertainment* offers '*He* [Pasquill] *lies downe, and faines himselfe dead*' (Q1, D2r); '*Mamon sings. Lantara, &c. Pasquill riseth, and striketh him*' (D2r). In *The Malcontent*, also by Marston, Mendozo 'Seems to poison Maleuole' (QA, H1v), making Celzo believe Malevole's death. Shortly after, to Celzo's great surprise, Malevole 'Starts vp and speakes' (H2r). Further, Heywood's *2 The Iron Age* has '*Synon who had before counterfeited death, riseth vp, and answereth*' (Q1, K3v). Finally, in Killigrew's *The Prisoners*, Gallippus uses the same ploy twice: '*Gallip. throwes his Sword at the King, & counterfeits and falls, then the King leaves him and pursues Lucanthe*' (D1, B7r); '*Gall.* Hell take thee: [*Exit*]' (B7r);[6] '*Gallippus lies downe by her, and counterfeits himselfe dead*' (C8r); '*Gallippus stirres and when he sees Hiparcus rises*' (C8v).⁷ It seems a reasonable speculation that the use of this ploy would have depended for its theatrical effectiveness on the fact that audiences had not been rendered blasé by the frequent sight of fictional corpses rising up and making their unaided way offstage.

It is also important to note that intervals between the acts were related in varying degrees to the fictional world. The reality of the fictional world was not wholly maintained throughout, and often the practical needs of the play required that it be breached. In hall theatres, for instance, pauses in the action were essential to give time for stage attendants to trim the candles that lit the stage or, if necessary, to replace them. The Induction to *The Staple of News*, a Jonson play acted by the King's Men at Blackfriars, has a stage direction '*The Tiremen enter to mend the lights*' (F2, 2A2v).⁸ In both indoor and open-air theatres, the time would have been used for stage hands to place or remove props for the next act. Some play texts reproduce book-keepers' instructions for such tasks performed during act-intervals. Examples include '*Whil'st the Act Plays, the Foot-step, little Table, and Arras hung up for the Musicians*' (Massinger, *The City Madam* Q1, K1r)⁹ and '*Six Chaires placed at the Arras*' (Fletcher and Rowley, *The Maid in the Mill* F1, 4A2v). The second direction is printed at the end of Act 1 of the play. The chairs were to be used for Don Julio and his guests as spectators at the country-sports masque in the middle of the second scene of Act 2: '*Jul.* Come, come; The Sports are coming on us: / Nay, I have more guests to grace it: Welcome / Don *Gostanco, Giraldo, Philippo:* Seat, seat all' (4A4r). Fredson Bowers observes: 'The placing of the chairs here, some 275 lines before they are required, would seem to indicate that the division between Act I and Act II was an interval, used to facilitate the mechanics of the performance.'¹⁰ On the other hand, various examples show that even during act-intervals the logic of the fictional world could control the stage space to the extent of preventing the departure of characters who were merely sleeping as well as those who were actually dead. In the F1 text of *A Midsummer Night's Dream*, which appears to have been influenced by a playbook marked up for a post-1609 revival of the play, the sleeping characters are instructed to remain onstage during the interval between Acts 3 and 4: '*They sleepe all the Act*' (TLN 1507). The actors were not allowed to walk off the stage at the end of Act 3 and then return at the beginning of Act 4 after taking a rest in the tiring-house during the interval.

The interval between acts was sometimes used to present in musical terms the event taking place in the play world during the time between the acts. In Fletcher and Massinger's *The Little French Lawyer*, the interval between Acts 4 and 5 was intended to be filled with the kind of music related to the story of the play, as we have seen in Chapter 3. In the Folio text of *King Lear*, which represents a post-1609 version, a stage direction marked near the end of Act 2 calls for '*Storme and Tempest*' (TLN 1584; 2.4.284), and the opening stage direction of Act 3 reads '*Storme still. Enter Kent, and a Gentleman, seuerally*' (TLN 1615; 3.1.0). It may well be that sound effects representing strong winds, rain and thunder filled the interval between Acts 2 and 3.[11] Something similar seems to have been required by an additional stage direction marked by the Cockpit book-keeper in the manuscript of *The Captives*: 'Act: 2 Storme contynewed' (MS, TLN 651). Furthermore, act-intervals were occasionally used to present fictional events in abbreviated form by means of a dumb-show device, as in the following instances:

Whilest the Act is a playing, Hercules and Tiberio enters, Tiberio climes the tree, and is receiued aboue by Dulcimel, Philocalia and a Priest: Hercules stayes beneath. (*Parasitaster, or the Fawn* Q1, H3r)

Here a passage ouer the Stage, while the Act is playing for the Marriage of Charalois with Beaumelle, &c. (Field and Massinger, *The Fatal Dowry* Q1, F1r)

In the Act time Deflores hides a naked Rapier. (*The Changeling* Q1, D3v)

From these examples it seems evident that the audience was expected to remain in the fictional world even during act-intervals.

In general we should dismiss the possibility that corpses walked off in view of the audience, while allowing that in those situations where the removal of the bodies by stage attendants would not have been the simpler and more elegant solution, the corpses might indeed have had to walk or crawl off the stage as unobtrusively as possible. The implications of this conclusion are that, despite the many non-realistic conventions of the early modern drama, and despite the frequency with which dramatists broke the illusion of a wholly separate play world, nevertheless for a corpse to get up and walk offstage in the middle of the play was in every sense a step too far. It would have represented too radical a disruption of the illusion on which the play world depended. But different rules apply in the middle of the play from those that obtain at the end, and in the latter case, as I shall argue later, the spectacle of a corpse coming to life and leaving the stage was more readily accepted.

CONCEALED BY HANGINGS

The following examples illustrate the inventive ways in which playwrights and players used the discovery area for solving the staging problems of the disposal of the corpses without disrupting the reality of the fictional world. As mentioned above, in the Q2 and F1 texts of *Hamlet*, in the dumb show to the *Gonzago* play, the player king's dead body is carried away from the stage by some minor players. Interestingly, the Q1 text, which some scholars think reflects London performances,[12] does not mention the removal of the corpse.

Enter in a Dumbe Shew, the King and the Queene, he sits downe in an Arbor, she leaues him: Then enters Lucianus with poyson in a Viall, and powres it in his eares, and goes away: Then the Queene commeth and findes him dead: and goes away with the other. (Q1, F3r)

The significant point is that the Q1 text directs the king to sit down in an arbour, as opposed to the Q2 and F1 texts which have him lie on a bank: '*he lyes him downe vpon a bancke of flowers*' (Q2, H1v; 3.2.135); '*Layes him downe vpon a Banke of Flowers*' (F1, TLN 1994). On the Globe stage, the arbour could easily have been represented by the discovery space. In the Q1 staging, the dead body of the player king could therefore have been concealed by the stage curtains.[13] It is by no means certain that the Q1 staging was actually adopted at the Globe, but on the assumption that it was, the use of stage curtains would have been a convenient means of avoiding the necessity for bringing on bearers to remove the corpse.

Two of Shakespeare's love tragedies require at their conclusion the use of the discovery space. The final scene of *Othello* has as its opening stage direction '*Enter Othello, and Desdemona in her bed*' (F1, TLN 3239; 5.2.0). The bed with Desdemona lying in it would have been pushed out from the discovery area on to the stage, rather than merely 'discovered', because the tragedy's most important events were to take place either on or near the bed.[14] Most notably, it is where Othello strangles Desdemona. Then, Emilia, who is stabbed by Iago, dies beside Desdemona. Finally, Othello stabs himself and falls on the bed. It was not necessary for their bodies to be borne out at the end of the play. Instead, on Lodovico's instruction, 'Let it be hid' (TLN 3679; 5.2.365), either the bed curtains would have been closed, or the bed would have been drawn into the discovery space and concealed by the stage curtains. The last scene of *Romeo and Juliet*, which takes place in Capulet's monument, is likely to make use of the discovery space for Juliet's tomb, although it is also possible that the stage trap could represent it.[15] (Earlier in the play, when Juliet drinks Friar Lawrence's potion, the space must have been used for either thrusting out or revealing her bed. The actors could have visually emphasised the miscarriage of her hopes by using the same place for staging both her bed and her tomb.[16]) In the finale, Paris, Romeo and Juliet are found dead near the tomb. Supposing that the tomb was represented by the discovery space, the three bodies could have been placed in it and concealed by the stage hangings, perhaps at the end of the play immediately before the general exit, or possibly when the Prince orders, 'Seale vp the mouth of outrage for a while' (Q2, L4v; 5.3.216).[17]

Marston's *Antonio's Revenge*, performed by the Children of Paul's, provides a further intriguing example. The curtains of the upper playing level and the curtains of the main stage level are both used in the last sequence of scenes. On the main stage, Antonio and other revengers, who have disguised themselves as masquers, dance a measure to celebrate Piero's marriage to Maria. During the dance, the ghost of Andrugio positions himself in the central space on the upper level: '*While the measure is dauncing, Andrugios ghost is placed betwixt the musick houses*' (Q1, K1v). Piero then orders sweetmeats to be brought in. The revengers persuade him to dismiss Galeatzo, senators and others from the stage. The moment the unwitting victim sits down at table, they '*binde Piero, pluck out his tongue, and tryumph ouer him*' (K2r). After tormenting him by showing the dish that contains his son Julio's flesh, the revengers stab him one by one, and then '*They run all at Piero with their Rapiers*' (K3r). The ghost of Andrugio, who has derived great satisfaction from the sight, makes his final exit, being covered with the upper curtains: '*The curtaines being drawne, Exit Andrugio*' (K3r). As for the removal of Piero's body, the lower curtains are drawn to cover it: '*The curtaines are drawne, Piero departeth*' (K4r). It may be that the table of sweetmeats was revealed by means of the stage curtains, and that Piero was stabbed to death in the discovery space. The stage direction's use of the verb '*departeth*' may, however, indicate that the corpse should be carried into the discovery space, perhaps by one or two of the characters who have returned with Galeatzo and the senators.

The Spanish Tragedy, 4.2 consists of the mad Isabella's soliloquy, which ends with her violent action against herself. The 1592 Quarto (Q1), which is the sole authority for the play, and the 1602 Quarto (Q4), which reproduces 'new additions' (Q4, A1r), differ about the placing of the direction 'She stabs her selfe' (Q1, K2r); '*She stabs her selfe*' (Q4, L1v). The Q1 text places the direction before the last line of her soliloquy, while the Q4 edition prints the direction after her last line. It is not certain whether in the Q1 version Isabella is really intended to stab herself one line earlier. The placing may be related to the fact that the direction takes two lines in the margin at the foot of the page (K2r). Philip Edwards suggests the possibility that Isabella dies offstage, saying that 'if she is to drag herself, wounded, off-stage, she has one line to speak as she does so'.[18] Even if we adopt the earlier timing of when she stabs herself, however, it may be that she does not begin to move until after delivering her last line. In any event, although neither text provides an actual direction for Isabella, she might have made a stumbling exit,[19] but it is equally possible that she was intended to die onstage, regardless of the fact that no such direction as '*she dies*' occurs in either text. In the beginning of the scene, Isabella, having entered with a weapon, says 'I will reuenge my selfe vpon this place, / Where thus they murdered my beloued Sonne' (Q1, K2r); 'I will reuenge my selfe vpon this place, / Where they murdered my beloued sonne' (Q4, L1r), and, as instructed by the stage direction, 'She cuts downe the Arbour' (Q1, K2r); '*She cuts downe the Arbour*' (Q4, L1r). The property arbour used for Horatio's hanging earlier in the play would probably have been set up in the central discovery space between the flanking doors, and so she might well die in it near the arbour. In both versions, Isabella's scene-ending suicide is followed by Hieronimo's scene-opening arrival: 'Enter *Hieronimo*, he knocks vp the curtaine' (Q1, K2v); '*Enter* Hieronimo, *He knocks vp the curtaine*' (Q4, L1v). Hieronimo, in fictional terms, makes a curtained space so that he can conceal his dead son's body in order to reveal it later, but the curtain could also permit the actor playing Isabella to stand up and walk off out of sight of the audience.

2 Edward IV, usually attributed to Heywood, has a scene dealing with the murder of the late King Edward's two sons in the Tower.[20] The two princes, Edward and Richard, say their prayers and leave the stage, as Tyrrell makes his entrance: 'As the yong Princes go out, enter Tirill' (Q1, T2r). An offstage noise convinces the onstage Tyrrell that his subordinates have carried out the violent attack on the young princes: 'A noyse within' (T2r). Then the murderers, Dighton and Forrest, enter by opposing doors, each carrying one of the dead princes: 'Enter at one doore Dighton, with Edward vnder his arme, at the other doore Forrest with Richard' (T2r). 'They lay them downe' (T2v). As Tyrrell's scene-closing speech indicates, the three onstage characters make their joint departure, leaving the two bodies onstage: 'The priest here in the Towre will burie them, / Let vs away' (T2v). Since the succeeding scene, which takes place in Mistress Blage's house, has nothing to do with the murder of the princes, the corpses need somehow to be disposed of at the end of the scene. If Dighton and Forrest put the two corpses together in the central space between the doors through which they had brought them, the bodies could have been concealed by the stage hangings.

Greene's *Friar Bacon and Friar Bungay*, acted by the Queen's Men, has a scene where two Suffolk students visit Friar Bacon's cell in order to find out by means of his magic mirror how their respective fathers are faring. To their dismay, the magic mirror shows the fathers killing each other:

'*They fight and kill ech other*' (Q1, H2r). This act incites both sons to avenge their fathers' deaths, an aim they promptly achieve, each dying at the other's hand: '*The two schollers stab on another*' (H2r). Friars Bacon and Bungay have been onstage throughout the scene, which enables them plausibly to remove the sons' bodies. Disposing of their fathers' bodies is a more tricky matter, because so far as the drama is concerned, they are not actually there at all; Friar Bacon had merely produced an image in his magic mirror of their fatal encounter, which took place elsewhere at Fressingfield. A hint as to how this might have been managed is contained in a stage direction earlier in the play: '*Enter Frier Bacon drawing the courtaines with a white sticke, a booke in his hand, and a lampe lighted by him, and the brasen head and miles, whith weapons by him*' (G1v). In response to the students' request, he could reveal his magic mirror by opening curtains – either the stage curtains (in a purpose-built theatre) or a free-standing property (where the stage equipment was not so complete).[21] The fathers would emerge on to the stage where the fight would take place, but at the moment of simultaneously killing each other they would fall back within the curtained space. Shortly afterwards, in remorse at the two extra deaths his mirror has indirectly caused, Friar Bacon '*breakes the glasse*' (H2r), and at this point he would close the curtains, concealing the fathers' dead bodies.

DEATHS ON THE UPPER GALLERY

Some death scenes involve the use of the upper playing level. Consider, for example, More's execution, which takes place in the finale of *Sir Thomas More*. On arriving at the place of execution, he says, 'Oh, is this the place? / I promise ye it is a goodly Scaffolde' (MS, TLN 1911–12). After 'going vp the stayres' (TLN 1920), he says 'Truely heers a moste sweet Gallerie' (TLN 1926), while 'walking' (TLN 1926) up and down. It may be that a scaffold was meant to be brought onstage at the beginning of the scene, although the playbook contains no stage direction calling for it. But it seems more likely that the scaffold was intended to be represented by the upper playing level, against which the stairs could have been set up. In that case, the executioner would have entered above directly from the tiring-house. When More finally lays his head on the block, after saying 'No eye salute my trunck with a sad teare, / Our birthe to heauen should be thus: voide of feare' (TLN 1981–2), an '*exit*' direction is given for his action (TLN 1982). Suppose that the upper gallery served as the scaffold. Since this area was continuous to the upper floor of the tiring-house, the actor playing More could exit into the inside of the upper level where his execution takes place out of sight of the audience.²² It is possible that a similar procedure was adopted for the hanging of Lincoln, which takes place much earlier in the same play. In that scene, a 'Iibbit' is 'set vp' on the stage (TLN 584). Lincoln is directed to mount the ladder to the gibbet: 'he goes vp' (TLN 613). When he is executed, the stage direction for him reads 'he leapes off' (TLN 636). No cue is provided in the text for the removal of his body, and this presents us with two alternatives. It may be that the gibbet is set up against the tiring-house façade so that Lincoln can jump into the inside of the upper level. It is equally possible that he is actually hanged on the stage and that his body is carried off at the end of the scene. We shall return to this question after examining some more execution scenes.

Hanging scenes were fairly common on the early modern stage. *The Spanish Tragedy* has two onstage hangings. In the first arbour scene Horatio's murderers 'hang him in the Arbor' (Q1, D2v). In the scene of Pedringano's execution, some scaffolding would have been brought on. He mounts the ladder, and the hangman 'turnes him off' the ladder (F3v). In each case, as the text informs, the corpse is borne out from the stage: 'Heere he [Hieronimo] throwes it from him and beares the body [of Horatio] away' (D4r); '*Depu.* So Executioner, conuay him [Pedringano] hence, / But let his body be vnburied' (F3v). Yarington's *Two Lamentable Tragedies* also offers an execution scene. The scene's opening direction reads '*Enter* Merry *and* Rachel *to execution with officers with Halberdes, the Hangman with a lather. &c.*' (Q1, K1v). Merry is hanged first ('*Goe vp the lather*' (K1v); '*Turne of the Lather*' (K2r)), and then Rachel climbs up the ladder ('*Rach.* . . . Come let me clime these steps that lead to heauen' (K2v)). This execution scene ends with an officer's instruction, 'Cut downe their bodies, giue hers funerall, / But let his body be conueyed hence, / To Mile-end greene, and there be hang'd in chaines' (K2v). These and other hanging scenes imply that the early modern theatre had devised a reliable harness of some kind for the actor to wear to ensure that he could be 'hanged' safely. According to John H. Astington, the use of body harness for hanging scenes was a staging practice inherited from the medieval cycle plays.²³

Fletcher and Massinger's tragedy of *Sir John van Olden Barnavelt*, which survives in a playhouse manuscript, ends with the beheading of the titular character. The manuscript contains a stage direction that calls for a scaffold to be brought on: '*Enter Prouost Barnauelt: Lords: Guard. (a Scaffold put out). Execution*' (TLN 2849–54). Just after ascending the scaffold, Barnavelt says: 'Thus high yo^u raise me, a most glorious kindnes / for all my Cares, for my most faithful service / for yo^u, and for the State, thus ye promote me' (TLN 2858–60). He prays to heaven, and his execution is finally carried out. (Some device would have been used for the effect of the decapitation.²⁴) A lord then orders the executioner to 'draw in the body' (TLN 2998), and a second lord makes a brief comment on his end: 'Farwell, great hart: full low thy strength now lyes, / he that would purge ambition this way dies' (TLN 3002–3). It may be that the scaffold with Barnavelt's supposedly headless body lying on it was intended to be conveyed into the discovery area. It is equally possible that the second lord's words imply that Barnavelt's body has been removed from the scaffold and put on the stage so as to be carried off. Sir Thomas More's execution, mentioned already, is unusual though not unique among execution scenes because of its symbolic resonance. More's final exit on the upper level might very well have suggested his execution as being a glorious victory over earthly power and authority.[25] Given the importance of this symbolic effect, we can surmise that the execution of Lincoln earlier in the *Sir Thomas More* play would not have involved the use of the upper level.

Act 4, scene 5 of Fletcher's *Bonduca* is a siege scene, in which Romans occupy the main stage and Britons appear on the upper level: '*Enter Swetonius, Iunius, Decius, Demetrius, Curius, and Souldiers: Bonduca, two daughters, and Nennius, above. Drum and Colours*' (F1, 4H4v). When Bonduca refuses to yield to the Romans and forces her daughters to die with her, the upper position gives her death the aspect not just of an honourable end but of a symbolic victory over those who have vanquished her. Swetonius appropriately says, 'Give her fair Funeral; / she was truely noble, and a Queen' (4I1v). There are some more scenes involving deaths on the upper gallery. In *1 Henry VI*, 1.4, Salisbury and Gargrave are shot dead when they are '*on the Turrets*' with Talbot and Glansdale (F1, TLN 487; 1.4.22).[26] In *3 Henry VI*, 5.6, Richard of Gloucester stabs Henry VI to death '*on the Walles*' of the Tower of London (F1, TLN 3073; 5.6.0).[27] *Two Lamentable Tragedies* has the stage direction '*Then being in the vpper Rome* Merry *strickes him in the head fifteene times*' (Q1, B4r). In these cases, however, unlike the ceremonial death of Sir Thomas More and the symbolic triumph of Bonduca, the effect of the upper location may have been merely to emphasise the victims' helplessness and isolation. Regardless of its theatrical effect, one thing we may say for certain is that the upper playing area was a convenient place from which to dispose of the corpse.

THE USE OF THE STAGE TRAP

The stage trap was another useful means for disposing of dead bodies. This can be seen in two drowning scenes in *Locrine*, a revenge play written possibly by Peele, or, more probably by Greene, and published as 'Newly set foorth, ouerseene and corrected, By *W. S.*' (Q1, A2r).[28] In Act 4, scene 5, the defeated Scythian King Humber, alone onstage, commits suicide after saying 'And gentle *Aby* take my troubled corps, / Take it and keep it from all mortall eies' (H4r). The stage direction 'Fling himselfe into the riuer' (H4r) suggests that the actor was intended to jump into the stage trap. Immediately after this action, the ghost of Humber's victim, Albanact enters, perhaps from the trapdoor, although the direction only says 'Enter the ghoast of *Albanact*' (H4v). He expresses great joy and returns to the underworld: 'Vnbind *Ixion* cruell *Rhadamanth*, / And laie proud *Humber* on the whirling wheele / Backe will I post to hell mouth *Tanarus*' (H4v). The use of the trap door in both cases would certainly have reinforced in the audience's mind its status as gateway to the underworld. In the finale of the play, Locrine's young daughter Sabren, when captured by his father's enemies, kills herself after saying 'And that which *Locrines* sword could not perform, / This pleasant streame shall present bring to passe' (K4r). The stage direction 'She drowneth her selfe' (K4r) indicates that she would also have used the stage trap.

Some river scenes involve multiple murders. In a scene in *The Devil's Charter*, a Globe play, Caesar Borgia, aided by Frescobaldi, murders the Duke of Candy, his brother, and throws the corpse into the river Tiber: 'Helpe *Frescobaldi* let vs heaue him ouer, / That he may fall into the riuer *Tiber*' (Q1, F4r). No sooner is this done than 'Caesar *casteth* Frescobaldi *after*' into the river, in order to get rid of all evidence of the crime. By using the trap as the river, Caesar could avoid carrying off the two dead bodies. *The Hector of Germany*, acted at the Red Bull and at the Curtain by young London citizens, has a scene in which Young Fitzwater enters with three scoundrels, and contrives to bring about the deaths of all of them. Before leaving the stage at the end of the scene, he says, 'But I must cast you all into the Riuer. / Yes, swords and all, to cleare mee from suspect' (Q1, G3v). Here too the river was most likely represented by the stage trap, through which Young Fitzwater could have disposed of the three men's bodies and their weapons.

In the penultimate scene of Marlowe's *Edward II*, the prisoner King is finally murdered by Lightborn, Matrevis and Gurney. At the end of the scene, after stabbing Lightborn to keep his silence, Gurney says to Matrevis: 'Come let vs cast the body in the mote, / And beare the kings to *Mortimer* our lord, away' (Q1, M1r). They might throw Lightborn's body into the stage trap, especially if the King has appeared from there as if from the dungeon which is 'the sincke, / Wherein the filthe of all the castell falles' (L4r). However it is equally possible that the moat is offstage. Since the King's murder involves the use of a bed, Gurney and Matrevis could have utilised the curtained space to get rid of Lightborn's body as well as the King's. In *Macbeth*, 3.3, Banquo is attacked and killed by the three murderers hired by Macbeth. They were probably expected to bear the body offstage at the end of the scene, even though the text contains no stage direction or speech indicating how it should be removed. In the succeeding scene, however, before the beginning of the banquet, the first Murderer says to Macbeth that Banquo is 'safe in a ditch' (F1, TLN 1285; 3.4.25), and this speech may suggest that the murderers were intended to throw Banquo's body into the stage trap. It is perhaps worth mentioning here that the term 'ditch' occurs in a few stage directions, referring to the space below the stage, and that one of these directions can be found in a play ascribed by some scholars to Shakespeare: 'Then Shakebag falls into a ditch' (*Arden of Faversham* Q1, G2v)[29]; '*Shee fals downe vnder the Stage, and he followes her, and fals into the ditch*' (*The Valiant Welshman* Q1, D4v). If Banquo's corpse was disposed of by means of the stage trap, his ghost might have used the same place for his entrances and exits in the banquet scene. The stage directions for its appearances, however, say merely '*Enter the Ghost of Banquo, and sits in Macbeths place*' (*Macbeth* F1, TLN 1299; 3.4.36) and '*Enter Ghost*' (TLN 1363; 3.2.87), and this question would depend largely on the positions of the banquet table and the chairs on the stage.[30]

Marlowe and Nashe's *Dido, Queen of Carthage*, acted by the Children of the Chapel,[31] ends with three suicides. First, Dido makes Iarbas help her to create a fire, dismisses him and then casts herself into the flames.

Now *Dido*, with these reliques burne thy selfe,
And make *Aeneas* famous through the world,
For periurie and slaughter of a Queene: (Q1, G2r)

Iarbas returns and kills himself in despair, having been tricked by Dido's words, 'after this is done, / None in the world shall haue my loue but thou' (G2r). Finally, Anna follows him by killing herself. It appears that the staging of fire sometimes utilised the stage trap, and sometimes the discovery space. In the following four stage directions, the first two indicate the use of the trap, while the other two indicate the use of the discovery space:

Thunder, and the Gulfe opens, flames issuing; and Ophioneus ascending, with the face, wings, and taile of a Dragon; a skin coate all speckled on the throat. (Chapman, *Caesar and Pompey* Q1, C3v)

The Devills sinck roaring; a flame of fier riseth after them. (*The Two Noble Ladies* MS, TLN 1860–1)

Let there be a brazen Head set in the middle of the place behind the Stage, out of the which, cast flames of fire . . . (Greene, *Alphonsus, King of Aragon* Q1, F1v)

Enter Harpax in a fearefull shape, fire flashing out of the study. (*The Virgin Martyr* Q1, L1r)

It is therefore very likely that Dido used either the stage trap or the discovery area for her final exit. As for the deaths of Iarbas and Anna, the text provides no precise information as to how they kill themselves. It is possible that they also burned themselves in the same manner as Dido.[32] If, however, we take Anna's last words literally, she and Iarbas seem to have stabbed themselves; before killing herself, she says to the dead Iarbas, 'But *Anna* now shall honor thee in death, /And mixe her bloud with thine' (G2v).[33] In that case, the play would have ended with two corpses onstage, requiring removal or some other device. Another play by Marlowe offers a further example. In *2 Tamburlaine the Great*, Act 3, scene 4, the Captain of Balsera dies from a bullet wound while flying from Scythians with his wife and son. Olympia, his wife, stabs the son to death ('She stabs him' (O1, H6r)) and burns the two corpses, as indicated in the subsequent dialogue: 'ther. How now Madam, what are you doing?'; 'Olim. Killing my selfe, as I haue done my sonne, / Whose body with his fathers I haue burnt, / Least cruell Scythians should dismember him' (H6v). For this scene, either the trap or the discovery space would have been used.

Shirley's *1 St Patrick for Ireland*, written for an Irish company, offers a further fire scene, where Milcho sacrifices his life for the sake of his pagan religion. After saying to St Patrick 'I choose to leap into these fires / Rather than heare thee preach thy cursed faith. / Y'are sure to follow me' (Q1, G2v), '*He burnes himselfe*' (G2v). Since the text contains directions such as '*An altar discovered*' (C4v) and '*Sinks*' (I3v), Shirley, in writing this play, had evidently thought of the availability of a discovery space and a stage trap.[34] The fire scene is then succeeded by an altar scene. Its opening stage direction, '*Recorders. The Altar prepar'd with Ferochus and Endarius, as before*' (G2v), suggests the use of the discovery space for placing the altar. Taken together, these matters seem to confirm that Milcho was intended to use the stage trap for his self-immolation, it being the most appropriate exit-point for him, because of its associations with hell. As for the exit of St Patrick and other onstage characters, the stage direction simply reads '*Exeunt*' (G2v). They would not follow Milcho. Led by St Patrick's guardian angel Victor, St Patrick, the Queen and a bard would exit from one of the stage doors, as suggested by St Patrick's speech 'Oh Tyrant, cruell to thy selfe, but we / Must follow our blest Guide and holy Guardian: / Lead on, good Angell' (G2v).

AT THE END OF THE PLAY

By examining a variety of onstage deaths, we have observed how efficiently Shakespeare and his contemporaries utilised the curtained space, the gallery over the stage and the stage trap so as to present visually impressive and symbolically meaningful killings and deaths and also to avoid the necessity of bringing on bearers for the corpses. Some of these examples occur in the middle of plays, and others occur towards the ends. But only as it reaches its conclusion do we sometimes see the use of a device that is never employed in the main body of the play. The ending of *The Changeling*, Beatrice and De Flores being already dead onstage, consists of an epilogue spoken by Alsemero:

> EPILOGUE
> ALS. *All we can doe, to Comfort one another,*
>   *To stay a Brothers sorrow, for a Brother;*
>   *To Dry a Child, from the kinde Fathers eyes*
>   *Is to no purpose, it rather multiplies:*
>   *Your only smiles have power to cause re-live*
>   *The Dead agen, or in their Rooms to give*
>   *Brother a new Brother, Father a Child;*
>   *If these appear, All griefs are reconcil'd.*
>
>   Exeunt omnes.
>   (Q1, I3v)

The actor of Alsemero is here speaking directly to the audience, making the conventional plea for applause. The general exit marked after the epilogue indicates that all the other actors are still onstage while the epilogue is being spoken. When they make their departure, it is just possible that the bodies of Beatrice and De Flores could have been borne away by their fellow actors, but Alsemero's speech has deliberately broken the illusion of the alternative reality of the play world, and so it is much more likely that they would have walked off like every one else. The words, '*Your only smiles have power to cause re-live / The Dead agen*' are particularly significant, because it seems to represent, rather gracefully, the cue for the actors playing Beatrice and De Flores to stand up and acknowledge the applause along with the other actors before leaving the stage.

Heywood's *2 The Iron Age* ends with nine corpses onstage: Pyrhus, Orestes, Pillades, Diomed, Menelaus, Thersites, Cethus, Synon and Hellena. Scarcely has Hellena killed herself when Ulysses enters alone and delivers the play's closing speech. It is noticeable that he speaks its first lines within the play world and then speaks the rest of the speech directly to the audience:

In thee they are punisht: of all these Princes,
And infinite numbers that opposed *Troy*,
And came in *Hellens* quarrell (saue my selfe)
Not one [suruiues], . . .
And since I am the man soly reseru'd,
Accept me for the Authors Epilogue.
If hee haue beene two bloody? tis the Story,

Truth claimes excuse, and seekes no farther glory,
Or if you thinke he hath done your patience wrong
(In teadious Sceanes) by keeping you so long,
Much matter in few words, hee bad me say
Are hard to expresse, that lengthned out his Play.

(Q1, K4v)

Here it seems incontestable that the nine onstage corpses were expected to walk off at the end of the play, since anything else would have been completely impractical. A short time earlier in the same scene, Synon, who had been assumed to be dead, stood up, fought with Cethus, and died: 'Synon *who had before counterfeited death, riseth vp, and answereth*' (K3v); '*They* [Cethus and Synon] *fight, and kill one another*' (K4r). Now, at the end of the play, after Ulysses has spoken the epilogue on behalf of the author, the nine dead bodies, including Synon's corpse, would stand up as living actors, without the risk of causing confusion for any of the less attentive members of the audience.

A university play, *Orestes*, written by an Oxford student, Thomas Goffe, suggests that academic dramatists came to the same conclusion as professional playwrights regarding solving the problem of how to arrange the departure of dead characters. In Act 5, scene 2, where Strophius and Electra are alone onstage, Strophius dies first, and then Electra stabs herself. In scenes 4 and 5, their corpses are still onstage. The text gives no information as to whether the corpses should remain onstage until the end of the play or whether they should be carried away before Act 5, scene 7, in which another killing takes place. In Act 5, scene 7, which is the penultimate scene of the play, Orestes and Pylades arrive '*with naked rapiers*' (Q1, I2v), '*run at one another*' twice (I2v), and they finally '*fall downe dead, embracing each other*' (I3r). When, in the last scene, Tyndarus enters with lords and others, at least two corpses, possibly four, lie onstage. He delivers his play-closing speech directly to the audience:

Then now is *Argos* Court like to some stage,
When the sad plot fills it with murdred Trunckes,
And none are left aliue but onely one,
To aske the kinde spectators (*plaudite*)
All else haue bid (*valete*) to the world,
The man reseru'd for that, is *Tyndarus*,
. . .
And as these friends ioin'd hands to beare their Fate;
So we desire you to imitate.
Who since they all are dead, we needs must craue
Your gentle hands to bring them to their graue.

(I3r–I4r)

At the end of the play 147

Tyndarus and others might have carried the bodies offstage, though if there were four of them – and the phrase 'since they all are dead' suggests more than two – this could have been a cumbersome and time-consuming procedure. It seems at least as likely that, after Tyndarus makes his request for applause, the corpses would have got up, bowed and made their way to their offstage 'grave'.[35]

It is relevant to cite here Robert Weimann's discussion of epilogues. Dealing with the epilogues to *As You Like It*, *All's Well That Ends Well* and *The Tempest*, he observes that in each case 'the epilogue gracefully helps to displace or at least tone down a sense of abruptness in the perception of an abiding gulf between represented roles and performing actors'.[36] His analysis of the epilogue to *As You Like It* is especially useful: he traces the transition from fictional representation to theatrical reality by showing how the actor begins the epilogue speaking from within the role of Rosalind ('It is not the fashion to see the Ladie the Epilogue' (F1, TLN 1776–7; Epilogue.1–2)), gradually distances the assimilated role, and ends up pledging, 'If I were a Woman, I would kisse as many of you as had beards that pleas'd me' (TLN 2791–3; Epilogue.18–19).[37] Michael Shapiro suspects that 'this change was signaled or accompanied by a physical gesture such as the removal of a wig or some article of female attire'.[38] As to the endings of *The Changeling*, *2 The Iron Age* and *Orestes*, it is certain in each case that the epilogue helps the audience to register the gap between the fictional event and the physical reality and allows the onstage corpses to return to the actual bodies of the actors. As Tiffany Stern has plausibly argued, most prologues and epilogues may very well have been ephemeral. But the epilogues to these three plays suggests that at least in some cases the epilogue was integral to the play's ending and therefore virtually the same epilogue would have been used for the play's revivals.

We should also consider the endings of plays that have no epilogues. In the finale of *Hamlet*, there are four dead bodies onstage: Hamlet, Claudius, Gertrude and Laertes. In both Q2 and F1 versions, Horatio asks Fortinbras to give 'order that these bodies / High on a stage be placed to the view' (Q2, O2r (O2 missigned 'G2') / F1, TLN 3872–3; 5.2.377–8). In both versions, he responds to Horatio's request by saying 'Let foure Captaines / Beare *Hamlet* like a souldier to the stage' (Q2, O2r; 5.2.395–6); 'Let foure Captaines / Beare *Hamlet* like a Soldier to the Stage' (F1, TLN 3895–6). But then the two versions differ about the number of bodies to be carried away: 'Take vp the bodies' (Q2, O2r; 5.2.401); 'Take vp the body' (F1, TLN 3902). The Q2 text is agreed to have been printed from the author's manuscript, while the F1 text appears to derive from a transcript of a theatrical manuscript. The difference may possibly imply that, for practical reasons, Shakespeare finally intended the actors playing Claudius, Gertrude and Laertes to stand up and leave the stage after the end of the play. Like F1, the Q1 text, which is thought to reflect actual performances, perhaps at the Globe, adopts the singular form: 'Take vp the bodie' (I4r). Whereas the dead body of Hamlet was treated with dignity and respect, the disregarded dead bodies of Claudius and the others sprawled on the stage would have made an effective contrast. The F1 text specifically instructs that the funeral march be followed by an offstage sound: '*Exeunt Marching: after the which, a Peale of Ordenance are shot off*' (TLN 3905–6; 5.2.403). Fortinbras's eulogy on the hero, the funeral march and the offstage cannon salute – these bring the play to a sombre and ceremonial conclusion, following which the corpses could stand up and go offstage without in any way disrupting the emotional power of the ending.[39]

King Lear offers a similar case. Towards the end of the play, the bodies of Goneril and Regan are brought on and then Lear enters with Cordelia's body in his arms before expiring himself, so that at the end of the play the bodies of Lear and his three daughters are on stage. The wounded Edmond having been carried away to die offstage, the tragedy ends with the sad reunion of Lear and his three daughters.[40] When Albany says 'Beare them from hence' (F1, TLN 3293; 5.3.319), it is not certain that he orders the removal of all four corpses. It is possible that he refers only to Lear and Cordelia, excluding Goneril and Regan, whose faces he has had covered ('couer their faces' (TLN 3199; 5.3.243)). In practice, four would have been too many to be borne out ceremoniously with respect. It is therefore very likely that only Lear and Cordelia were carried away in the funeral procession accompanied '*with a dead March*' (TLN 3302; 5.3.327). Until after the funeral march ended, the dead bodies of Goneril and Regan would therefore have remained onstage, waiting for their departure as living actors.

As a final example of how the number of corpses onstage can grow at a prodigious rate in a short space of time, consider what happens at the end of *The Duchess of Malfi*. The Q1 text employs the massed entry technique, and the initial stage direction of the play's last scene reads: '*Cardinall (with a Booke) Bosola, Pescara, Malateste, Rodorigo, Ferdinand, Delio, Seruant with Antonio's body*' (N2r). The last scene actually begins with the Cardinal's entrance, followed shortly by the arrival of Bosola and a servant bearing Antonio's body. After killing the servant, Bosola stabs the Cardinal. Then Ferdinand enters and '*He wounds the Cardinall, and (in the scuffle) giues Bosola his death wound*' (N3r). Bosola in turn kills Ferdinand. Shortly Pescara, Malateste, Roderigo and Grisolan, who have been above, come down and see the fatally wounded Cardinall and Bosola die one after the other. Finally, Delio arrives with Antonio's son. In short, at the end of the play, there are five dead bodies and six living characters on the stage. The text provides no indication that the living characters should bear away any of the corpses, not even the virtuous Antonio who is presumably the subject of the proverb-like couplet with which Delio ends the play: '*Integrity of life, is fames best friend, / Which noblely (beyond Death) shall crowne the end*' (N4r), an allusion to Horace's famous ode 'Integer vitae scelerisque purus ...' and also to the proverbial idea that 'the end crowns all'.[41] We must conclude that the audience's applause, which would crown the performance, would also serve as a cue for the five dead bodies to come to life and leave the stage with the living characters.[42]

PHYSICAL REALITY AND THE FICTIONAL WORLD

As the performance commences, the fictional world is created on the stage. The doorways in the stage wall and the actors' comings and goings through them greatly contribute to the audience's consciousness that the fictional world extends behind the stage. During the performance, the stage is the dual presence of the physical reality (stage-as-stage) and the imaginary world of the play (stage-as-fictional-world). Actors, onstage, represent characters in a variable role/actor balance.[43] There are moments when attention is directly called to the physical reality of the stage space and performing actors. Even in such moments, the fictional world created on the stage still remains and, as Bernard Beckerman has aptly remarked, the audience experiences a double image.[44] Take, for example, the scene-closing exit of *Macbeth*, Act 1, scene 1. After saying together 'Houer through the fogge and filthie aire' (F1, TLN 13; 1.1.12), the three witches would most probably leave the stage on foot through a flaking doorway, though we cannot entirely rule out the possibility that they exit flying through the use of the descent machinery.[45] Either manner of the actors' departure would draw attention to their physical limitations, but the revelation of the gap between the fictional and theatrical events (characters' journey to another fictional place/ actors' departure from the playing space) would not utterly destroy the fictional world. With dead bodies, however, it is quite another story. If an onstage corpse should walk off in the middle of a play, the role/actor balance would break down and the imaginary world would be shattered: the corpse should therefore either be borne out as if to another fictional place that is supposed to exist behind the stage or it should simply be hidden in order to prevent it becoming a visual distraction. Different expectations are generated, however, at the end of the play, as we return from the fictional world to the real world. Authoritative figures' formal concluding speeches, ceremonial general exits and particularly epilogues function as the declaration that the play is ending. Once the action of the play is completed, the logic of the fictional world stops functioning, and the stage therefore becomes no more than a stage. Only at this point does it become appropriate for onstage corpses to reanimate themselves as actors belonging to the real world.

Conclusion: the Shakespearean stage space and stage directions

The preceding chapters have considered several questions concerning early modern staging practices and stage directions. We have examined scenes involving offstage voices and sounds, together with several kinds of scene setting, including outside a house, inside a house and in a garden; and lastly, we have looked at scenes involving onstage deaths. In the process we have seen how early modern playwrights and players used the structure of the stage for different purposes: to ensure the audibility of offstage voices and sounds; to control the visibility of characters; to convey fictional locales; to create specific moods and atmospheres; and to maintain a frequently shifting balance between fictional and theatrical realities.

Before summarising what we have learned, it is important to emphasise that the early modern theatre made no simple, clear distinction between onstage and offstage. The structural relation between the main stage and the spaces behind, above and below provided Shakespeare and his contemporaries with a wide range of possibilities for different aural and visual effects. The openings in the *frons scenae* could connect the tiring-house and the stage not only as passages for entrances and exits but also both visually (by showing the presence of a character offstage to the characters onstage and to the audience) and aurally (by transmitting voices and sounds efficiently from off to onstage). Similar effects could be achieved in respect of both the stage balcony and the stage trap. How the openings in the tiring-house façade were disposed during the performance is an important matter, particularly whether the flanking doors and the central hangings were left open or closed, and whether the balcony was even equipped with curtains. These issues all bear directly on how characters managed their entrances and exits, as well as on the related question of whether offstage characters were visible to the audience.

The surviving play texts provide good reasons for believing that the stage doors were shut only in those scenes where they serve as doors in the fictional world. But in most scenes, including not only those located in open spaces and unlocalised scenes but also many indoor scenes, they were likely kept open throughout the scenes, remaining neutral stage doors. Opening or closing a stage door was likely therefore to be a significant action. Stage doors could be useful properties, especially at those moments when the action would benefit through making the location more specific. Beginning a scene with opening the entry door may have been a common device by which the actor suggested the locale or situation of the new scene, giving the impression that the character has just come out of the house represented by the tiring-house façade. Playwrights and players were often eager to extend the stage space, visually as well as aurally, using the visibility of the positions behind the stage doors. It is important to be clear, however, that extending the stage space in this way was not done because the existing space was insufficiently large. Not only plays acted on the small stages of private theatres but also those performed on the comparatively large stages of public theatres offer numerous scenes involving the use of positions either on or immediately behind the threshold of doorways. In both indoor and open-air theatres these positions would have been only partially visible to most spectators. They were particularly useful for presenting those fictional events which could not easily be shown on the stage, such as a large crowd. A common pattern of entrance involving two characters or groups is that the first character/group comes forward while the second remains either on or immediately behind the threshold of the doorway, as in the stage direction '*Enter Leucippus and Ismenus: the people within stoppes*' (*Cupid's Revenge* Q1, I4v). A few minor actors visible in a doorway could represent a crowd, a troop or the like. The position just behind a doorway was also a useful means of enabling characters to make entrances on to the stage that were unobtrusive, but at the same time, dramatically significant. A hesitant or partial entrance could illustrate something of the state of mind of the entering character, or maybe of their attitude towards other characters already onstage. One example is the hesitant entry Helen makes when summoned to the presence of the King of France in *All's Well That Ends Well*, 2.1. An entry of an entirely different kind is that made by Dol in *The Alchemist*, 2.3; her appearance is clearly undertaken with the coquettish aim of whetting Mammon's appetite.

Regarding the use of upper curtains, it is likely that the Globe theatre installed a curtained music room above the stage around 1609 after the King's Men acquired the Blackfriars theatre and that other adult companies gradually followed suit. In the case of private-theatre plays and post-1609 public-theatre plays, we should therefore consider whether the upper curtains were open or closed in these scenes. On the other hand, even in early public theatres, when appropriate for the fictional situation, musicians would have used either the upper playing area or the tiring-house upstairs as a temporary music room, because Shakespeare and his colleagues attached great importance to spatial meanings of the areas above, behind and below the stage. In both public and private theatres, through the early modern period, not only the stage balcony but also the space behind it was occasionally used for acting. In the first balcony scene in *Romeo and Juliet*, the Nurse's voice calling 'Madam' (Q2, D4r; 2.2.149, 151) would have been heard from the tiring-house upstairs as if from the inside of Juliet's bed-chamber. When *Pericles* was first performed at the Globe, the 'Musicke of the Spheres' (Q1, I1v; 5.1.229) that Pericles hears when he has regained his peace of mind might very well have been played on the upper floor of the tiring-house.

The meanings and usage of basic theatrical terms were closely related to the ways in which Shakespeare and his colleagues used the stage space and facilities, accommodating the fictional reality of the dramatic world to the physical reality of the theatre. '*Within*' is an inexact stage direction. This familiar theatrical term could refer to anywhere within the tiring-house, whether at the stage level or at the upper level. In practice, however, there were only a few locations that regularly served as '*within*'. Where an offstage voice is involved, the actor probably delivered the speech from behind one of the three openings in the tiring-house façade. In particular, when an actor speaks many speeches from '*within*', as in certain echo scenes and prison scenes, he might well have positioned himself in the central space behind the stage hangings for the purpose of better audibility. A character located '*within*' was not necessarily out of sight of the audience. If, for example, the stage door was open at that moment, the actor standing just behind it could, and in some cases would, have been visible to the audience. In *Twelfth Night*, 4.2, the imprisoned Malvolio would have occupied the curtained space, and Feste might have revealed him by opening the curtains, after or while saying 'What hoa, I say, Peace in this prison' (F1, TLN 2003; 4.2.18) – that is, at or around the very moment indicated by the Folio stage direction '*Maluolio within*' (TLN 2005; 4.2.19). Some entry stage directions suggest that an actor could '*enter*' by showing himself either immediately behind or almost on the threshold of a stage door. To *enter*, to stand *at the door* and to be *within* could sometimes be the same thing. At the upper level, as well as at the main stage level, the playing area could extend behind, at least in aural terms. It follows that '*above*', the most common term for the upper performance area, might sometimes refer to the space behind it. Since '*within*' could refer to the tiring-house upstairs, '*within*' could also be '*above*', and vice versa.

Even when clearly requiring the use of particular locations such as immediately behind, or almost on, the threshold of a stage door or behind the upper performance area out of sight of the audience, playwrights seldom bothered to give specific instructions; detailed stage directions like '*enter to the door within*', '*show oneself at the door*', '*above within*' and '*unseen above*' are rare. Even in such cases they tended to give bare, general instructions, using either '*enter*' or '*within*' or '*above*' only. When in *Measure for Measure*, 3.1 Isabella makes her pre-entry call 'What hoa? Peace heere' (F1, TLN 1249; 3.1.44) from behind the threshold of a stage door, which is probably kept open throughout the scene, the stage direction simply reads '*Enter Isabella*' (TLN 1248; 3.1.43). In a hospital scene in *The Changeling* two cries are heard from 'the upper room' (Q1, E1r) where the madmen are incarcerated, and the stage directions for the voices are both '*within*' (E1r, E2r). Thus, the same term could indicate different actions and positions, while different stage directions might indicate the same action or location. Table 1 lists the findings about '*enter*', '*within*' and '*above*', showing how the meanings of these stage directions overlap. In each case, we have to try to identify what might have been actually indicated by the stage direction while taking into account the fictional locale or situation of the scene and the stage conditions in the playhouse where the version of the play was performed.

It has been recognised that the bare stage did not impose limitations on dramatists and actors. On the contrary, the absence of scenery on the stage and the lack of curtains between the stage and the auditorium made fluent scene changes possible. A verbal reference to the scene's place-setting could establish the scene's locality. An entering character could convey the scene's locale visually by making his entrance in a distinctive manner, as in the stage direction '*Enter Brutus in his Orchard*' (*Julius Caesar* F1, TLN 616; 2.1.0). At the beginning of 2.1, Brutus would have opened the stage door, as if entering from his house, and strolled on an imaginary walk, thereby creating the sense of a garden on the bare stage of the Globe. For such a moment to work, the audience would have had to exercise their imagination, co-operating with and bringing to life what the dramatist had indicated in the briefest and most perfunctory manner. This is not to say that early modern plays overtaxed spectators' imaginations. They were not expected to imagine picturesque scenes but were only required to accept whatever location was being conveyed by a verbal or non-verbal signal. They did not have to keep the locality in mind throughout the scene: the scene's locale might become vague as the scene proceeds, and even a change in locale could take place during the scene. The audience were accustomed to making such efforts. They were

Conclusion

Table 1: *Positions which might be referred to by the stage directions* 'enter', 'within' *and* 'above'

Stage Direction	Possible Positions (The Visibility of the Character). Notes on the Door/Curtains. Examples.
Enter	**On the stage (Visible)** In most cases, the entry door has already been opened; in some cases the door is closed and either the entering character himself or another character already onstage opens the door. '*Enter* Lorenzo *senior.* / *Lo.se.* Oh heare it is, I am glad I haue found it now' (*Every Man In* Q1, K2v); '*Enter Brutus in his Orchard*' (*Julius Caesar* F1, TLN 615; 2.1.0); '*Porter.* . . . Anon, anon, I pray you remember the Porter. / *Enter Macduff, and Lenox*' (*Macbeth* F1, TLN 762–3; 2.3.20–1). **Behind the threshold of a flanking doorway (Visible/Invisible)** In most cases the door has already been opened; in some cases either the character himself or another character onstage opens the door; in other cases it is closed. '*Laf.* Nay, come your waies. / *Enter Hellen.* / . . . / *Laf.* Nay, come your waies' (*All's Well* F1, TLN 698–701; 2.1.93–4); '*Enter Tib.* / *Tib.* I am within sir, whats your pleasure?' (*Every Man In* Q1, K2v); '*Fri.* . . . Who knocks so hard? whence come you? whats your will? / *Enter Nurse.* / *Nur.* Let me come in, and you shal know my errant' (*Romeo and Juliet* Q2, G4v; 3.3.78–9); '*Enter Nurse, and knocke*' (*Romeo and Juliet* Q2, G4v; 3.3.70). **In the discovery space (Visible/Invisible)** In most cases either the discovery-space curtains are drawn open or there is a gap between them; in some cases they are closed. '*Enter Faustus in his Study*' (*Doctor Faustus* QA, A2v); '*Enter king within*' (*When You See Me* Q1, B4v). **On the upper performance area (Visible)** Where there is a curtained music room above the stage, the curtains would be presumably opened either before or when an actor enters there. '*Enter the Countesse.* / . . . / *Mo*: . . . Deare Aunt discend and gratulate his highnes' (*Edward III* Q1, B1v–B2v; 1.2.0-87); '*Enter Palamon, and Arcite in prison*' (*Two Noble Kinsmen* Q1, D2r; 2.2.0). **From the trapdoor (Visible)** '**Enter** the ghoast of *Albanact*' (*Locrine* Q1, H4v); '*Enter the Ghost of Banquo, and sits in Macbeths place*' (*Macbeth* F1, TLN 1299; 3.4.36).
Within	**Behind the threshold of a flanking doorway (Invisible/Visible)** Where '*within*' is involved, the door is mostly closed; in some cases the door has already been opened; in other cases either the character himself or another character onstage opens it. '*Emillia calls within*' (*Othello* Q1, M2r; 5.2.85); '*2. Ser. within.* Come in Sir' (*Love's Pilgrimage* F1, 8A4r); '*The Clowne bounce at the gate, within.* / . . . / *A Seruant.* Why how now Maisters, what a coyle is there?' (*Doctor Faustus* QB, G1r-v). **In the discovery space (Invisible/Visible)** In most cases the discovery-space curtains are closed; in some cases either they are drawn open or there is a gap between them. '*Rousa.* Ooh. – *Within*' (*Atheist's Tragedy* Q1, K2v); '*Boy wthin* oh' (*Olden Barnavelt* MS, TLN 1671); '*Maluolio within*' (*Twelfth Night* F1, TLN 2005; 4.2.19).

Table 1: *(cont.)*

Stage Direction	Possible Positions (The Visibility of the Character). Notes on the Door/Curtains. Examples.
	On the upper performance area (Invisible/Visible) Where there is a curtained music room above the stage, when *'within'* is involved, the curtains are mostly kept closed. In some cases the curtains are open. *'Lute sounds within. / . . . / Sing within a little'* (*Chances* F1, 3A4r); *'Old merri. within.* If you will sing and daunce' (*Knight of the Burning Pestle* Q1, G3r).
	Behind the upper performance area (Invisible) In any theatre, whether it has a curtained music room above or not, there may be a set of hangings concealing the space behind the upper playing area. *'[Nurse] Within:* Madam' (*Romeo and Juliet* F1, TLN 952; 2.2.149); *'Madman within.* Bounce, bounce, he falls, he falls' (*Changeling* Q1, E1r).
	Already on the stage (Visible) *'Enter Monsieur la Writ within'* (*Little French Lawyer* F1, H4v)
Above	**On the upper performance area (Visible/Invisible)** Where there is a curtained music room above the stage, when the action takes place *above*, the music-room curtains are presumably opened, unless the action benefits from having them closed. *'Mad-men above*, some as birds, others as beasts' (*Changeling* Q1, E2r); *'Str.* Helpe, helpe, here helpe – ha – *Vnseen Above'* (*Court Beggar* O1, Q5r).
	Behind the upper performance area (Invisible) In any theatre, whether it has a curtained music room above or not, there may be a set of hangings concealing the space behind the upper playing area. *'Pind. Aboue.* O my Lord' (*Julius Caesar* F1, TLN 2506; 5.3.26); *'Str.* Helpe, helpe, here helpe – ha – *Vnseen Above'* (*Court Beggar* O1, Q5r).

NB: This table summarises discussions in the preceding chapters: it does not show all possible positions.

constantly required to do so because of the opportunities afforded the dramatist by the very flexibility of the English Renaissance stage, a circumstance whose significance it is impossible to over-emphasise. According to need, the stage could remain neutral; it could also, when desired, become specific; and it could also alter from the one to the other with extreme rapidity. The tiring-house façade provided visual support not only to outside-a-house and inside-a-house scenes but also to other kinds of indoor and outdoor settings, such as prison scenes and garden scenes. Because of their physical features and their locations in relation to the main stage and the tiring-house façade, it was frequently the case that stage doors, the curtained space, the upper gallery, the stage trap and stage posts could all serve as various kinds of place, structure or objects in the fictional world, such as the street door of a house, a prison cell, a window, trees, or even a river.

Although the stage structure was always visible to the audience and the plays made use of many non-realistic conventions, in general the playwrights endeavoured to maintain the illusion of the fictional world during the performance. Scenes involving onstage deaths show that there was a clear distinction between what could be shown to the spectators and what should be concealed from them. Shakespeare and his fellow dramatists usually arranged for the removal of corpses by characters in the play world and sometimes utilised the stage hangings, the upper gallery and the stage trap so that they could make visually impressive and symbolically meaningful death scenes while also preventing the departure of the corpses being seen by the audience. Even during intervals between the acts the logic of the fictional world could control the stage, and neither dead nor sleeping characters were allowed to walk off the stage at the end of the acts. Only at the end of the play, when the completion of the play is declared in some form or other, the logic of the fictional world stops functioning, and the stage becomes no more than a stage. Only at this point could onstage corpses return to living actors belonging to the real world. The stage direction 'Exeunt omnes' marked after the epilogue to *The Changeling* implicitly calls for the actors playing Beatrice and De Flores to stand up, bow to the audience in gratitude for their applause that has had the '*power to cause re-live / The Dead agen*' (Q1, I3v), and then leave the stage with the other actors.

However careless or casual some of the surviving stage directions may seem at first glance, we make a serious error if we conclude from this apparent indifference that the Shakespearean theatre was a place of primitive techniques, capable only of crude and unsophisticated theatrical effects. On the contrary, the stage directions, properly understood, offer a reasonably faithful indicator of how the plays were staged. The great achievement of early modern playwrights and players was to make full use of both the separation and the connection between onstage and offstage spaces and of the versatility of the stage structure so as to present a truly remarkable variety of fictional events and situations.

Notes

CHAPTER 1

1 See John Orrell, *The Human Stage: English Theatre Design, 1567–1640* (Cambridge University Press, 1988), pp. 20–9; Herbert Berry, 'The First Public Playhouses, Especially the Red Lion', *Shakespeare Quarterly*, 40 (1989), 133–45; Herbert Berry (ed.), 'Playhouses, 1560–1660', in Glynne Wickham, Herbert Berry and William Ingram (eds.), *English Professional Theatre, 1530–1660* (Cambridge University Press, 2000), pp. 290–4.
2 For the results and interpretations of the Rose excavations, see Julian M. C. Bowsher, 'The Rose and Its Stages', in *Shakespeare Survey 60* (Cambridge University Press, 2007), pp. 36–48; Julian Bowsher and Patricia Miller, *The Rose and the Globe—Playhouses of Tudor Bankside, Southwark: Excavations 1988–91* (Museum of London, 2009), chapters 3 and 5.
3 Henslowe's *Diary* contains a reference to the performance of 'the Jewe of malltuse' on 26 February 1592 by Lord Strange's Men at the Rose. See R. A. Foakes (ed.), *Henslowe's Diary*, 2nd edn (Cambridge University Press, 2002), p. 16. Until 1594, when the Lord Chamberlain and the Lord Admiral set up a pair of playing companies, and the Theatre and the Rose were officially allotted to the two companies, no company and no playwright had any reason to expect a play to be staged exclusively at any one playhouse. *The Jew of Malta* was therefore not written specifically for performance at the Rose, while *The Downfall of Huntingdon* was probably written with the enlarged Rose's stage specifically in mind. See Andrew Gurr, *Shakespeare's Opposites: The Admiral's Company 1594–1625* (Cambridge University Press, 2009), pp. 143–4.
4 See Foakes (ed.), *Henslowe's Diary*, p. 7.
5 See Bowsher, 'The Rose and Its Stages', p. 37; Bowsher and Miller, *The Rose and the Globe*, p. 47.
6 For a useful discussion of the design and facilities of the Theatre, see Gabriel Egan, 'The Theatre in Shoreditch, 1576–1599', in Richard Dutton (ed.), *The Oxford Handbook of Early Modern Theatre* (Oxford University Press, 2009), pp. 168–85.
7 Julian M. C. Bowsher, 'Twenty Years On: The Archaeology of Shakespeare's London Playhouses', *Shakespeare*, 7 (2011), 457.
8 For an important discussion of this point, see R. A. Foakes, 'Henslowe's Rose/Shakespeare's Globe', in Peter Holland and Stephen Orgel (eds.), *From Script to*

Stage in Early Modern England (Basingstoke: Palgrave Macmillan, 2004), pp. 16–23.

9 Reconsidering the location of the lords' room, Gabriel Egan has suggested that it was more likely to be in the lowest gallery, in the section nearest the stage. Regarding the phrase 'ouer the stage, i'the Lords roome' in Carlo's speech, he writes: 'if he [Carlo] is making a gesture it is possible that "ouer the stage" means "across the stage", in other words "over there"'. Egan, 'The Situation of the "Lords Room": A Revaluation', *Review of English Studies*, 48 (1997), 303.

10 Bowsher and Miller, *The Rose and the Globe*, p. 90.

11 See John Orrell, 'Beyond the Rose: Design Problems for the Globe Reconstruction', in Franklin J. Hildy (ed.), *New Issues in the Reconstruction of Shakespeare's Theatre* (New York: Peter Lang, 1990), pp. 95–100.

12 See Bowsher and Miller, *The Rose and the Globe*, pp. 127–8.

13 Foakes (ed.), *Henslowe's Diary*, p. 213.

14 Foakes (ed.), *Henslowe's Diary*, pp. 307–8.

15 See Orrell, 'Beyond the Rose', pp. 111–16. See also Franklin J. Hildy, 'Reconstructing Shakespeare's Theatre', in Hildy (ed.), *New Issues*, pp. 13–17.

16 For recent discussions of this and related questions, see Tim Fitzpatrick and Wendy Millyard, 'Hangings, Doors and Discoveries: Conflicting Evidence or Problematic Assumptions?', *Theatre Notebook*, 54 (2000), 2–23; Andrew Gurr, 'Doors at the Globe: The Gulf between Page and Stage', *Theatre Notebook*, 55 (2001), 59–71; Tim Fitzpatrick, 'Playwrights with Foresight: Staging Resources in the Elizabethan Playhouses', *Theatre Notebook*, 56 (2002), 85–116; Tim Fitzpatrick, *Playwright, Space and Place in Early Modern Performance: Shakespeare and Company* (Farnham: Ashgate, 2011).

17 In Fitzpatrick's view, this entry direction merely functions to ensure that Farnezie ends up between the other two characters and does not require three separate entrance-points. See 'Playwrights with Foresight', p. 90; *Playwright, Space and Place*, pp. 259–60. His book and articles offer different interpretations from mine, both here and in many other examples, where his argument is generally built on the assumption that there were only two doorways to the stage. In the present example, everything turns on how one interprets this admittedly somewhat ambiguous direction, in particular the use of 'in the mid'st'. Rather than describing Farnezie's final position on stage between Urcenze and Onophrio, as Fitzpatrick believes, and even given its odd and awkward phrasing, in my view it simply refers to the character's entry through the central opening.

18 For a similar comment, see Bernard Beckerman, 'The Use and Management of the Elizabethan Stage', in C. Walter Hodges, S. Schoenbaum and Leonard Leone (eds.), *The Third Globe: Symposium for the Reconstruction of the Globe Playhouse, Wayne State University, 1979* (Wayne State University Press, 1981), pp. 161–2. Cf. Fitzpatrick, *Playwright, Space and Place*, pp. 280–1.

19 Foakes (ed.), *Henslowe's Diary*, p. 308.

20 R. A. Foakes, 'Playhouses and Players', in A. R. Braunmuller and Michael Hattaway (eds.), *The Cambridge Companion to English Renaissance Drama*, 2nd edn (Cambridge University Press, 2003), pp. 17–18.

21 See Andrew Gurr, *The Shakespearean Stage: 1574–1642*, 4th edn (Cambridge University Press, 2009), p. 170.
22 See Herbert Berry, *The Boar's Head Playhouse* (Washington: Folger Shakespeare Library, 1986), pp. 106–19; Berry (ed.), 'Playhouses, 1560–1660', pp. 453, 488–92.
23 See Berry, *The Boar's Head Playhouse*, p. 57.
24 For an analysis of the scene that contains these three correlated directions, see Chapter 2.
25 For a reproduction of the building contract for the Hope, see E. K. Chambers, *The Elizabethan Stage*, 4 vols. (Oxford: Clarendon Press, 1923), II, 466–8.
26 See Reavley Gair, *The Children of Paul's: The Story of a Theatre Company, 1553–1608* (Cambridge University Press, 1982), pp. 44–58.
27 Herbert Berry, 'Where was the Playhouse in which the Boy Choristers of St. Paul's Cathedral Performed Plays?', *Medieval and Renaissance Drama in England*, 13 (2001), 101–16. See also Roger Bowers, 'The Playhouse of the Choristers of Paul's, c.1575–1608', *Theatre Notebook*, 54 (2000), 70–85.
28 See Gair, *The Children of Paul's*, pp. 58–60.
29 For the dimensions of the first and the second Blackfriars theatres, see Irwin Smith, *Shakespeare's Blackfriars Playhouse: Its History and Its Design* (London: Peter Owen, 1964), pp. 134–43, 164–74.
30 See Smith, *Shakespeare's Blackfriars Playhouse*, pp. 247–50.
31 Hereafter I generally refer to the theatre built by James Burbage in the Blackfriars precinct in 1596 simply as the Blackfriars, and not as the second Blackfriars. Richard Farrant's Blackfriars theatre is always referred to as the first Blackfriars.
32 See Andrew Gurr, *The Shakespearian Playing Companies* (Oxford: Clarendon Press, 1996), pp. 116–17, 296–7. For a different view about the use of the two playhouses, see Roslyn Knutson, 'Two Playhouses, Both Alike in Dignity', *Shakespeare Studies*, 20 (2002), 111–17.
33 See Gurr, *The Shakespearean Stage*, p. 200.
34 Jean MacIntyre, 'Production Resources at the Whitefriars Playhouse, 1609–1612', *Early Modern Literary Studies*, 2.3(1996), 2.1–35, paragraphs 3, 13–21.
35 See Kelly Christine Steele, 'Terra Incognita: A Theoretical Reconstruction of the Whitefriars Stage', unpublished PhD thesis, University of Birmingham (2009), pp. 240–52. See also Smith, *Shakespeare's Blackfriars Playhouse*, pp. 394–6.
36 Richard Hosley suggests that the 'tree' Tiberio climbs is 'either a property tree set up against the tiring-house façade or one of the columns of the tiring-house façade'. Hosley, 'The Playhouses', in Clifford Leech and T. W. Craik (gen. eds.), *The Revels History of Drama in English*, 8 vols. (London: Methuen, 1975–1983), III, 223.
37 See Iain Mackintosh, 'Inigo Jones – Theatre Architect', *TABS*, 31 (1973), 99–105.
38 See John Orrell, *The Theatres of Inigo Jones and John Webb* (Cambridge University Press, 1985), pp. 39–77.
39 See John Harris and Gordon Higgott, *Inigo Jones: Complete Architectural Drawings* (New York: The Drawing Center, 1989), pp. 266–8.

40 Gordon Higgott, 'Reassessing the Drawings for the Inigo Jones Theatre: A Restoration Project by John Webb?' (paper based on a lecture given at a conference at Shakespeare's Globe, 13 February 2005).
41 See Gurr, *The Shakespearean Stage*, pp. 197, 201.
42 I am grateful to Andrew Gurr for sharing his latest view with me.
43 Franklin J. Hildy, 'Keeping up with the Jones', *Around the Globe*, 30 (Summer 2005), 27.
44 For analyses of the drawings, see Orrell, *The Human Stage*, pp. 186–203; John Orrell, 'The Theaters', in John D. Cox and David Scott Kastan (eds.), *A New History of Early English Drama* (Columbia University Press, 1997), pp. 100–1.
45 James Wright in *Historia Histrionica* (1699) says, 'The *Black-friers, Cockpit,* and *Salisbury-court* ... were all three Built almost exactly alike, for Form and Bigness' (Q1, B4r). John Orrell thinks Wright reliable, while Herbert Berry is sceptical. See Orrell, *The Human Stage*, pp. 188–90; Berry (ed.), 'Playhouses, 1560–1660', p. 629.
46 In the identification of extant manuscript playbooks, I follow those enumerated in William B. Long, '"Precious Few": English Manuscript Playbooks', in David Scott Kastan (ed.), *A Companion to Shakespeare* (Oxford: Blackwell, 1999), pp. 414–33.
47 There are arguments against this manuscript's status as a playbook. Grace Ioppolo, for example, describes it as a foul-paper text (rough draft) showing Heywood at work. She writes: 'This manuscript lacks the censor's license, suggesting instead that a fair copy of it was made for him to read, and certainly it remains often too illegible to have served for the book-keeper in the theatre.' Ioppolo, *Dramatists and Their Manuscripts in the Age of Shakespeare, Jonson, Middleton and Heywood: Authorship, Authority and the Playhouse* (London: Routledge, 2006), pp. 95–6. See also Ioppolo, '"The foule sheet and ye fayr": Henslowe, Daborne, Heywood and the Nature of Foul-Paper and Fair-Copy Dramatic Manuscripts', *English Manuscript Studies 1100–1700*, 11 (2002), 143–51. Even if the book-keeper might have annotated Heywood's manuscript for subsequent transcription, the annotated manuscript could still show how the book-keeper treated the author's stage directions. For an argument for its use as a playbook, see James Purkis, 'Foul Papers, Promptbooks, and Thomas Heywood's *Captives*', *Medieval and Renaissance Drama in England*, 21 (2008), 128–56.
48 Long, '"Precious Few"', p. 417.
49 Examples include: '*the two houres trafficque of our Stage*' (*Romeo and Juliet* Q2, A2r; Prologue.12); 'the space of two houres and an halfe, and somewhat more' (Jonson, *Bartholomew Fair* F2, A5r; Induction); 'three howres of mirth' (Dekker, *If It Be Not a Good Play, the Devil Is in It* Q1, M4r; Epilogue).
50 See Michael J. Hirrel, 'Duration of Performances and Lengths of Plays: How Shall We Beguile the Lazy Time?', *Shakespeare Quarterly*, 61 (2010), 159–82.
51 For a description of the cuts in the Folger copy of *The Two Merry Milkmaids*, see Leslie Thomson, 'A Quarto "Marked for Performance": Evidence of What?', *Medieval and Renaissance Drama in England*, 8 (1995), 184–8. For an analysis of

the cuttings in the Padua *Macbeth* and *Measure for Measure*, see Stephen Orgel, *The Authentic Shakespeare, and Other Problems of the Early Modern Stage* (New York: Routledge, 2002), pp. 23–32.
52 Orgel, *The Authentic Shakespeare*, p. 21.
53 Orgel, *The Authentic Shakespeare*, pp. 21–2.
54 See Andrew Gurr, 'Maximal and Minimal Texts: Shakespeare v. the Globe', in *Shakespeare Survey 52* (Cambridge University Press, 1999), pp. 68–87.
55 See Gurr, 'Maximal and Minimal Texts', p. 76.
56 See Andrew Gurr (ed.), *The First Quarto of King Henry V* (Cambridge University Press, 2000), p. 9.
57 See Richard Dutton, '*The Famous Victories* and the 1600 Quarto of *Henry V*', in Helen Ostovich, Holger Schott Syme and Andrew Griffin (eds.), *Locating the Queen's Men, 1583–1603: Material Practices and Conditions of Playing* (Farnham: Ashgate, 2009), pp. 135–44.
58 See Lukas Erne, *Shakespeare as Literary Dramatist* (Cambridge University Press, 2003), chapters 8 and 9.
59 See Tiffany Stern, 'Re-patching the Play', in Holland and Orgel (eds.), *From Script to Stage*, pp. 151–77; Stern, *Making Shakespeare: From Stage to Page* (London: Routledge, 2004), pp. 113–22; Stern, '"A small-beer health to his second day": Playwrights, Prologues, and First Performances in the Early Modern Theater', *Studies in Philology*, 101 (2004), 172–99; Stern, *Documents of Performance in Early Modern England* (Cambridge University Press, 2009).
60 Stern, *Documents of Performance*, pp. 253–4.
61 Andrew Gurr, 'A New Theatre Historicism', in Holland and Orgel (eds.), *From Script to Stage*, p. 71.
62 For citation, I will choose one of the substantive texts, unless the choice influences the discussion. For a Shakespearean play, the one serving as the copy text for the *Riverside Shakespeare* edition shall be used, where the difference between the authoritative texts does not much matter. G. Blakemore Evans (gen. ed.), *The Riverside Shakespeare*, 2nd edn (Boston: Houghton Mifflin, 1997).
63 Stanley Wells and Gary Taylor with John Jowett and William Montgomery, *William Shakespeare: A Textual Companion* (Oxford: Clarendon Press, 1987), p. 2.
64 Richard Hosley, 'The Gallery over the Stage in the Public Playhouse of Shakespeare's Time', *Shakespeare Quarterly*, 8 (1957), 16–17.
65 For a similar view, see David Bradley, *From Text to Performance in the Elizabethan Theatre: Preparing the Play for the Stage* (Cambridge University Press, 1992), p. 77.
66 For comments on 'fictional' terms in the theatrical plots, see Michela Calore, 'Elizabethan Plots: A Shared Code of Theatrical and Fictional Language', *Theatre Survey*, 44 (2003), 249–61; Stern, *Documents of Performance*, p. 228.
67 See Alan C. Dessen and Leslie Thomson, *A Dictionary of Stage Directions in English Drama, 1580–1642* (Cambridge University Press, 1999), entries for 'walls' and 'window'.
68 Examples include: '*Enter Faustus in his Study*' (Marlowe, *Doctor Faustus* QA, A2v); '*Enter Theophilus in his study, Bookes about him*' (*The Virgin Martyr* Q1,

K3r); '*Enter Guadagni in his Study. A Taper, Baggs, Books, &c.*' (Brome, *The Novella* O1, H7v).
69 See Alan C. Dessen, *Recovering Shakespeare's Theatrical Vocabulary* (Cambridge University Press, 1995), pp. 139–40. It must also be noted that, as Dessen suggests, some '*Enter in his study*' directions may well be understood as '*Enter as if in his study*': e.g., '*Enter* Soranzo *in his study reading a Booke*' (Ford, *'Tis Pity She's a Whore* Q1, C4v). See *Recovering Shakespeare's Theatrical Vocabulary*, pp. 160–4.
70 For a useful discussion of the staging of prison scenes, see Alan C. Dessen, *Elizabethan Stage Conventions and Modern Interpreters* (Cambridge University Press, 1984), pp. 97–100.
71 See Dessen, *Recovering Shakespeare's Theatrical Vocabulary*, pp. 142–4. See also Dessen and Thomson, *Dictionary of Stage Directions*, entry for 'tent'.
72 The plot of *2 The Seven Deadly Sins* had traditionally been assigned to a performance by Strange's Men in the early 1590s but Scott McMillin suggested that it actually belonged to the Chamberlain's Men in the later 1590s. More recently, David Kathman has argued effectively that it originated with the Chamberlain's Men, *c*.1597–98. See McMillin, 'Building Stories: Greg, Fleay, and the Plot of *2 The Seven Deadly Sins*', *Medieval and Renaissance Drama in England*, 4 (1989), 53–62; Kathman, 'Reconsidering *The Seven Deadly Sins*', *Early Theatre*, 7 (2004), 13–44. For a counter-argument, see Andrew Gurr, 'The Work of Elizabethan Plotters and *2 The Seven Deadly Sins*', *Early Theatre*, 10 (2007), 67–87. See also Kathman, '*The Seven Deadly Sins* and Theatrical Apprenticeship', *Early Theatre*, 14 (2011), 121–39.
73 Michael Hattaway suggests that 'j wooden canepie', which is listed in Henslowe's inventory, may have been the frame for a stage tent. See Hattaway, *Elizabethan Popular Theatre: Plays in Performance* (London: Routledge and Kegan Paul, 1982), p. 38; Foakes (ed.), *Henslowe's Diary*, p. 319.
74 See Bernard Beckerman, *Shakespeare at the Globe: 1599–1609* (New York: Macmillan, 1962), p. 95.
75 See Gurr, *The Shakespearean Stage*, p. 184. In this connection, it is noteworthy that in Middleton and Dekker's *The Roaring Girl*, the stage direction '*The three shops open in a ranke ... to them enters* Laxton, Goshawke *and* Greenewit' (Q1, C3r) may indicate the use of the discovery space for all the three shops.
76 In the Q1 text of the play, the corresponding stage direction reads 'Achilles *and* Patro *stand in their tent*' (F4v). Although this direction does not include the word '*enter*', it indicates virtually the same action as the F1 entry direction: Achilles and Patroclus appear from a stage door representing the entrance of Achilles' tent.
77 Regarding '*The Drumme playing, and Trumpet sounding*', Michael Hattaway says: 'There is no way of telling whether this is theatrical short-hand for a battle "off" ... or part of a processional entrance.' Hattaway (ed.), *The Third Part of King Henry VI* (Cambridge University Press, 1993), p. 160n. It seems to me more likely that the sounds would have represented the offstage battle. For one thing, the corresponding direction in the Octavo text of the play reads 'Alarmes' (D5v).

78 For discussions of '*passing over the stage*', see Mariko Ichikawa, *Shakespearean Entrances* (Basingstoke: Palgrave Macmillan, 2002), chapter 7; Leslie Thomson, '"*Pass over the stage*" – Again', in Lena Cowen Orlin and Miranda Johnson-Haddad (eds.), *Staging Shakespeare: Essays in Honor of Alan C. Dessen* (University of Delaware Press, 2007), pp. 23–44.
79 Antony Hammond, 'Encounters of the Third Kind in Stage-Directions in Elizabethan and Jacobean Drama', *Studies in Philology*, 89 (1992), 81.
80 See Peter Holland (ed.), *A Midsummer Night's Dream* (Oxford University Press, 1994), p. 169n; Foakes (ed.), *Henslowe's Diary*, p. 320.
81 See R. A. Foakes (ed.), *A Midsummer Night's Dream* (Cambridge University Press, 1984), p. 74n.
82 Thomas North's translation of Plutarch's *Lives of the Noble Grecians and Romans* (1579) provides: 'Nowe Brutus having passed a litle river, walled in on either side with hie rockes, and shadowed with great trees, being then darke night, he went no further, but stayed at the foote of a rocke with certaine of his Captaines and frends that followed him'. Geoffrey Bullough (ed.), *Narrative and Dramatic Sources of Shakespeare*, 8 vols. (London: Routledge and Kegan Paul, 1957–1975), v, 129. I am grateful to Raymond Powell for calling my attention to this passage.
83 See Arthur Humphreys (ed.), *Julius Caesar* (Oxford University Press, 1984), p. 227n.
84 See Foakes (ed.), *Henslowe's Diary*, p. 319.
85 For a similar view, see David Daniell (ed.), *Julius Caesar* (Walton-on-Thames: Thomas Nelson and Sons, 1998), p. 316n.
86 A cave could have been represented by a trapdoor, and so the devilish Caliban could emerge with symbolic appropriateness from the trap. But he speaks from '*within*' before making his entrance: 'There's wood enough within' (TLN 451; 1.2.314). This confirms that the location of his rock-den is within the tiring-house, not under the stage, and so rules out the use of the trapdoor. The usage of '*within*' is fully discussed in Chapters 2 and 3.
87 For similar comments, see Stephen Orgel (ed.), *The Tempest* (Oxford University Press, 1987), p. 118n; Roger Warren (ed.), *Cymbeline* (Oxford University Press, 1998), pp. 161–2n.
88 In the Q1 text of *Richard III*, the First Murderer refers to the malmsey butt as being in the next room in both cases: 'And then we wil chop him in the malmsey But in the next roome' (D2r; 1.4.155–6); 'I thus, and thus: if this wil not serue. / Ile chop thee in the malmesey But, in the next roome' (D3v; 1.4.269–70).
89 For similar comments, see Alan Brissenden (ed.), *As You Like It* (Oxford University Press, 1994), p. 101n; Michael Hattaway (ed.), *As You Like It* (Cambridge University Press, 2000), p. 76n; Juliet Dusinberre (ed.), *As You Like It* (London: Thomson Learning, 2006), p. 155n.
90 See *The Oxford English Dictionary*, prepared by J. A. Simpson and E. S. C. Weiner, 2nd edn, 20 vols. (Oxford University Press, 1989), sense 1.a for 'orchard'.
91 See Bullough (ed.), *Narrative and Dramatic Sources*, II, pp. 166–7.

92 See Ernest Schanzer (ed.), *The Winter's Tale* (Harmondsworth: Penguin, 1969), p. 210.
93 See Stephen Orgel (ed.), *The Winter's Tale* (Oxford University Press, 1996), p. 168n. See also Susan Snyder and Deborah T. Curren-Aquino (eds.), *The Winter's Tale* (Cambridge University Press, 2007), p. 184n; John Pitcher (ed.), *The Winter's Tale* (London: A & C Black, 2010), p. 259n.
94 See Andrew Gurr, *Playgoing in Shakespeare's London*, 3rd edn (Cambridge University Press, 2004), p. 36; Gurr, *The Shakespearean Stage*, p. 19.
95 For comments on these references, see Orrell, *The Human Stage*, p. 90; Egan, 'The Situation of the "Lords Room"', pp. 299–300.
96 For a more detailed discussion of this question, see Leslie Thomson, 'Playgoers on the Outdoor Stages of Early Modern London', *Theatre Notebook*, 64 (2010), 3–11.

CHAPTER 2

1 John H. Astington, 'Malvolio and the Dark House', in *Shakespeare Survey 41* (Cambridge University Press, 1988), pp. 55–62.
2 Astington, 'Malvolio and the Dark House', p. 55.
3 Astington, 'Malvolio and the Dark House', p. 62.
4 Dessen and Thomson's *Dictionary of Stage Directions* provides the following explanation for '*within*': 'widely used (roughly 800 examples) to indicate the location of a sound or the presence of a figure within the tiring house and therefore offstage out of sight of the playgoer'.
5 This example occurs in one of the additional passages included in the fourth quarto (1602) of *The Spanish Tragedy*. According to recent attribution studies, Shakespeare is the likeliest author of the 1602 additions. See Warren Stevenson, *Shakespeare's Additions to Thomas Kyd's 'The Spanish Tragedy': A Fresh Look at the Evidence Regarding the 1602 Additions* (Lewiston, NY: Edwin Mellen Press, 2008); Hugh Craig, 'The 1602 Additions to *The Spanish Tragedy*', in Hugh Craig and Arthur F. Kinney (eds.), *Shakespeare, Computers, and the Mystery of Authorship* (Cambridge University Press, 2009), pp. 162–80; Brian Vickers, 'Shakespeare and Authorship Studies in the Twenty-First Century', *Shakespeare Quarterly*, 62 (2011), 107–11, 141–2.
6 There are numerous '*knock within*' and '*knocking within*' directions that do not include '*at the door*' or the like. We cannot be sure that these directions implicitly call for the use of a stage door for producing the offstage sound. For example, *Macbeth*, 2.2 provides '*Knocke within*' (F1, TLN 717; 2.2.54), which is followed by Macbeth's comment on the sound: 'Whence is that knocking? / How is't with me, when euery noyse appalls me?' (TLN 718–19; 2.2.54–5). When another knocking is heard ('*Knocke*' (TLN 727; 2.2.62)), Lady Macbeth says 'I heare a knocking at the South entry' (TLN 728; 2.2.62–3). More knockings are heard: '*Knocke*' (TLN 732; 2.2.66); '*Knocke*' (TLN 737; 2.2.70). It seems unlikely that these sounds would have come from behind a stage door. The next scene, usually known as the Porter's scene, has '*Knocking within*' (TLN 743; 2.3.0) and five more '*Knock*' directions (TLN 746, 749, 754, 757, 761; 2.3.3, 7, 12, 15, 19). Since

knockings began in the previous scene, these continual sounds might come from the same unidentified offstage place as in 2.2. It is more likely that they would come from behind the stage door which is shortly to be opened by the Porter for the entrance of Macduff and Lennox ('*Enter Macduff, and Lenox*' (TLN 763; 2.3.21)). For relevant discussions, see Frances Ann Shirley, *Shakespeare's Use of Off-stage Sounds* (University of Nebraska Press, 1963), p. 13; Fitzpatrick, *Playwright, Space and Place*, pp. 68–9.

7 As E. A. J. Honigmann suggests, 'Ooh' functions more as a stage direction than a speech, directing the actor to make a noise appropriate to the situation. See Honigmann, 'Re-enter the Stage Direction: Shakespeare and Some Contemporaries', in *Shakespeare Survey 29* (Cambridge University Press, 1976), p. 123.

8 At the very beginning of the same scene, the discovery space is used as a closet: '*Musicke. A Clozet discouer'd. A Seruant sleeping with lights and money before him*' (K1v). But this would not have prevented the actors from using the curtained space later in the scene for thrusting forth the bed. There is a slight change of location during the scene.

9 For a similar view, see Suzanne Gossett (ed.), *Bartholomew Fair* (Manchester University Press, 2000), pp. 17–18.

10 Some editions place Ursla onstage when '*She calls within*'. Perhaps, the editors thought that '*within*' is used in the sense of 'towards within'. See E. A. Horsman (ed.), *Bartholomew Fair* (Harvard University Press, 1960), p. 58; Edward B. Partridge (ed.), *Bartholomew Fair* (University of Nebraska Press, 1964), p. 56. I agree with Suzanne Gossett that '[at 2.4.62] In reaction to Mooncalf's comments on the progress of the cooking, Ursula goes into the booth, from which she calls at 2.5.44.' Gossett (ed.), *Bartholomew Fair*, p. 83n.

11 For the shares of the two dramatists in *The Virgin Martyr*, see Fredson Bowers (ed.), *The Dramatic Works of Thomas Dekker*, 4 vols. (Cambridge University Press, 1953–1961), III, 368–74.

12 See Dessen and Thomson, *Dictionary of Stage Directions*, entry for 'end'.

13 See N. W. Bawcutt (ed.), *The Control and Censorship of Caroline Drama: The Records of Sir Henry Herbert, Master of the Revels 1623–73* (Oxford: Clarendon Press, 1996), pp. 171–2.

14 See Philip Edwards and Colin Gibson (eds.), *The Plays and Poems of Philip Massinger*, 5 vols. (Oxford University Press, 1976), III, 293–302.

15 For useful comments on this manuscript, see Long, '"Precious Few"', pp. 429–30; Ioppolo, *Dramatists and Their Manuscripts*, pp. 136–40.

16 See Bawcutt (ed.), *The Records of Sir Henry Herbert*, p. 175.

17 See Alan B. Farmer and Zachary Lesser, 'Vile Arts: The Marketing of English Printed Drama, 1512–1660', *Research Opportunities in Renaissance Drama*, 39 (2000), 89–91.

18 It must be noted that in the scene in *Believe as You List*, three characters appear on the upper level and observe from there the event taking place on the main stage. The manuscript contains both Massinger's and the book-keeper's directions for them: 'Enter Metellus. flaminivs. Sempronivs. aboue' (MS, TLN

1958–9 (Massinger's corrected direction, deleted by the book-keeper)); '*Ent: Metellus fflaminius: & Sempronius (Aboue)*' (TLN 1960–3 (the book-keeper's)); 'Enter aboue flaminivs. metellus. sempronivs' (TLN 1982–3 (Massinger's original direction, deleted by the book-keeper)). As for the warning in *The City Madam*, Richard Hosley argues that 'the musicians were required to vacate the music room above so that it might be used for the discovery of Plenty and Lacy as "statues" in a raised playing-area'. Hosley, 'Was There a Music-Room in Shakespeare's Globe?', *Shakespeare Quarterly*, 13 (1960), 116. But this view is questionable. Since Plenty and Lacy have been directed to be '*ready behind*' earlier in the scene (Q1, L2v), they should be discovered there behind the arras at the stage level. When they are ordered by Sir John to 'Descend' (L4r), just as Hermione is instructed to do by Paulina in the finale of *The Winter's Tale* (F1, TLN 3307; 5.3.99), Plenty and Lacy would have descended from the statues' plinths and come forth from the discovery space.

19 For a full discussion of this question, see Bruce R. Smith, *The Acoustic World of Early Modern England: Attending to the O-Factor* (University of Chicago Press, 1999), pp. 206–17.

20 For this stage direction, the Folio text reads '*Enter two Servants, Rowl: Ashton.*' There is, however, no speech spoken by or to or about a third servant, and the action does not require his presence. The second servant would therefore enter alone. '*Enter two Servants*' is most probably an error for '*Enter 2. Servant.*' The names '*Rowl: Ashton*' must have been a book-keeper's warning for the two players to prepare to enter shortly, carrying Sanchio in a chair: '*Enter Leonardo, and Don Zanchio (carried by two Servants in a chair.)*' (F1, 8A4r). See L. A. Beaurline (ed.), *Love's Pilgrimage*, in Fredson Bowers (gen. ed.), *The Dramatic Works in the Beaumont and Fletcher Canon*, 10 vols. (Cambridge University Press, 1966–1996), II, 674.

21 See Wells and Taylor with Jowett and Montgomery, *Textual Companion*, p. 618.

22 See, for example, Stanley Wells and Gary Taylor (gen. eds.), *William Shakespeare: The Complete Works* (Oxford: Clarendon Press, 1986), p. 1373; Jay L. Halio (ed.), *King Henry VIII* (Oxford University Press, 1999), p. 195; Gordon McMullan (ed.), *King Henry VIII* (London: Thomson Learning, 2000), p. 400n.

23 See Foakes (ed.), *Henslowe's Diary*, p. 206.

24 For a description of the manuscript, see T. H. Howard-Hill, ed., *Sir John van Olden Barnavelt*, Malone Society Reprints (Oxford University Press, 1980), pp. iv–x.

25 There are also some stage directions including the phrase '*within the curtains*': '*She fals vpon her bed within the Curtaines*' (*Romeo and Juliet* Q1, I1r); 'they ... sit downe within the curteines' (*The Downfall of Robert, Earl of Huntingdon* Q1, A2v); 'they ... sit downe within the curteins' (A3r); '*He drawes the Curtaines and sits within them*' (Chapman, *Sir Giles Goosecap* Q1, I2v). The first direction may, however, refer to the bed curtains and not to the stage hangings.

26 For the authorship of the play, see Robert Kean Turner (ed.), *The Little French Lawyer*, in Bowers (gen. ed.), *The Dramatic Works in the Beaumont and Fletcher Canon*, IX, 329–30.

27 Turner (ed.), *The Little French Lawyer*, p. 387.
28 See W. W. Greg (ed.), *Bonduca*, Malone Society Reprints (Oxford University Press, 1951), pp. v–vi. For an important discussion of the term 'foul papers', see Paul Werstine, 'The Continuing Importance of New Bibliographical Method', in *Shakespeare Survey 62* (Cambridge University Press, 2009), pp. 30–45.
29 In the F1 text, the corresponding stage directions read respectively: '*Enter 2^d Daughter and a Servant*' (4G4r); '*Enter Judas and his people to the door*' (4H3v); '*Enter Drusus and Regulus, with souldiers. / Sould.* Kill him, kill him, kill him' (4H4v).
30 See W. W. Greg, *Dramatic Documents from the Elizabethan Playhouses*, 2 vols. (1931; repr. Oxford: Clarendon Press, 1969), 1 (Commentary), 322.
31 For critical comments on the conjecture that *Troilus and Cressida* was written to be performed at one of the Inns of Court, see David Bevington (ed.), *Troilus and Cressida* (Walton-on-Thames: Thomas Nelson and Sons, 1998), pp. 87–90; Anthony B. Dawson (ed.), *Troilus and Cressida* (Cambridge University Press, 2003), pp. 7–9; Dawson, 'Staging Evidence', in Holland and Orgel (eds.), *From Script to Stage*, pp. 98–102; Gurr, *The Shakespeare Company, 1594–1642* (Cambridge University Press, 2004), p. 129. On the other hand, it is certainly possible that *Troilus and Cressida* was performed at an Inn of Court as well.
32 For a useful textual analysis, see Bevington (ed.), *Troilus and Cressida*, pp. 398–429.
33 For a similar view, see Bevington (ed.), *Troilus and Cressida*, p. 367.
34 The phrase '*acted publikely*' did not necessarily mean 'acted at a public open-air theatre'. Andrew Gurr observes that the formal distinction between 'public' and 'private' lost its point once the boy companies came under the authority of the Master of the Revels in 1606 or thereabouts and the adjectives became fuzzier. See Gurr, *The Shakespeare Company*, p. 160. As Gurr notes, Carlell's *The Deserving Favourite* Q1 (1629) was published as 'Acted, first before the Kings Maiestie, and since publickely at the BLACK-FRIERS' (A1r).
35 In the playbook of *The Second Maiden's Tragedy*, which is a fair copy written by a scribe, the playwright's stage directions are all left untouched by the book-keeper except that he adds the names of two players to roles (TLN 1723, 1929). See Long, '"Precious Few"', p. 425.
36 The use of stage doors is fully discussed in Chapter 4.
37 Another example involving '*enter*' and '*within*' requires a comment. Samuel Rowley's *When You See Me, You Know Me* provides '*Enter king within*' (Q1, B4v). This stage direction is followed by another direction for the King, '*Call within*' (B4v). An onstage character's response suggests that he perceives the King's offstage presence only aurally: 'Harke, the king cals' (C1r). He makes another onstage character exit to answer the King's call (C1r), presumably through one of the flanking doors. It is therefore most likely that the King would remain unseen behind the central curtains. For a discussion of such 'invisible entrances', see Ichikawa, *Shakespearean Entrances*, pp. 130–1.
38 Turner (ed.), *The Little French Lawyer*, p. 359.
39 See Turner (ed.), *The Little French Lawyer*, p. 332.

40 Plautus's *Menaechmi* is Shakespeare's principal source for *The Comedy of Errors*. He had enough Latin to read it in the original, but it is possible that he had seen its translation by Warner in manuscript. See Bullough (ed.), *Narrative and Dramatic Sources*, 1, pp. 3–4; Charles Whitworth (ed.), *The Comedy of Errors* (Oxford University Press, 2002), pp. 23–4.
41 See George Walton Williams (ed.), *The Woman Hater*, in Bowers (gen. ed.), *The Dramatic Works in the Beaumont and Fletcher Canon*, 1, pp. 150–1. The Q1 scene numbers do not match up with those in Williams's edition.
42 F1's 'Scaen. 2' is clearly an error for 'Scaen. 4'.
43 It should however be noted that early modern plays provide shouts of joy, applause or the like which offstage soldiers or people give, responding to something onstage that logically it is impossible they could know. As David Carnegie argues, these offstage shouts are designed to reinforce the dramaturgy of the moment and the logic of realism does not apply to them. See Carnegie, 'Mutinous Soldiers and Shouts [Within]: Stage Directions and Early Modern Dramaturgy', in Brian Boyd (ed.), *Words That Count: Essays on Early Modern Authorship in Honor of MacDonald P. Jackson* (University of Delaware Press, 2004), pp. 222–38.
44 The ascription of the play to Shakespeare both in the Stationers' Register (1605) and on the title-page of the first (1608) and second (1619) quartos is probably a deliberate fraud. Detailed studies of the play's linguistic and other features have strengthened the case that Middleton wrote most or, more probably, all of it. See Gary Taylor and John Lavagnino (gen. eds.), *Thomas Middleton and Early Modern Textual Culture: A Companion to the Collected Works* (Oxford: Clarendon Press, 2007), pp. 355–6.
45 See John Russell Brown (ed.), *The Duchess of Malfi* (London: Methuen, 1964), p. xxxv. For a similar view, see Leah S. Marcus (ed.), *The Duchess of Malfi* (London: A & C Black, 2009), p. 327n.
46 Since the two consecutive scenes (TLN 1725–1876, TLN 1877–1983) take place in the same location, one might wish to treat them as one continuous scene. In the manuscript of the play, only act divisions are provided and scene divisions are not marked. It is, however, noticeable that most scene-opening directions are centred, while mid-scene entries are generally marked in margins. Judging, therefore, from the fact that the stage direction '*Enter Gouianus in black, a booke in his hand, his page carying a Torche before hym*' (TLN 1877–8) is centred, the arrival of Govianus and his page was treated as the beginning of a new scene.
47 See Brown (ed.), *The Duchess of Malfi*, p. xxxvn.
48 R. B. Graves, '*The Duchess of Malfi* at the Globe and Blackfriars', *Renaissance Drama*, n.s. 9 (1978), 199.
49 Unfortunately, the Q1 text shows the compositor's confusion of the speech prefixes for Echo, and, as for 'Eccho within', the word 'within' is not properly printed as a stage direction.
50 See Bowers (ed.), *The Dramatic Works of Thomas Dekker*, 1, pp. 107–8.
51 As for the validity of the title-page attribution, Scott McMillin and Sally-Beth MacLean observe as follows: 'There is no reason not to think that *Clyomon and*

Clamydes was being performed by the Queen's Men and that they released it for publication, just as the title-page says. (This leaves open the possibility that it was an old play which the Queen's Men took over and refurbished.)' McMillin and MacLean, *The Queen's Men and Their Plays* (Cambridge University Press, 1998), p. 89.

52 David Kathman observes that 'most of the evidence we have suggests that the preferred playing venues for the Queen's Men in London were four inns within the City limits that served as part-time playhouses in the last quarter of the sixteenth century'. Kathman, 'London Inns as Playing Venues for the Queen's Men', in Ostovich, Syme and Griffin (eds.), *Locating the Queen's Men*, p. 65.

53 It should however be noted that playing conditions in provincial venues may not necessarily have been primitive. Leslie Thomson argues that the considerable number of discovery scenes in plays that could have been performed in the provinces provides support for the belief that 'a provincial venue would typically have included a stage and tiring house ... with provision for hanging curtains'. Thomson, 'Staging on the Road, 1586–1594: A New Look at Some Old Assumptions', *Shakespeare Quarterly*, 61 (2010), 542. As Barbara D. Palmer suggests, the hall screen of a great hall could well serve as a tiring-house façade. See Palmer, 'On the Road and on the Wagon', in Ostovich, Syme and Griffin (eds.), *Locating the Queen's Men*, pp. 27–8, 32–3. It is, however, by no means certain whether travelling players acted in front of the hall screen, since, as David Bevington notes, they may have wished to be closer to the lord of the manor and his chief guests at the hall's upper end. See Bevington, *This Wide and Universal Theatre: Shakespeare in Performance Then and Now* (University of Chicago Press, 2007), p. 34.

54 I agree with Michela Calore about Clamydes's possible use of half-open hangings. See Calore, '*Enter out*: Perplexing Signals in Some Elizabethan Stage Directions', *Medieval and Renaissance Drama in England*, 13 (2001), 128–30.

55 Alan C. Dessen has concluded that to present a prison, Elizabethans did not introduce a set of bars on the stage. As he argues, the stage direction '*Mellida goes from the grate*' could easily be fictional. See Dessen, *Elizabethan Stage Conventions and Modern Interpreters*, pp. 96–8. It may be worth noting that William Rowley's *A New Wonder: A Woman Never Vexed* has a scene in which a prisoner begs for money from the upper playing level: '*Old Foster, and above at the grate, a box hanging downe*' (Q1, H3r). In this example, the balcony balustrade would have served as the grate.

56 See Reavley Gair (ed.), *Antonio's Revenge* (Manchester University Press, 1978), pp. 27, 93–4.

57 Fletcher's *The Woman's Prize* offers another example that requires the use of a stage door including a grate or grille. In Act 3, scene 5 Maria has Petruchio locked in his house, because she believes him to be infected with the plague. The stage direction '*Petruchio within*' (F1, 5O4v) is printed before Petruchio's first offstage speech: '*Petru*. Doe you heare my Masters: ho, you that locke the doores up' (5O4v). Including this speech, Petruchio delivers twelve speeches (some 40 lines altogether) from *within*, that is, behind the door. When he says 'If any man

misdoubt me for infected, / There is mine arme, let any man looke on't' (5O4v), he would thrust his hand from the grate in the door, because a doctor arrives at that very moment with an apothecary and feels Petruchio's pulse: '*Enter Doctor and Pothecary.* / . . . / *Doct.* It [his pulse] beats with busiest, / And shews a general inflammation, / Which is the symptome of a pestilent feaver, / Take twenty ounces from him' (5O4v). (The surviving manuscript, which seems to have been copied from a theatre playbook for a private collector, lacks the doctor's arrival with the apothecary and his attempt to diagnose Petruchio.) *The Woman's Prize* is usually dated to 1610–11 and it has often been assumed that because the play was performed by the King's Men in 1633 it must originally have been performed at the Globe and/or Blackfriars. For the earliest known reference to the play, see Bawcutt (ed.), *The Records of Sir Henry Herbert*, pp. 182–3. Celia R. Daileader and Gary Taylor argue, however, that it was probably first performed between December 1609 and April 1610 at the Whitefriars theatre by the Children of the Queen's Revels. See Daileader and Taylor (eds.), *The Tamer Tamed, or The Woman's Prize* (Manchester University Press, 2006), pp. 3, 8–10, 25. Meg Powers Livingston, on the other hand, suggests the period between late January and September 1611 as the most likely time for the play's composition. See Livingston (ed.), *The Woman's Prize*, Malone Society Reprints (Manchester University Press, 2008), pp. vii–viii. Lucy Munro observes that there is no external or internal evidence to settle the date and venue matter. See Munro (ed.), *The Tamer Tamed* (London: A & C Black, 2010), pp. xv–xvii.

58 See also Andrew Gurr and Gabriel Egan, 'Prompting, Backstage Activity, and the Openings onto the Shakespearean Stage', *Theatre Notebook*, 56 (2002), 139–40.

59 In their edition of the play, C. H. Herford and Percy Simpson add the direction '*Security appears at the grate*' at the moment when Security begins to speak. Herford and Simpson (eds.), *Ben Jonson*, 11 vols. (Oxford: Clarendon Press, 1925–1952), IV, 606. See also R. W. Van Fossen (ed.), *Eastward Ho* (Manchester University Press, 1979), p. 192n.

60 David Carnegie, '"*Maluolio within*": Performance Perspectives on the Dark House', *Shakespeare Quarterly*, 52 (2001), 409.

61 For useful discussions of the effect of keeping him out of sight, see Alan C. Dessen, *Elizabethan Drama and the Viewer's Eye* (University of North Carolina Press, 1977), pp. 151–2; Carnegie, '"*Maluolio within*"', pp. 409–14.

62 For comments on the possibility that the play was acted in front of the hall screen, see T. J. King, *Shakespearean Staging, 1599–1642* (Harvard University Press, 1971), pp. 98, 149–50; Bevington, *This Wide and Universal Theatre*, p. 34.

CHAPTER 3

1 See M. M. Mahood, *Playing Bit Parts in Shakespeare* (London: Routledge, 1998), pp. 86–7.

2 Charles R. Forker (ed.), *King Richard II* (London: Thomson Learning, 2002), p. 464n.

3 Since the music is used to intensify the melancholy mood of the scene, its performance should not be poor. I agree with David Lindley that 'some small hesitation prompts Richard's comment, but the music thereafter perhaps should be expertly played'. Lindley, *Shakespeare and Music* (London: Thomson Learning, 2006), p. 123.
4 *The Thracian Wonder* was first published in 1661 as '*Written* by John Webster *and* William Rowley' (Q1, A1r) but has been listed as an anonymous play with suggested dates ranging between 1590 and 1600. Michael Nolan, however, has recently proposed Rowley and Heywood's authorship, suggesting a later date of 1611–12. See Nolan (ed.), *The Thracian Wonder by William Rowley and Thomas Heywood: A Critical Edition* (Salzburg: Institut für Anglistik und Amerikanistik, Universität Salzburg, 1997), pp. xxxv-lvii. He offers some interesting observations, but more systematic analysis of the play itself and the works by Rowley and Heywood would be needed for the proposed view to be considered seriously. See also David Carnegie's review of Nolan's edition, *Modern Language Review*, 94 (1999), 160–1; David Nicol, 'The Date of *The Thracian Wonder*', *Notes and Queries*, 253 (2008), 223–5.
5 See Chambers, *The Elizabethan Stage*, III, 96.
6 We must nevertheless treat this illustration with some care. As John H. Astington points out, 'the picture was made after the Restoration, and the anthology of dramatic pieces it prefaces are claimed to have been produced during the Commonwealth – although the claim was not made until 1673 – while the plays from which most of them are drawn were all written before 1642'. He asserts at one point that '*The Wits* picture is merely a visual collage, a *jeu d'esprit* showing a theatre that never was', but his final judgement is that, 'While far from being a meticulous or realistic recorder, Chantry [a principal candidate for the maker of the plate] drew from his knowledge of what the theatres of his time were like.' Astington, '*The Wits* Illustration, 1662', *Theatre Notebook*, 47 (1993), 122, 139. Although the illustration lacks authority as the depiction of an actual theatre, it very probably shows the normal placement of upper curtains at pre-Restoration theatres.
7 For important discussions of act-intervals, see Wilfred T. Jewkes, *Act Division in Elizabethan and Jacobean Plays: 1583–1616* (1958; repr. New York: AMS Press, 1972); Gary Taylor, 'The Structure of Performance: Act-Intervals in the London Theatres, 1576–1642', in Gary Taylor and John Jowett, *Shakespeare Reshaped: 1616–1623* (Oxford: Clarendon Press, 1993), pp. 3–50.
8 Richard Hosley, 'Was There a Music-Room in Shakespeare's Globe?', *Shakespeare Quarterly*, 13 (1960), 113–23.
9 Hosley thinks that the stage direction '*Musicke heere descends*' (Rowley, *A Shoemaker a Gentleman* Q1, C4r) suggests that the Red Bull had a music room over the stage by about 1608. See Hosley, 'Was There a Music-Room in Shakespeare's Globe?', p. 113. However, the 1638 Quarto text, printed as 'Acted at the *Red Bull* and other Theaters' (A2r), appears to reflect later revivals and is therefore not reliable for the play's first performance at the Red Bull. See Taylor, 'The Structure of Performance', pp. 4, 32.

10 For some more occurrences of '*music above*', see Dessen and Thomson, *Dictionary of Stage Directions*, entry for 'above'. It is also noteworthy that 'musique aloft' occurs twice in the surviving manuscript playbook of *The Launching of the Mary* (TLN 245, 2793). Both instances are made by the author himself, the amateur Walter Mountfort, and not by the book-keeper.
11 The Q1 text's inclusion of stage directions such as '*Chaire out*' (D4v) and '*Chaire at the Arras*' (E4v) suggests a playhouse manuscript's influence on the text. Before and after the stage direction '*She dies. still Musicke aboue*' are printed instructions as to the musical performance: '*Recorders: Sadly*' (I1v); '*Cease Rec.*' (I1v). The direction '*She dies. still Musicke aboue*' is very likely authorial and the directions mentioning recorders must be annotations marked by the book-keeper. Two more King's Men plays, both co-written by Fletcher and Massinger, have scenes where 'Celestiall Musick' (*The Double Marriage* F1, 5C4v) and 'Musick from the Spheres' (*The Prophetess* F1, 4D4r) are played, although the stage directions for the music include neither '*above*' nor its equivalent: '*still Musick*' (*The Double Marriage* F1, 5C4v); '*Musick*' (*The Prophetess* F1, 4D4r).
12 See Dessen and Thomson, *Dictionary of Stage Directions*, entry for 'without'.
13 *Richard II* F1 is thought to have mostly been printed from a copy of Q3 (reprinted from Q2, itself a reprint of Q1) annotated with reference to a theatre playbook. Q1 is agreed to have been printed from authorial papers. Q1's corresponding direction, most probably written by Shakespeare, reads '*The trumpets sound, Richard appeareth on the Walls*' (F4v; 3.3.61). It calls only for a parley from the stage, and does not call for an answer from offstage or a fanfare announcing the royal entry. Q3's corresponding direction (F4r) is substantially the same as the Q1 direction. For a textual analysis, see Forker (ed.), *King Richard II*, Appendix 1.
14 On the trumpeters' possible entrance, see Forker (ed.), *King Richard II*, p. 344n.
15 Richard Hosley's conjecture is that '*Fedele and Fortunio*, having been performed at the [first] Blackfriars during the early winter of 1583–84, was performed at Court on 6 January or 2 February of 1584 by Oxford's Boys under the name of one of their component companies, the Children of the Queen's Chapel'. Hosley (ed.), *A Critical Edition of Anthony Munday's Fedele and Fortunio* (New York: Garland, 1981), p. 94. Hosley believes that his conclusion is confirmed by Q1's inclusion of stage directions for music between the acts: 'The first Act beeing ended, the Consorte of Musique soundeth a pleasant Galliard' (C2r); 'The second Act beeing ended, the Consorte soundeth again' (D4v); 'The third Act being doone, the Consort sounds a sollemne Dump' (E3v); 'The fourth Act being ended, the Consort soundeth a pleasant Allemaigne' (G1r); 'The fift Act being done, let the Consort sound a cheerefull Galliard, and euery one taking handes together, departe singing' (H1r). As he says, these directions may suggest that the play was written to be performed at a private theatre. It is, however, equally possible that the directions were related to the court performance. See Taylor, 'The Structure of Performance', pp. 27–9; Tracey Hill, *Anthony Munday and Civic Culture: Theatre, History and Power in Early Modern London* (Manchester University Press, 2004), p. 123.
16 As John Jowett notes, a 1582 Catholic pamphlet contains a reference to Munday's first occupation as a player: 'munday, who first was a stage player ...' (Thomas

Alfield, *The Death of Campion* O1, D4v). See Jowett (ed.), *Sir Thomas More* (London: Methuen, 2011), pp. 10–11. See also Chambers, *The Elizabethan Stage*, II, 330, III, 444; Hill, *Anthony Munday and Civic Culture*, p. 123.

17 In the F1 text Rodorigo's speech reads 'Ho, Governor'. 'Governor' is clearly an error for 'Gunner'. The F2 text of the play reads 'Gunner' for 'Governor' (L3r).
18 See Joost Daalder (ed.), *The Changeling* (London: A & C Black, 1990), p. xliv; Taylor and Lavagnino (gen. eds.), *Thomas Middleton and Early Modern Textual Culture*, p. 1095.
19 For the shares of the two playwrights in *The Changeling*, see Taylor and Lavagnino (gen. eds.), *Thomas Middleton and Early Modern Textual Culture*, pp. 422–3.
20 Although in Q1 the line '*Come aloft Boyes, aloft*' is printed as part of the preceding song, this line is usually treated as an ordinary speech in modern editions. For a note on the line, see Michael Hattaway (ed.), *The Knight of the Burning Pestle* (London: Ernest Benn, 1969), p. 81n. Andrew Gurr, on the other hand, observes that it is a line from a sea shanty. (I am grateful to him for sharing his view with me.)
21 For similar comments, see Astington, 'Malvolio and the Dark House', p. 61; Hattaway (ed.), *The Knight of the Burning Pestle*, p. 78n; Leslie Thomson, 'Window Scenes in Renaissance Plays: A Survey and Some Conclusions', *Medieval and Renaissance Drama in England*, 5 (1990), 236.
22 For comments on some of these special cases, see Hosley, 'Was There a Music-Room in Shakespeare's Globe?', p. 116.
23 See Humphreys (ed.), *Julius Caesar*, p. 220n; Marvin Spevack (ed.), *Julius Caesar* (Cambridge University Press, 1988), p. 139n.
24 Daniell, ed., *Julius Caesar*, p. 308n.
25 Unfortunately, the only architectural evidence for the backstage stairs leading to the upper level seems to be the Jones/Webb drawings of two playhouses: Worcester College H & T 10, 11 (Gotch 1/7B, 1/7C) (Figures 3a and 3b); H & T 4 (Gotch 1/27). Supposing that H & T 10 and 11 show a realised Renaissance commercial theatre, if not the Cockpit in Drury Lane, in this theatre the backstage staircase was constructed behind the central bay some 15 feet away from the plane of the *frons scenae* (measured to the newel). An actor proceeding to the stage balcony after exiting by a stage door walked the distance from the stage door to the foot of the stairs, climbed them and then walked the distance from the head of the stairs to the balcony. Two and a half or so lines would have been far from sufficient for an offstage ascent. I am indebted to John Orrell for providing me with his analysis of the backstage arrangements shown in the drawings.
26 Beckerman, *Shakespeare at the Globe*, p. 230.
27 See Smith, *Shakespeare's Blackfriars Playhouse*, pp. 412–14; Orgel (ed.), *The Tempest*, p. 164n; Cirus Hoy (ed.), *The Double Marriage*, in Bowers (gen. ed.), *The Dramatic Works in the Beaumont and Fletcher Canon*, IX, 102.
28 See Gurr, *The Shakespearean Stage*, p. 195.
29 The specification of the musical instruments '*Sackbut & Troup musick*' must have been an annotation by the company book-keeper for the authorial direction '*A strange Musick*'. See Turner (ed.), *The Little French Lawyer*, pp. 332, 410.

30 It must be noted that there is a stage direction for gentlemen thieves to '*Peepe above*' (K4r), marked only four lines after the direction '*Lowder*'. It is, however, unlikely that the musicians would hastily vacate the music room so that the actors might just peep from there. They would rather be required to stay and peep from between the music-room curtains, since they are also acting gentlemen thieves, when delivering strange music and irritating noise.
31 It should be noted that, as Andrew Gurr says, trumpets, an army's instrument for signalling to cavalry and for calling attention at ceremonies, were not considered to be primarily musical instruments. See Gurr, *The Shakespeare Company*, p. 78.
32 See Wells and Taylor with Jowett and Montgomery, *Textual Companion*, p. 543; Nicholas Brooke (ed.), *Macbeth* (Oxford University Press, 1990), pp. 64–6; Stephen Orgel, 'Macbeth and the Antic Round', in *Shakespeare Survey 52* (Cambridge University Press, 1999), pp. 144–5; Stern, *Making Shakespeare*, pp. 32–3.
33 For a similar view, see Brooke (ed.), *Macbeth*, p. 163n.
34 Hosley, 'Was There a Music-Room in Shakespeare's Globe?', p. 119.
35 See Hosley, 'Was There a Music-Room in Shakespeare's Globe?', pp. 117–19.
36 See Foakes (ed.), *Henslowe's Diary*, p. 21.
37 For a similar view, Eugene M. Waith (ed.), *Titus Andronicus* (Oxford University Press, 1984), p. 176n.
38 Hosley, 'The Gallery over the Stage', p. 31. Although questions have been asked about the upper location of the lords' room, the gallery over the stage was certainly used regularly for spectators.
39 G. K. Hunter interprets it as a reference to the introductory concert of music which, when the Duke of Stettin-Pomerania visited the Blackfriars in 1602, lasted 'for a whole hour preceding the play'. See Hunter (ed.), *Malcontent* (London: Methuen, 1975), pp. lii-liii; Hunter, 'Were There Act-Pauses on Shakespeare's Stage?', in Standish Henning, Robert Kimbrough and Richard Knowles (eds.), *English Renaissance Drama: Essays in Honor of Madeleine Doran and Mark Eccles* (Southern Illinois University Press, 1976), p. 19.
40 For a comment on F1's placement of this stage direction, see Jay L. Halio (ed.), *The Merchant of Venice* (Oxford University Press, 1993), pp. 148–9n.
41 See Gurr, *The Shakespearean Stage*, p. 192.
42 For some comments on the music, see David Bevington (ed.), *Henry IV, Part 1* (Oxford University Press, 1987), pp. 219–20n; Herbert Weil and Judith Weil (eds.), *The First Part of King Henry IV* (Cambridge University Press, 1997), p. 141n; David Scott Kastan (ed.), *King Henry IV, Part 1* (London: Thomson Learning, 2002), p. 254n.
43 For similar views, see John H. Long, *Shakespeare's Use of Music: The Final Comedies* (University of Florida Press, 1961), pp. 46–7; Doreen Delvecchio and Antony Hammond (eds.), *Pericles* (Cambridge University Press, 1998), p. 185n. See also Suzanne Gossett (ed.), *Pericles* (London: Thomson Learning, 2004), pp. 411–12.
44 For a useful discussion of the specific call for the sound of hautboys, see Wes Folkerth, *The Sound of Shakespeare* (London: Routledge, 2002), pp. 37–43.

45 Hugh Macrae Richmond, *Shakespeare's Theatre: A Dictionary of His Stage Context* (London: Continuum, 2002), entry for 'music room'.

CHAPTER 4

1. See Gabriel Egan, '"Geometrical" Hinges and the *Frons Scenae* of the Globe', *Theatre Notebook*, 52 (1998), 62–4.
2. See Andrew Gurr, 'Stage Doors at the Globe', *Theatre Notebook*, 53 (1999), 8–18; Fitzpatrick and Millyard, 'Hangings, Doors and Discoveries'; Tiffany Stern, 'Behind the Arras: The Prompter's Place in the Shakespearean Theatre', *Theatre Notebook*, 55 (2001), 110–18.
3. See Dessen and Thomson, *Dictionary of Stage Directions*, entry for 'chamber'.
4. Two plays provide interesting examples in this connection. James Shirley's *Love's Cruelty*, acted at the Cockpit in Drury Lane, has the stage direction '*Hippo. seemes to open a chamber doore and brings forth Eubel*' (Q1, G2v). This stage direction probably indicates that the actor, rather than just opening one of the flanking doors, makes as if to unlock it. For a comment on the usage of '*seems*', see Dessen, *Recovering Shakespeare's Theatrical Vocabulary*, pp. 250–1. It is, however, also possible that Hippolito opens the curtains covering the discovery space as if they were a door. The manuscript of *1 Richard II, or Thomas of Woodstock* contains a scene involving the use of curtains as a door. Early in the scene Lapoole '*drawes the curtaynes*' (MS, TLN 2432), revealing Woodstock sleeping in his bed. While it is just possible that these were the bed curtains, it is more likely that they were those concealing the discovery space. The bed would have been thrust out on to the main stage, since the action around the bed continues for a good 200 lines. When the two murderers have finally strangled Woodstock, Lapoole orders them to dispose of the corpse, saying 'take it vp gently, lay hime in his bed. / then shutt the doore as if he ther had dyd' (TLN 2629–30). The murderers would have pushed the bed with Woodstock's corpse on it back into the discovery space, and then they would have closed the curtains to represent the bedchamber door. For a similar view, see Peter Corbin and Douglas Sedge (eds.), *Thomas of Woodstock* (Manchester University Press, 2002), p. 170n. Although MacD. P. Jackson has recently suggested that *Woodstock* was written by Samuel Rowley after Shakespeare's *Richard II*, the majority view is still that *Woodstock* was among Shakespeare's sources for *Richard II*. See Jackson, 'Shakespeare's *Richard II* and the Anonymous *Thomas of Woodstock*', *Medieval and Renaissance Drama in England*, 14 (2002), 17–65, and 'The Date and Authorship of *Thomas of Woodstock*: Evidence and Its Interpretation', *Research Opportunities in Renaissance Drama*, 46 (2007), 67–100. For some other recent discussions of the authorship and date of the play, see Corbin and Sedge (eds.), *Thomas of Woodstock*, p. 4; Michael Egan (ed.), *The Tragedy of Richard II Part One: A Newly Authenticated Play by William Shakespeare*, 4 vols. (Lewiston, NY: Edwin Mellen Press, 2006), 1, 3–494.
5. Later in the same scene, there is the stage direction '*Enter foure over the stage with Beaupre and Verdoone bound and halters about their necks*' (K4r). Here '*foure*' clearly

means 'four gentlemen', since the exit direction for the same characters reads '*Exit Verta. Beaup. and Gent.*' (K4r). '*Verta.*' in the exit direction is clearly a compositorial error for '*Verdo.*' The F2 text of the play reads 'Ver.' for '*Verta.*' (2Z3r).

6 June Schlueter and James P. Lusardi, 'Offstage Noise and Onstage Action: Entrances in the Ophelia Sequence of *Hamlet*', in Hardin L. Aasand (ed.), *Stage Directions in 'Hamlet': New Essays and New Directions* (Fairleigh Dickinson University Press, 2003), p. 39.

7 Tailor's *The Hog Hath Lost His Pearl*, performed at Whitefriars by 'certaine LONDON *Prentices*' (Q1, A2r), begins with a scene of type 1. Although very little is known about the author and the company of apprentices, the play's opening entry direction is important in that it clearly indicates that the entering character crosses the stage to the door opposite the one by which he has entered: '*Enter* Lightfoote *a country gentleman passing ouer the stage and knocks at the other dore*' (B1r).

8 Dekker and Webster's *Westward Ho* provides a useful example in this connection. In the play's last scene Monopoly '*Lookes out*' (Q1, H4v), answering an onstage knock. He would open the door and show himself but would remain offstage. Since, however, he is given an '*Exit*' (H4v) several lines later, 'looking out' was counted as an entrance.

9 In the Folio version of the play, Jonson adds the stage direction '*Shee spies her husband come: and runnes to him*' (F1, F1r).

10 Other important scenes of type 1 include the opening scene of *The Country Girl*, a possible King's Men play. In this scene, three suitors to the young widow named Lady Mosely and her own brother come to see her one after another, but they are all refused admittance by Master William, who is probably her steward. What is interesting about this scene is that each time the steward exits, rejecting the new visitor, he is specifically directed to shut the door after him: '*Exit Shut*' (Q1, B1r); '*Exit Shut*' (B1v); '*Exit shut*' (B1v); '*Exit* shut' (B3r).

11 Most texts of Jonson's plays use the neo-classical system of scene-division. Under this system, scenes change with the arrival of new characters. Of the texts cited in this chapter, *Volpone* F1, *Epicoene* F1 and *The Alchemist* F1 use the neo-classical system, while *Every Man in His Humour* Q1 uses the departure of all characters as the end of each scene.

12 As Dessen and Thomson observe, Jonson's use of '*without*' rather than '*within*' for directing knocking and other offstage sounds is noticeable. See Dessen and Thomson, *Dictionary of Stage Directions*, entry for 'without'. This must be related to the predominance of indoor scenes in *Volpone*, *The Alchemist* and *Epicoene*.

13 *Volpone* contains three more scene-sequences belonging to type 2: 2.5–2.7 (which takes place in Corvino's house); 3.3–3.9 (in Volpone's house); 5.1–5.3 (in Volpone's house).

14 *The Massacre at Paris* has a similar example: '*Enter the* Guise *and knocketh*' (O1, C7r).

15 Until quite recently it has been generally thought that Q1 derives from the memory of an actual performance but some scholars have argued that *Romeo*

and Juliet Q1 is a deliberate abridgement of Shakespeare's original and not a reported text. See, for example, Jay L. Halio, 'Handy-Dandy: Q1/Q2 *Romeo and Juliet*', in Jay L. Halio (ed.), *Shakespeare's 'Romeo and Juliet': Texts, Contexts, and Interpretation* (University of Delaware Press, 1995), pp. 123–50. Jill L. Levenson, the recent Oxford editor of the play, treats Q1 as 'a script in print'. See Levenson (ed.), *Romeo and Juliet* (Oxford University Press, 2000), p. 61. Lucas Erne observes that 'The first quarto of *Romeo and Juliet* . . . probably takes us as close as we can get to the play as it would have been performed by Shakespeare and his fellow players in London and elsewhere.' Erne (ed.), *The First Quarto of 'Romeo and Juliet'* (Cambridge University Press, 2007), p. 25. Regarding the stage directions in Q1, however, it has been argued that they derive from the printing process rather than the theatre or the author. See John Jowett, 'Henry Chettle and the First Quarto of *Romeo and Juliet*', *Papers of the Bibliographical Society of America*, 92 (1998), 53–74.

16 Other important scenes of type 2 include *The Second Maiden's Tragedy*, Act 3 (MS, TLN 1170–461), in which offstage knockings drive Govianus's Lady to kill herself so as to avoid becoming the Tyrant's wife. Shirley's *The Traitor* shows his careful control of the closing and opening of stage doors. At the very beginning of the opening scene of Act 3, while entering, Depazzi tells his page Rogero to 'Make fast the Chamber-doore' (Q1, E2r). Towards the end of the same scene '*Knockes*' are heard from offstage (E4r). Similarly, at the very start of the first scene of Act 5, Sciarrha says to Amidea that 'The doores are fast' (I2v). Towards the end of the scene, there are the stage directions 'Florio *knockes*' (K1r) and 'Florio *breakes ope the doore*' (K1r).

17 Such a differentiation between the central and marginal areas of the stage can be observed in the final scene of the play, when the Friar, after having entered, orders Balthazar to 'Go with [him] to the Vault' (Q2, L3v; 5.3.131).

18 See *The Oxford English Dictionary*, sense 2 for 'shut'. I am grateful to Franklin J. Hildy for calling my attention to the possibility that the phrase 'shut the door' meant 'lock the door'.

19 In the Q1 text of the play, the stage direction '*within*' is not attached to the first speech prefix for Pandarus, and the entry direction for him is omitted (H1v). It is therefore not clear whether he speaks his first speech from offstage or after having entered.

20 Anne Lancashire, the Revels editor of the play, thinks that '*a farder dore*' either is a door situated at a distance from the tomb or, alternatively, it is at a distance from the door by which he went out at the end of the previous scene. See Lancashire (ed.), *The Second Maiden's Tragedy* (Manchester University Press, 1978), p. 55.

21 In contrast, in a tomb scene in *The Knight of Malta*, by Fletcher, Field and Massinger, a stage door, with a key in its keyhole, continues to represent the door of the church after being opened at the beginning of the scene. In the middle of the scene, Miranda, Norandine and Collonna have scarcely exited by the door, carrying off the already awake but still faint Oriana, when Rocca, Mountferrat and Abdella enter '*With a dark lanthorn*' by the same door (F1, 5M1r). In this case, the entering characters' conversation makes clear that,

although the groups passed each other offstage, in the darkness they did not recognise each other: '*Mount.* What were those past by?'; '*Roc.* Some scout of Souldiers, I think.'; '*Mount.* . . . They saw not us I hope' (5M1r).
22 See George Walton Williams (ed.), *The Island Princess*, in Bowers (gen. ed.), *The Dramatic Works in the Beaumont and Fletcher Canon*, v, 541.
23 Leslie Thomson, 'Marlowe's Staging of Meaning', *Medieval and Renaissance Drama in England*, 18 (2005), 35.
24 For an account of this performance, see Evans (gen. ed.), *The Riverside Shakespeare*, Appendix C, Number 14.
25 Although *James IV* has been commonly attributed to the Queen's Men, Scott McMillin and Sally-Beth MacLean exclude it from their plays. See McMillin and MacLean, *The Queen's Men and Their Plays*, p. 92.
26 The Trinity Manuscript provides no stage direction for their entrance. The Archdale Manuscript (Folger Shakespeare Library, MS V.a.231), which is a Ralph Crane transcript close to Middleton's early draft of the play, suggests that Middleton's original idea was to have only the Black Queen's Pawn and the Black Bishop's Pawn enter in the Induction, when Loyola says 'I see my Son, and Daughter' (Archdale MS, p. 4; 'I see my Sonne and daughter' (Trinity MS, TLN 79)) and that the first thought was later revised to bring on both Houses in their entirety. The Archdale Manuscript contains both the original direction, deleted, and its replacement: 'Enter y^e Bl. Qu^s Pawne & Bl. Bp$^{s'}$ (p. 4); 'Musick – En< > (seuerally) the Wh< > & Black-hous< > as they are sett f< > y^e Game' (p. 3). For comments on these stage directions, see Taylor and Lavagnino (gen. eds.), *Thomas Middleton and Early Modern Textual Culture*, pp. 876, 880.
27 The Induction begins with the discovery of Loyola and Error: 'Ignatius Loyola appearing, Error at his foote as asleepe' (Trinity MS, TLN 13–14) / 'Ignatius discovered; and Error, a-sleepe' (Archdale MS, p. 1). At the end of the Induction, the Trinity Manuscript provides no exit for them and other onstage characters, while the Archdale Manuscript has 'Exeun< >' (p. 5).
28 In addition to the examples cited above, Munday's *Fedele and Fortunio* provides 'Enter Crackstone out of Victoriaes house' (Q1, E3r); 'Enter Pedante disguised, comming forth of Victoriaes house' (E4v). The first direction derives evidently from Pasqualigo's *Il Fedele*, which has, in the corresponding episode, 'Frangipetra esce fuor di casa di Vittoria' (O1, F3v). These two examples in *Fedele and Fortunio* also require the entering characters to open the door that represents the door of Victoria's house.
29 Because of its inclusion of '*as*' Richard Rowland deals with this direction as a piece of evidence for Heywood's involvement in *How a Man May Choose*. See Rowland, *Thomas Heywood's Theatre, 1599–1639: Locations, Translations, and Conflict* (Farnham: Ashgate, 2010), pp. 86–7.
30 For a useful account of the relationship of *The Shrew* and *A Shrew*, see Ann Thompson (ed.), *The Taming of the Shrew*, updated edn (Cambridge University Press, 2003), pp. 172–82.
31 See Peter Thomson, *Shakespeare's Theatre*, 2nd edn (London: Routledge, 1992), pp. 44–5.

32 For a useful discussion of such outside-inside transitions, see Dessen, *Elizabethan Stage Conventions*, pp. 86–8.
33 The Children of the Whitefriars who appeared there in 1609 were granted a new royal patent on 4 January 1610. Richard Dutton has argued that they were not a continuation of the old Queen's Revels Children but were actually a new entity, engineered as such by the Revels Office. See Dutton, 'The Revels Office and the Boy Companies, 1600–1613: New Perspectives', *English Literary Renaissance*, 32 (2002), 339–40.
34 Similar situations also occur in plays performed at open-air amphitheatres. For instance, *The Merry Wives of Windsor*, 2.2 contains Bardolph's speech, 'Sir *Iohn*, there's one Master *Broome* below would faine speake with you' (F1, TLN 906–7; 2.2.144–5). In this scene, which is located upstairs, the stage doors might well have been kept open. It should however be noted that the early modern use of locale is very flexible and inconsistent. There are scenes where the locale changes from upstairs to downstairs during the scene. Take, for example, *2 Henry IV*, 2.4, an Eastcheap tavern scene. When a drawer enters and announces Pistol's arrival, it becomes clear that the scene is located upstairs: 'Sir, Antient pistol's belowe, and would speake with you' (Q1, D3v; 2.4.69–70). Towards the end of the scene, however, when a knocking is heard and Peto enters with news, his entry door appears to represent the entrance door of the tavern: '*Peyto knockes at doore*' (E3v; 2.4.351). This door would need to be closed sometime before the offstage knocking occurs.
35 As Tim Fitzpatrick suggests, it appears more likely that what Truewit refers to as 'this gallerie/lobby' is the stage, rather than the curtained space. See Fitzpatrick with Johnston, 'Spaces, Doors and Places in Early Modern English Staging', *Theatre Notebook*, 63 (2009), 3–4; Fitzpatrick, *Playwright, Space and Place*, pp. 47–8. Cf. Richard Dutton (ed.), *Epicene* (Manchester University Press, 2003), p. 55. It is perhaps noteworthy that in *Hamlet*, 2.1 Polonius refers to the stage as a lobby with a hiding place covered by an arras: 'You know sometimes he walkes foure houres together / Heere in the Lobby. . . . / At such a time, Ile loose my daughter to him, / Be you and I behind an Arras then, / Marke the encounter' (Q2, E4v-F1r; 2.1.160–4). F1 is essentially the same as Q2. Interestingly, Q1 has Corambis say 'The Princes walke is here in the galery ...' (D4v). Jean MacIntyre suggests that Jonson's description of flanking doors as 'studies' characterises the actual features of the Whitefriars. See MacIntyre, 'Production Resources at the Whitefriars Playhouse', paragraphs 16–17; MacIntyre, 'Additional to "Production Resources at the Whitefriars Playhouse, 1609–1612"', *Early Modern Literary Studies*, 3.3 (1998), 8.1–3.
36 See Fitzpatrick, *Playwright, Space and Place*, pp. 54–61; Fitzpatrick with Johnston, 'Spaces, Doors and Places', pp. 13–16.
37 Fitzpatrick with Johnston, 'Spaces, Doors and Places', pp. 13–14. See also Fitzpatrick, *Playwright, Space and Place*, pp. 55–6.
38 I am indebted to John H. Astington for these important points about the Jonson title-page.
39 Tarlton was a member of Sussex's Men before being chosen as a founding player of the Queen's Men in 1583. For histories of the two troupes, lists of their

playing venues in London and records of the companies' appearances in different parts of the country on tour and their appearances at court, see Gurr, *The Shakespearian Playing Companies*, pp. 174–7, 182–4, 196–217. R. A. Foakes takes the view that the verse refers to Tarlton's popularity both at court and in the provinces. See Foakes, 'Playhouses and Players', pp. 39–40. Tarlton's technique for making a comic entrance as described in *Thalia's Banquet* was no doubt perfected in the London theatre, but it seems to have proved equally successful when he was on tour with the Queen's Men. Thomas Nashe makes a brief allusion to it in *Pierce Penniless* (1592): 'Amongst other cholericke wise Iustices, he was one, that hauing a play presented before him and his Towneship, by Tarlton & the rest of his fellowes her Maiesties seruants, and they were now entring into their first merriment (as they call it) the people began exceedingly to laugh, when Tarlton first peept out his head' (Q1, E3r-v).

40 In the Q1 text of the play, there are only two stage directions: one is '*DOL is seene*' (E2v; 2.3); the other is '*WITHIN*' (C4v; 2.1).

41 As F. H. Mares thinks, the central curtained space might well have been associated with the alchemist's secret laboratory. See Mares (ed.), *The Alchemist* (Harvard University Press, 1967), p. xlvii.

42 For similar views, see Hattaway (ed.), *The Third Part of King Henry VI*, p. 74n; John D. Cox and Eric Rasmussen (eds.), *King Henry VI, Part 3* (London: Thomson Learning, 2001), p. 188n.

43 See Hattaway (ed.), *The Third Part of King Henry VI*, p. 75n; Cox and Rasmussen (eds.), *King Henry VI, Part 3*, p. 189n; Randall Martin (ed.), *Henry VI, Part Three* (Oxford University Press, 2001), p. 153n.

44 For a similar view, see Martin (ed.), *Henry VI, Part Three*, p. 161n. For an alternative assessment of the number of actors, see Cox and Rasmussen (eds.), *King Henry VI, Part 3*, Appendix 2.

45 See, for example, Evans (gen. ed.), *The Riverside Shakespeare*, p. 599; N. W. Bawcutt (ed.), *Measure for Measure* (Oxford University Press, 1991), pp. 149–50; Brian Gibbons (ed.), *Measure for Measure* (Cambridge University Press, 1991), pp. 129–30.

46 Even if the door is kept closed and Isabella is therefore not visible at the moment indicated by the entry direction, its placement is not necessarily too early. It is also possible to think that the direction indicates an invisible but audible entrance, like the direction '*Enter Nurse, and knocke*' (*Romeo and Juliet* Q2, G4v; 3.3.70).

CHAPTER 5

1 See Wells and Taylor with Jowett and Montgomery, *Textual Companion*, pp. 386–8; Evans (gen. ed.), *The Riverside Shakespeare*, pp. 1178–9. For a different view, see Daniell (ed.), *Julius Caesar*, pp. 121–9.

2 In the following list, an asterisk indicates that although the scene contains no specific reference to its locality, it is probably a garden scene. These probable garden scenes are not counted among the nineteen. *1 Henry VI*, 2.4; *2 Henry VI*,

1.4*, 2.2, 4.10; *Edward III*, 2.1; *Titus Andronicus*, 4.1*; *The Taming of the Shrew*, 2.1; *King John*, 5.7; *Richard II*, 3.4; *Romeo and Juliet*, 2.2, 2.3*, 3.5; *2 Henry IV*, 5.3; *Much Ado About Nothing*, 2.3, 3.1; *Julius Caesar*, 2.1; *As You Like It*, 1.1; *Twelfth Night*, 1.1*, 2.5, 3.1; *Troilus and Cressida*, 3.2; *Measure for Measure*, 4.1*; *Cymbeline*, 1.1; *The Two Noble Kinsmen*, 2.2.

3 See Evans (gen. ed.), *The Riverside Shakespeare*, plate 24 (following p. 1386).

4 Ralph Agas, *Civitas Londinum: Facsimile from the Original in the Possession of the Corporation of the City of London* (London: Adams and Francis, 1874). R. A. Foakes observes that the Agas map appears to have been based in part on the Braun and Hogenberg map of London (published 1572). See Foakes, *Illustrations of the English Stage: 1580–1642* (Stanford University Press, 1985), p. 4.

5 Nan Fairbrother, *Men and Gardens* (New York: Alfred A. Knopf, 1956), p. 61.

6 Fairbrother, *Men and Gardens*, p. 56.

7 Biblical quotations are taken from *The Geneva Bible: A Facsimile of the 1560 Edition*, with an introduction by Lloyd E. Berry (University of Wisconsin Press, 1969).

8 For a book-length study of the literary tradition of the enclosed garden, see Stanley Stewart, *The Enclosed Garden: The Tradition and the Image in Seventeenth-Century Poetry* (University of Wisconsin Press, 1966).

9 Terry Comito, *The Idea of the Garden in the Renaissance* (Rutgers University Press, 1978).

10 'In happy houre he doth a garden plot espye, / From which, except he warely walke, men may his love descrye, / For lo, it fronted full upon her leaning place, / Where she is woont to shew her heart by cheerefull frendly face' (*Romeus and Juliet*, lines 451–4). Bullough (ed.), *Narrative and Dramatic Sources*, 1, pp. 297–8.

11 It must however be noted that the F1 text has an initial '*Actus Primus. Scoena Prima*' (TLN 1), though there is no subsequent act or scene division.

12 *Richard II* is also likely to have been first acted at the Theatre. In 3.4, the Queen says to her attendants, 'But stay, here come the gardeners, / Lets step into the shadow of these trees' (Q1, G2v; 3.4.24–5), but she and her attendants might have only retired to a side position on the stage.

13 Rosalie L. Colie, *Shakespeare's Living Art* (Princeton University Press, 1974), p. 145.

14 Terry Comito, 'Caliban's Dream: The Topography of Some Shakespeare Gardens', *Shakespeare Studies*, 14 (1981), 24–5.

15 Mark Rose's comment on the design of the scene is worth quoting here: 'In the design of the scene, the lovers are literally surrounded by uncomprehending callers, strangers to their special, transformed world, and these pressures from the impinging outside world help to establish their isolation and perhaps suggest, too, the fragility of their love's creation.' Rose, *Shakespearean Design* (Harvard University Press, 1972), pp. 70–1.

16 David Bevington locates the scene in 'Friar Laurence's monastery garden'. See Bevington (ed.), *The Complete Works of Shakespeare*, 5th edn (New York: Pearson Education, 2004), p. 1023n. It is equally likely that the Friar is near his 'close cell' (Q2, D4v; 2.2.188) in some indeterminate outdoor location where he is gathering weeds and wild flowers for their medicinal value.

17 See Eugene M. Waith (ed.), *The Two Noble Kinsmen* (Oxford University Press, 1989), p. 109n. On the possibility that Palamon and Arcite descended to the main stage for 2.2, see Lois Potter (ed.), *The Two Noble Kinsmen* (Walton-on-Thames: Thomas Nelson and Sons, 1997), p. 63. There are other examples where a bare '*Enter*' indicates the use of the upper location even at the beginnings of scenes. *Edward III*, 1.2, reasonably attributed to Shakespeare, offers one such example. (For Shakespeare's part in *Edward III*, see Giorgio Melchiori (ed.), *King Edward III* (Cambridge University Press, 1998), pp. 16–17.) This scene takes place before the gates of the Countess's castle. The scene-opening entry reads merely '*Enter the Countesse*' (Q1, B1v; 1.2.0), but since later in the same scene she is requested by Montague to 'discend' (B2v; 1.2.87), the Countess is clearly meant to appear on the upper playing level. The 1616 Quarto of *Doctor Faustus* has '*Thunder. Enter Lucifer and 4 deuils, Faustus to them with this speech*' (QB, B1r). As modern editions usually indicate, to the sound of thunder, Lucifer and the four devils would very likely enter on the upper level so that they might observe Faustus without his being aware of their presence. A similar point can be made about another direction in the same text: '*Thunder. Enter Lucifer, Belzebub, and Mephostophilis*' (G4v). See, for example, Fredson Bowers (ed.), *The Complete Works of Christopher Marlowe*, 2nd edn, 2 vols. (Cambridge University Press, 1981), II, 168, 221; David Scott Kastan (ed.), *Doctor Faustus: A Two-Text Edition* (New York: W. W. Norton, 2005), pp. 63, 116. The surviving manuscript of Heywood's *The Captives* supplies another example. The author's direction for the opening entrance of 'Actus 4^a. Scena 3^a' (TLN 2395) reads 'Enter, Dennis wth the ffryar vpon his backe' (TLN 2396). Interestingly, there is an additional instruction marked by the Cockpit bookkeeper above this entry direction: 'from aboue' (TLN 2395). As his speech suggests, Dennis would descend from the upper playing space to the main stage by means of a ladder. It may be that the author simply forgot to specify whence Dennis enters. It is equally likely that he thought his stage direction sufficient, since Dennis's use of the upper level could be easily inferred from his own speech. In this connection, the entrances of Luce and Adriana in *The Comedy of Errors*, 3.1, usually known as the 'lock-out' scene, require a comment: '*Enter Luce*' (F1, TLN 679; 3.1.47); '*Enter Adriana*' (TLN 706; 3.1.60). Although they are directed to enter, they should remain unseen by Antipholus and Dromio of Ephesus, who are standing with two other characters in front of the stage door representing the street door of the Phoenix. They might join Dromio of Syracuse, who is acting the role of porter behind this stage door. In other words, the women might make audible but invisible entrances. There is another possibility. Towards the end of the preceding scene (2.2), Adriana mentioned her intention to have dinner upstairs with her supposed husband, while leading him off the stage: 'Husband Ile dine aboue with you to day' (TLN 603; 2.2.207). Her appearance on the upper level would suggest the intimate atmosphere of the dinner that is taking place while her real husband is seeking admission. As for Luce, since she does not appear anywhere else in the play, this is her only opportunity to be visible to the audience. Her main function would

seem to be to reinforce the comic effect of not only the mistress but also her maid throwing insults at the master and his man from the upper location.
18 See, for example, Waith (ed.), *The Two Noble Kinsmen*, p. 113; Potter (ed.), *The Two Noble Kinsmen*, p. 188n.
19 Richard Proudfoot has suggested a similar view, which is cited by Lois Potter in her edition of *The Two Noble Kinsmen*, p. 64.
20 'The grete tour, that was so thikke and stroong, / Which of the castel was the chief dongeoun / (Ther as the knyghtes weren in prisoun / Of which I tolde yow and tellen shal), / Was evene joynant to the gardyn wal / Ther as this Emelye hadde hir pleyynge.' *The Canterbury Tales*, in Larry D. Benson (gen. ed.), *The Riverside Chaucer* (Oxford University Press, 1987), 1 (A) 1056–61. According to Eugene M. Waith, 'Fletcher presumably read Chaucer in Thomas Speght's *The Workes of our Antient and Learned English Poet, Geffrey Chaucer*, first published in 1598, and then, revised and enlarged, in 1602.' Waith (ed.), *The Two Noble Kinsmen*, p. 26.
21 Similarly, in the middle of *The Taming of the Shrew*, 2.1, before allowing Petruchio to woo Katherina, Baptista speaks a speech implying that the scene is located in his garden: 'We will go walke a little in the Orchard, / And then to dinner' (F1, TLN 976-7; 2.1.111-12). Despite the garden setting, however, the eccentric Petruchio's wooing of the shrewish Katherina is far from romantic.
22 See Martin Butler (ed.), *Cymbeline* (Cambridge University Press, 2005), p. 79n.
23 See Harold N. Hillebrand (ed.), *Troilus and Cressida: A New Variorum Edition of Shakespeare*, supplemented by T. W. Baldwin (Philadelphia: J. B. Lippincott, 1953), pp. 147–8. The Song of Solomon, 6.1–2 reads: 'My welbeloued is gone downe into his garden to the beds of spices, to fede in the gardens, and to gather lilies. / I am my welbeloueds, and my welbeloued is mine, who fedeth among the lilies.'
24 In *Richard II*, 3.4, the Gardener and his men would be dressed in distinctive costumes and carrying gardening tools. Act 3 (scenes 1–11) of Brome's *The Sparagus Garden* takes place in the Asparagus Garden of the play's title. Immediately on the arrival of the Gardener and his wife at the beginning of 3.1 ('*Enter Gardner, and Martha his wife*' (Q1, E3v)), the locality would be established because of the gardener costume he is most probably wearing. For common situations involving veils, see Dessen and Thomson, *Dictionary of Stage Directions*, entry for 'veil, veiled, unveil'.
25 *Measure for Measure*, 4.1 offers an interesting passage, in which Isabella reports to the Duke how she has promised Angelo to meet him at midnight in his 'Garden circummur'd with Bricke' (F1, TLN 1799; 4.1.28). The secretive and illicit nature of the meeting is reinforced by the specification of the enclosed garden. In his edition of the play, J. W. Lever notes that 'No mention of a garden assignation appears in the sources.' Lever (ed.), *Measure for Measure* (London: Methuen, 1965), p. 97n.
26 See Melchiori (ed.), *King Edward III*, p. 17.
27 Consider also *2 Henry IV*, 5.3, which takes place in Shallow's orchard. At the beginning of the scene, Shallow leads Falstaff and others on to the stage, while saying to him, 'Nay you shall see my orchard, where, in an arbour we will eate a last yeeres pippen of mine owne graffing, with a dish of carrawaies and so forth'

(Q1, K1v–K2r; 5.3.1–3). It seems, however, unlikely that a property arbour would have been brought on for this scene. The most that is needed is a table and chairs or benches.

28 Incidentally, *The Oxford English Dictionary* cites a sentence that includes the phrase 'the Banketting howse in the garden'. See sense 2.b for 'banqueting'.

29 For a similar view, see Claire McEachern (ed.), *Much Ado About Nothing* (London: Thomson Learning, 2006), p. 204n. See also F. H. Mares (ed.), *Much Ado About Nothing* (Cambridge University Press, 1988), p. 81n.

30 Genesis, 3.8 reads: 'Afterwarde they heard the voyce of the Lord God walking in the garden in the coole of the day, and the man and his wife hid them selues from the presence of the Lord God among the trees of the garden.' For a comment on the allusion, see McEachern (ed.), *Much Ado About Nothing*, p. 293n.

31 It should, however, be noted that as R. A. Foakes observes, 'the illustration as a whole may have no direct connection with stage performances'. Foakes, *Illustrations of the English Stage*, p. 105.

32 It is also noteworthy that early modern plays provide at least one stage direction specifically requiring the discovery of an arbour: 'An Arbor discovered shepherds and shepherdesses discovered. Iupiter lyke a woodman wth semele' (Heywood, *The Escapes of Jupiter* MS, TLN 1061–2).

33 A similar effect can be observed in the conjuration scene in *2 Henry VI* (1.4). No specific location is indicated in the chief sources for this scene, i.e., Edward Hall's *The Union of the Two Noble and Illustre Families of Lancaster and York* (1548) and Raphael Holinshed's *The Chronicles of England, Scotland and Ireland* (2nd edn, 1587). (See Bullough (ed.), *Narrative and Dramatic Sources*, III, 87–154.) However, the Q1 text, which appears to reflect actual performances, has the Duchess of Gloucester specify the place earlier (1.2): 'And on the backside of my Orchard heere, / There cast their Spelles in silence of the night' (B1v). In 1.4, the witch Margery Jordan and wizards conjure up a spirit on the main stage, while the Duchess is observing them from the upper level. Suddenly, York and Buckingham rush in with their guard and arrest the Duchess and the conjurers. It is noteworthy that the F1 stage direction specifically directs them to break in: '*Enter the Duke of Yorke and the Duke of Buckingham with their Guard, and breake in*' (TLN 669-70; 1.4.40). Although Q1's corresponding direction simply reads 'Enter the Duke of *Yorke*, and the Duke of *Buckingham*, and others' (C1r), their entry door might well have been burst open in theatrical performances.

34 The same point can be made about several other garden scenes. In Garter's interlude, *The Most Virtuous and Godly Susanna*, Sensualitas and Voluptas hide in Susanna's orchard in order to corrupt her there: 'Here they [Sensualitas and Voluptas] go afore into the Orchard, and Susanna and her two maydes come vpon the stage' (Q1, C3v). In the anonymous two-part play called *The Troublesome Reign of John, King of England*, the poisoning of the King takes place in the orchard of Swinstead, i.e., Swineshead Abbey: '*Frier* . . . I meruaile why they dine heere in the Orchard' (*Part II* Q1, E1v). Incidentally, in Shakespeare's *King John*, the dying King is carried in the orchard: '*Hen.* Let him be brought into the Orchard heere' (F1, TLN 2615; 5.7.10). Although the date

of *King John* and its relation to *The Troublesome Reign* is a complex problem, one might have been somehow influenced by the other. Their ultimate source, Holinshed's *Chronicles* gives the location of the King's poisoning simply as 'the abbeie of Swineshead in Lincolnshire'. See Bullough (ed.), *Narrative and Dramatic Sources*, IV, 47. For recent discussions of the relationship between the two plays, see Brian Vickers, '*The Troublesome Raigne*, George Peele, and the Date of *King John*', in Boyd (ed.), *Words That Count*, pp. 78–116; Charles R. Forker, '*The Troublesome Reign*, *Richard II*, and the Date of *King John*: A Study in Intertextuality', in *Shakespeare Survey 63* (Cambridge University Press, 2010), pp. 127–48. (Both argue that *The Troublesome Reign* does antedate *King John*.)

35 Laetitia Yeandle has identified the handwriting as that of Sir Edward Dering. She says that Dering 'copied out, if not composed, three acts of a scenario of a plot set in Thrace and Macedon sometime after 1627 (Folger MS X.d.206)'. She also notes that his 'Booke of Expences' frequently refers to 'seeing a play' when in London. See Yeandle, 'Sir Edward Dering of Surrenden Dering and his "Booke of Expences" (1617–1628)', *Archaeologia Cantiana*, 125 (2005), 339–40. Dering's combined version of Shakespeare's *1* and *2 Henry IV* survives in a manuscript: *The History of King Henry the Fourth* (Folger MS V.b.34). George Walton Williams and Gwynne Blakemore Evans observe that this version 'discloses a more than casual concern for the technical aspects of production'. They therefore believe that 'His play could have been acted not only on the private stage at Surrenden but on the public stage in London'. See Williams and Evans (eds.), *The History of King Henry the Fourth, as revised by Sir Edward Dering, Bart.* (University Press of Virginia, 1974), p. xi. It is perhaps noteworthy that Dering's version has the stage direction '*Enter Northumberland: alone in his garden and Night-Cappe*' (4.9.0).

36 See Werner Habicht, 'Tree Properties and Tree Scenes in Elizabethan Theater', *Renaissance Drama*, n.s. 4 (1971), 76–7, 92. G. F. Reynolds suggests that a wood or forest would have been represented by two or three trees, and that trees might well have been onstage throughout performance. See Reynolds, '"Trees" on the Stage of Shakespeare', *Modern Philology*, 5 (1907), 153–68.

37 See R. A. Foakes (ed.), *Much Ado About Nothing* (Harmondsworth: Penguin Books, 1968), pp. 139–40; Waith (ed.), *The Two Noble Kinsmen*, p. 106n; Sheldon P. Zitner (ed.), *Much Ado About Nothing* (Oxford University Press, 1994), p. 129n; Roger Warren and Stanley Wells (eds.), *Twelfth Night* (Oxford University Press, 1994), p. 142n; Dusinberre (ed.), *As You Like It*, p. 149n; Keir Elam (ed.), *Twelfth Night* (London: Cengage Learning, 2008), p. 237n.

38 See Foakes (ed.), *Henslowe's Diary*, pp. 319–20.

39 See Foakes (ed.), *Henslowe's Diary*, p. 320n.

40 Different staging methods would have been adopted according to the equipment available at each performance. For some other possible methods, see McMillin and MacLean, *The Queen's Men and Their Plays*, p. 139. For references to *Friar Bacon*'s revivals, see Foakes (ed.), *Henslowe's Diary*, pp. 16–21.

41 The phrase '*like an Angell*' in the entry direction refers to the costume worn by Fame as she makes her entrance, not to the manner of her entering. (See Dessen and Thomson, *Dictionary of Stage Directions*, entry for 'like'.) This makes it on

balance more likely that the entrance would have taken place at stage level rather than by some form of angelic descent from the upper level.

42 The play's revivals at the reconstructed Rose and the Fortune could have employed the descent machine and the stage posts. In the extant theatrical plot of *The Battle of Alcazar*, made for a later production (*c*.1598–1601), properties and effects are marked in the margin. Unfortunately, however, the plot has been damaged and lacks Act 5.

43 See Dessen, *Elizabethan Stage Conventions*, pp. 93–101; *Recovering Shakespeare's Theatrical Vocabulary*, pp. 127–49.

44 For arguments for Chettle's co-authorship of the original *Sir Thomas More*, see John Jowett, 'Henry Chettle and the Original Text of *Sir Thomas More*', in T. H. Howard-Hill (ed.), *Shakespeare and 'Sir Thomas More': Essays on the Play and Its Shakespearian Interest* (Cambridge University Press, 1989), pp. 131–49; Jowett (ed.), *Sir Thomas More*, pp. 15, 415–23. See also MacDonald P. Jackson, 'Deciphering a Date and Determining a Date: Anthony Munday's *John a Kent and John a Cumber* and the Original Version of *Sir Thomas More*', *Early Modern Literary Studies*, 15.3 (2011), 2.1–24.

45 Scott McMillin has argued that the play was originally written for Strange's Men between the summer of 1592 and the summer of 1593 and revised for the Admiral's Men after 1603. See McMillin, *The Elizabethan Theatre and 'The Book of Sir Thomas More'* (Cornell University Press, 1987), chapters 3 and 4. Gary Taylor, on the other hand, has suggested that the play was revised after 1600, probably 1603–4, for the King's Men. See Taylor, 'The Date and Auspices of the Addition to *Sir Thomas More*', in Howard-Hill (ed.), *Shakespeare and 'Sir Thomas More'*, pp. 101–29. The most recent view, proposed by John Jowett, is that the original text was written *c*.1600 for Derby's Men and that the revisions, involving Worcester's/Queen Anne's Men, took place around 1603–4. See Jowett (ed.), *Sir Thomas More*, pp. 96–103, 424–33.

46 Heywood's *The English Traveller* has a scene in which Young Geraldine leads Master Wincott, Wincott's wife and her sister Prudentilla off to his father's garden, and then comes back with them shortly after. It is perhaps noteworthy that the stage direction for these people's re-entrance reads '*Enter againe as from Walking* Winc. Wife, Y. Ger. Prud.' (Q1, E3v), although in this example it is clear enough from the dialogue that '*as from Walking*' means '*as from Walking in the garden*'. It should also be noted that the dialogue requires Wincott's wife and her sister to re-enter with flowers in their hands: '*Winc.* See Master Geraldine, / How bold wee are, especially these Ladies / Play little better [then] the theeues with you, / For they haue robb'd your Garden' (E3v).

47 See Vittorio Gabrieli and Giorgio Melchiori (eds.), *Sir Thomas More* (Manchester University Press, 1990), p. 168n. See also Jowett (ed.), *Sir Thomas More*, pp. 38, 276n.

48 Werner Habicht offers a similar view: 'Garden scenes are sometimes suggested by movements of leisurely walking on imaginary paths, as when Iden in his garden is pleased to "enjoy such quiet walks as these": or else there is playful

movement, sportive action, or handling and strewing of flowers.' Habicht, 'Tree Properties', p. 79.
49 Preston's *Cambises*, an eight-actor troupe play, has a scene where the King spies a lady walking with a lord and playing music and falls in love with her. It is noteworthy that the stage direction for the lady and the lord reads 'heer trace vp & down playing' (Q1, E1v), although the scene is located in a field and not in a garden. I am grateful to Alan C. Dessen for providing me with this example.
50 See Cynthia Marshall (ed.), *Shakespeare in Production: As You Like It* (Cambridge University Press, 2004), p. 99n.
51 It is noteworthy that Lodge's *Rosalynde*, which was Shakespeare's major source for the play, provides a passage including the following sentences: 'The yong Gentleman [Orlando's counterpart] bare al with patience, til on a day walking in the garden by himself, he began to consider how he was the son of *John of Bourdeaux*'; 'As thus he was ruminating of his melancholie passions, in came *Saladyne* [Oliver's counterpart] with his men'. Bullough (ed.), *Narrative and Dramatic Sources*, II, 166–7.
52 For a similar comment, see Hattaway (ed.), *As You Like It*, p. 74n.
53 See Bullough (ed.), *Narrative and Dramatic Sources*, v, 95–9.
54 It is nevertheless possible that Brutus is wearing a nightgown, because, as Portia says, he has 'Stole from [her] bed' (TLN 879; 2.1.238). If, as Alan C. Dessen argues, Brutus enters in his nightgown as Caesar does in the next scene ('*Enter Iulius Caesar in his Night-gowne*' (TLN 984; 2.2.0)), the parallelism between 2.1 and 2.2 would become almost perfect. See Dessen, *Elizabethan Stage Conventions*, pp. 46–7. On the significance of the similarity between 2.1 and 2.2 of the play, see Norman Rabkin, *Shakespeare and the Common Understanding* (New York: Free Press, 1967), pp. 106–8; Jean E. Howard, *Shakespeare's Art of Orchestration: Stage Technique and Audience Response* (University of Illinois Press, 1984), pp. 144–7. Early modern English plays offer at least one stage direction including both 'gown' and 'unbraced': '*Antonio, in his night gowne, and a night cap, vnbrac'd, following after*' (Marston, *Antonio's Revenge* Q1, E3r). Another stage direction, from *2 Edward IV*, contains a combination of 'gown' and 'unbuttoned': 'Enter the two yong Princes, Edward and Richard, in their gownes and cappes vnbottond, and vntrust' (Q1, T1v). However, I am inclined to think that Brutus is already dressed, suggesting his half-readiness for participating in the enterprise.
55 On the Globe stage, this speech might have worked in straightforward theatrical terms rather than just in fictional terms. In other words, 'the Doore' might have meant the stage door behind which the actors were waiting for their entrance.
56 Assuming that he is already dressed, it would not matter whether he should go into his house for his formal robes before going out with Ligarius. Such realities would be sacrificed for the symbolic use of the stage door. (The actors playing Brutus and Ligarius would change costumes offstage before making their entrance in the next scene. This is, however, another question.) In contrast, at the end of the next scene, Caesar exits, leading the conspirators into his house: 'Good Friends go in, and taste some wine with me / And we (like

Friends) will straight way go together' (TLN 1125-6; 2.2.126-7). Caesar, in his nightgown, could not exit as if going directly to the Capitol.

CHAPTER 6

1 The comment Theseus makes at the end of the play-within-the-play in *A Midsummer Night's Dream* is worth citing: '*Moone-shine* and *Lyon* are left to bury the dead' (Q1, H3r; 5.1.348-9).
2 These cases include those in which the body might have been left onstage through the subsequent action after the end of the scene, although even in such cases, the corpse would have had to be removed sometime later. For useful discussions of such examples, see Homer Swander, 'No Exit for a Dead Body: What to do with a Scripted Corpse?', *Journal of Dramatic Theory and Criticism*, 5 (1991), 139-52; Dessen, *Recovering Shakespeare's Theatrical Vocabulary*, pp. 83-4.
3 What the direction '*Mustaffa* beate *Selimus* in' indicates is probably the two characters' passing over the stage, that is, entering by one of the flanking doors, crossing the stage and exiting by the other.
4 See Long, '"Precious Few"', p. 427.
5 For a similar comment on the anecdote, see A. R. Braunmuller (ed.), *Macbeth* (Cambridge University Press, 1997), p. 174n.
6 Gallippus is meant to rise up, cursing the king ('Hell take thee'), and leave the stage, since he is directed to re-enter later in the same scene ('*Enter Gallippus*' (B8r)).
7 I am grateful to Alan C. Dessen for providing me with the examples in *Jack Drum's Entertainment* and *The Prisoners*.
8 See Gurr, *The Shakespearean Stage*, p. 217.
9 Frederick Kiefer offers to explain why a stage direction should specify an '*Arras hung up for the Musicians*', if the central section of the tiring-house wall was already covered by hangings. He writes: 'The arras newly hung up probably portrays a figure or scene or colors in keeping with the dramatic action: the wondrous animation of the statues. Even though Renaissance theaters did not employ painted scenery in the modern fashion and certainly did not seek to achieve scenic illusion, the acting companies must have varied the hangings in order to match the mood of the action, as in *The City Madam*.' Kiefer, 'Curtains on the Shakespearean Stage', *Medieval and Renaissance Drama in England*, 20 (2007), 171.
10 Fredson Bowers (ed.), *The Maid in the Mill*, in Bowers (gen. ed.), *The Dramatic Works in the Beaumont and Fletcher Canon*, IX, 572.
11 Gary Taylor notes that the F1 text cuts eight of the Gentleman's lines, describing the storm, at the beginning of Act 3 (Q1, F3r-v; 3.1.7-15), and observes as follows: 'was the verbal description unnecessary, because the audience had just heard a prolonged aural representation of the storm?' Taylor, 'The Structure of Performance', pp. 49-50.
12 See, for example, Wells and Taylor with Jowett and Montgomery, *Textual Companion*, pp. 400-1; Erne, *Shakespeare as Literary Dramatist*, p. 219. Cf. Evans (gen. ed.), *The Riverside Shakespeare*, p. 1234.

13 For a similar view, see Ann Thompson and Neil Taylor (eds.), *Hamlet* (London: Thomson Learning, 2006), p. 307n.
14 For an important discussion of the staging of this scene, see Richard Hosley, 'The Staging of Desdemona's Bed', *Shakespeare Quarterly*, 14 (1963), 57–65.
15 For an argument for the use of the trap, see Andrew Gurr, 'The Date and the Expected Venue of *Romeo and Juliet*', in *Shakespeare Survey 49* (Cambridge University Press, 1996), p. 24.
16 For a useful discussion of the staging of *Romeo and Juliet*, see Leslie Thomson, '"With patient ears attend": *Romeo and Juliet* on the Elizabethan Stage', *Studies in Philology*, 92 (1995), 230–47.
17 For a similar view, see Levenson (ed.), *Romeo and Juliet*, p. 352n.
18 Philip Edwards (ed.), *The Spanish Tragedy* (Manchester University Press, 1977), pp. 109–10n.
19 For some more comments on Isabella's departure, see J. R. Mulryne (ed.), *The Spanish Tragedy* (London: A & C Black, 1989), p. 111n; David Bevington (ed.), *The Spanish Tragedy* (Manchester University Press, 1996), p. 118n; Emma Smith (ed.), *The Spanish Tragedy* (London: Penguin Books, 1998), p. 175.
20 For a recent discussion of Heywood's authorship of the play, see Richard Rowland, '"Speaking some words, but of no importance"?: Stage Directions, Thomas Heywood, and *Edward IV*', *Medieval and Renaissance Drama in England*, 18 (2005), 104–22. According to Herbert Berry, *1* and *2 Edward IV* could have been performed at the Boar's Head but were evidently written for performance at another place. See Berry, *The Boar's Head Playhouse*, p. 126.
21 On the use of a curtained enclosure by the Queen's Men, see McMillin and MacLean, *The Queen's Men and Their Plays*, pp. 139–41. See also Chapter 2, note 53.
22 For similar views, see Gabrieli and Melchiori (eds.), *Sir Thomas More*, p. 206n; McMillin, *The Elizabethan Theatre and 'The Book of Sir Thomas More*', p. 102. For a different view, see Jowett (ed.), *Sir Thomas More*, pp. 105–7.
23 See John H. Astington, 'Gallows Scenes on the Elizabethan Stage', *Theatre Notebook*, 37 (1983), 3–9.
24 W. J. Lawrence suggests the use of a dummy head. He refers to a scene in the 1616 text of *Doctor Faustus*, where the decapitation is preceded by the direction '*Enter Faustus with the false head*' (QB, F1v). See Lawrence, *Pre-Restoration Stage Studies* (Harvard University Press, 1927), pp. 245–50. See also Gurr, *The Shakespearean Stage*, pp. 224–5.
25 Vittorio Gabrieli and Giorgio Melchiori observe that 'The final exit of More, at gallery level, above the heads of the groundlings, "to the East" (V.iv.113) ["to the Easte" (MS, TLN 1977)] – the place of Christ's cross – turns execution into apotheosis.' Gabrieli and Melchiori (eds.), *Sir Thomas More*, pp. 30–1.
26 The entry direction for Salisbury and other English characters reads '*Enter Salisbury and Talbot on the Turrets, with others*' (F1, TLN 487–8; 1.4.22), and the subsequent dialogue makes clear that '*others*' include Gargrave and Glansdale. As Edward Burns suggests, no other actors might not enter above. Burns (ed.), *King Henry VI, Part 1* (London: Thomson Learning, 2000), p. 150n.

27 The scene's opening stage direction reads '*Enter Henry the sixt, and Richard, with the Lieutenant on the Walles*' (F1, TLN 3072–3; 5.6.0). On the possibility that the killing takes place on the main stage, see Hattaway (ed.), *The Third Part of King Henry VI*, p. 194n; Martin (ed.), *Henry VI, Part Three*, p. 316n; Cox and Rasmussen (eds.), *King Henry VI, Part 3*, pp. 359–60n.
28 Scott McMillin and Sally-Beth MacLean exclude *Locrine* from the Queen's Men canon. See McMillin and MacLean, *The Queen's Men and Their Plays*, p. 92. Roslyn L. Knutson, however, suggests adding it to their repertoire. See Knutson, 'The Start of Something Big', in Ostovich, Syme and Griffin (eds.), *Locating the Queen's Men*, p. 103. Sonia Massai takes the view that the epilogue to the play, a tribute to Queen Elizabeth universally ascribed to the reviser 'W. S.', was very possibly written for a revival of the play at court by the Queen's Men: 'So let vs pray for that renowned mayd, / That eight and thirtie yeares the scepter swayd' (K4v). See Massai, 'Shakespeare, Text and Paratext', in *Shakespeare Survey 62* (Cambridge University Press, 2009), p. 7. Tiffany Stern, however, questions the idea that a concluding prayer for the monarch indicates specifically a court production and suggests the possibility that the prayer was always spoken at the end of theatre performances, public or private. See Stern, 'Epilogues, Prayers after Plays, and Shakespeare's *2 Henry IV*', *Theatre Notebook*, 64 (2010), 122–9.
29 The most extensive argument in favour of Shakespeare's authorship of *Arden of Faversham* is presented by MacDonald P. Jackson. See, for example, 'Shakespeare and the Quarrel Scene in *Arden of Faversham*', *Shakespeare Quarterly*, 57 (2006), 249–93; 'Parallels and Poetry: Shakespeare, Kyd, and *Arden of Faversham*', *Medieval and Renaissance Drama in England*, 23 (2010), 17–33. See also Arthur F. Kinney, 'Authoring *Arden of Faversham*', in Craig and Kinney (eds.), *Shakespeare, Computers, and the Mystery of Authorship*, pp. 78–99. Brian Vickers, on the other hand, suggests Thomas Kyd as the likely author. See Vickers, 'Thomas Kyd, Secret Sharer', *Times Literary Supplement*, 18 April 2008, pp. 13–15. For an important review of the present state of attribution studies, see Vickers, 'Shakespeare and Authorship Studies in the Twenty-First Century'.
30 Dr Simon Forman's account of a Globe performance of *Macbeth* in 1611 contains a description of this scene, which reads 'And as he [Macbeth] thus did, standing up to drincke a Carouse to him [Banquo], the ghoste of Banco came and sate down in his cheirer behind him' (cited by Braunmuller in his edition of *Macbeth*, p. 58). Although this description is of the ghost's second appearance, and Forman does not describe its first appearance, his use of 'came' appears to suggest the ghost's use of a stage door for his entry. On the other hand, it is perhaps noteworthy that in Davenant's adaptation of *Macbeth* the ghost uses the trap door at least for his first exit and the second appearance in this scene: '*the Ghost descends*' (Q1, F3v); '*the Ghost of* Banq. *rises at his feet*' (F3v). For a useful discussion of this scene, see Stanley Wells, 'Staging Shakespeare's Ghosts', in Murray Biggs *et al.* (eds.), *The Arts of Performance in Elizabethan and Early Stuart Drama* (Edinburgh University Press, 1991), pp. 65–8.
31 The 1594 Quarto was printed as 'Played by the Children of her *Maiesties Chappell*. Written by Christopher Marlowe, and *Thomas Nash. Gent.*' (Q1,

A1r). It has been assumed that *Dido* was Marlowe's first play and it has sometimes been contended that it was composed for academic performance at Cambridge. Martin Wiggins has recently disputed the traditional assumption and argued persuasively that *Dido* was written in the late 1580s for the Children of the Chapel. See Wiggins, 'When Did Marlowe Write *Dido, Queen of Carthage?*', *Review of English Studies*, 59 (2008), 521–41.

32 Martin Wiggins thinks that all the three characters 'destroy themselves by disappearing downwards through the stage'. Wiggins, 'When Did Marlowe Write *Dido, Queen of Carthage?*', p. 539.

33 In some modern editions, while the stage direction for Dido reads '*Throws herself into the flames*', the directions for Iarbas and Anna read '*Kills himself*' and '*Kills herself*' respectively. See, for example, H. J. Oliver (ed.), '*Dido Queen of Carthage*' and '*The Massacre at Paris*' (London: Methuen, 1968), pp. 89–90; Bowers (ed.), *The Complete Works of Christopher Marlowe*, I, 58.

34 It seems reasonable to assume that the first performance of the play took place during the season of 1639–40 at the Dublin theatre in Werburgh Street that had opened in 1637. It is suggested that the Werburgh Street theatre may have had connections with the Phoenix in Drury Lane. See John P. Turner, Jr. (ed.), *A Critical Edition of James Shirley's St. Patrick for Ireland* (New York: Garland, 1979), pp. 33–45.

35 It is noteworthy that an academic moral play provides a similar example involving a sleeping character. In the finale of *Lingua*, by Thomas Tomkis, Appetitus is so fast asleep, dreaming of foods, that Anamnestes cannot wake him. Anamnestes finally seeks help from the spectators by speaking the epilogue: '*Ivdicious friends, it is so late at night, / I cannot waken hungrie Appetite: / Then since the cloase vpon his rising stands, / Let me obtaine this at your courteous hands, / Trie if the friendly opportunitie, / Of your good will, and gracious Plauditie, / With the thrice welcome murmure it shall keepe, / Can begge this prisoner from the bands of sleepe.*' The epilogue is followed by the stage direction 'Vpon the Plaudite, APPETITVS awakes, and runnes in after ANAMNESTES' (Q1, N1v).

36 Robert Weimann, *Author's Pen and Actor's Voice: Playing and Writing in Shakespeare's Theatre* (Cambridge University Press, 2000), p. 220.

37 See Weimann, *Author's Pen and Actor's Voice*, p. 221.

38 Michael Shapiro, *Gender in Play on the Shakespearean Stage: Boy Heroines and Female Pages* (University of Michigan Press, 1994), p. 132.

39 Perhaps, as Andrew Gurr suggests, they might start to dance a jig immediately after getting up. Taking account of the fact that 'up to at least 1600 jigs were the dominant tradition for closing performances in the open-air playhouse', Gurr thinks it 'tempting to ask whether the three corpses might not have sprung back to life to dance a final jig'. *The Shakespeare Company*, p. 75.

40 For a similar comment, see R. A. Foakes (ed.), *King Lear* (Walton-on-Thames: Thomas Nelson and Sons, 1997), p. 385n.

41 See Horace, *The Odes and Epodes*, with an English translation by C. E. Bennett (London: William Heinemann, 1914), Odes Book 1, Ode 22; Morris Palmer Tilley, *A Dictionary of the Proverbs in England in the Sixteenth and Seventeenth*

Centuries (University of Michigan Press, 1950), E116. For useful comments on the play-closing couplet, see Gurr, *Playgoing in Shakespeare's London*, pp. 100–1; David Gunby, David Carnegie and MacDonald P. Jackson (eds.), *The Works of John Webster: An Old Spelling Critical Edition*, 4 vols. (Cambridge University Press, 1995–), 1, 674.

42 I began this chapter with the treatment of the dead body in the dumb show presented prior to the *Gonzago* play in *Hamlet*, 3.2. It is worth mentioning here an example of the exit of a dead character at the end of a play-within-a-play. The play within *The Knight of the Burning Pestle* ends with the death of the Grocer Errant (Rafe's role): '*Raph*. . . . I die, flie, flie my soule to *Grocers* Hall. oh, oh, oh, &c.' (Q1, K3v). Then the Wife (Nell), who has been sitting on the stage with her husband (George) and the real Blackfriars gentlemen stool-sitters, praises Rafe's acting and tells him to bow and exit: 'Well said *Raph*, doe your obeysance to the Gentlemen and go your waies, well said *Raph*' (K3v). This speech is followed by the stage direction '*Exit Raph*' (K3v).

43 For a useful discussion of this subject, see Weimann, *Author's Pen and Actor's Voice*, pp. 180–215.

44 'Even when attention is directly called to the stage-as-stage, stage-as-fictional-world still remains. In such moments, the audience experiences a double image.' Beckerman, *Shakespeare at the Globe*, p. 66.

45 For a comment on the '*Exeunt*' direction for the witches (TLN 13), see Braunmuller (ed.), *Macbeth*, p. 103n. In Davenant's adaptation of *Macbeth*, the witches certainly made their exit flying: '*Ex. flying*' (Q1, A1r). It should, however, be noted that a contemporary describes Davenant's version as having 'new Scenes, Machines, as flyings for the witches' (John Downes, *Roscius Anglicanus* (1708), p. 33, cited by John Wilders in *Shakespeare in Production: Macbeth* (Cambridge University Press, 2004), p. 89n.)

Plays cited

Details about each play are given in the following order: title; author; date; company; theatre; and the text(s) cited.

Authorship attribution studies are offering new attributions and de-attributions, which I have chosen not to adopt unless they are confirmed by scholarly consensus.

Dates given are those of composition or first performance and no attempt is made to distinguish between them, on the assumption that a play was acted shortly after it was composed.

Sources for the information are Alfred Harbage, *Annals of English Drama, 975–1700*, revised by S. Schoenbaum, and Sylvia Stoler Wagonheim, 3rd edn (London: Routledge, 1989); Andrew Gurr, *The Shakespearean Stage: 1574–1642*, 4th edn (Cambridge University Press, 2009), Appendix: 'A Select List of Plays and Their Playhouses'; and research by modern editors.

Abbreviations

Dramatic Documents: W. W. Greg, *Dramatic Documents from the Elizabethan Playhouses*, 2 vols. (1931; repr. Oxford: Clarendon Press, 1969), II (Reproductions and Transcripts)

Huntington: *Shakespeare's Plays in Quarto: A Facsimile Edition of Copies Mainly from the Henry E. Huntington Library*, edited by Michael J. B. Allen and Kenneth Muir (University of California Press, 1981)

MSR: The Malone Society Reprints

Norton: *The Norton Facsimile: The First Folio of Shakespeare*, prepared by Charlton Hinman, 2nd edn (New York: W. W. Norton, 1996)

STC: Alfred W. Pollard and G. R. Redgrave, *A Short-Title Catalogue of Books Printed in England, Scotland, and Ireland, and of English Books Printed Abroad, 1475–1640*, revised by W. A. Jackson, F. S. Ferguson and Katharine F. Pantzer,

	2nd edn, 3 vols. (London: Bibliographical Society, 1976–1991)
Wing:	Donald Wing, *A Short-Title Catalogue of Books Printed in England, Scotland, Ireland, Wales, and British America, and of English Books Printed in Other Countries, 1641–1700*, revised and enlarged by Timothy J. Crist, John J. Morrison, Carolyn W. Nelson and others, 2nd edn, 4 vols. (New York: Modern Language Association of America, 1972–1998)

The Alchemist, Ben Jonson, 1610, King's Men, Blackfriars, Q1 (1612) [STC 14755]; F1 (1616) [STC 14751]

All's Well That Ends Well, William Shakespeare, 1602–03, Chamberlain's Men, Globe, F1 (1623) [Norton]

Alphonsus, King of Aragon, Robert Greene, 1587–88, Queen's Men? Unknown, Q1 (1599) [STC 12233]

Antonio's Revenge, John Marston, 1600–01, Paul's Children, Paul's, Q1 (1602) [STC 17474]

Antony and Cleopatra, William Shakespeare, 1606–07, King's Men, Globe, F1 (1623) [Norton]

Appius and Virginia, John Webster and Thomas Heywood, 1625–26, Unknown, Unknown, Q1 (1654) [Wing W1215]

Arden of Faversham, Anon., 1588–91, Unknown, Unknown, Q1 (1592) [STC 733]

As You Like It, William Shakespeare, 1599–1600, Chamberlain's Men, Globe/Court, F1 (1623) [Norton]

The Atheist's Tragedy, Cyril Tourneur, 1607–11, King's Men? Unknown, Q1 (1611) [STC 24146]

Bartholomew Fair, Ben Jonson, 1614, Lady Elizabeth's Men, Hope, Folio printed in 1631 (included in F2 (1640)) [STC 14754]

The Battle of Alcazar, George Peele, 1588–89, Admiral's Men? Unknown, Q1 (1594) [STC 19531]; MS plot (c.1598–1601) [Dramatic Documents]

Believe as You List, Philip Massinger, 1631, King's Men, Blackfriars/Globe, MS [MSR, ed. Charles J. Sisson, 1927 (1928)]

Bonduca, John Fletcher, 1610–14, King's Men, Globe/Blackfriars, MS [MSR, ed. W. W. Greg, 1951]; F1 (1647) [Wing B1581]

Brennoralt, Sir John Suckling, 1639–41, King's Men, Blackfriars, Q1 (1642) [Wing S6125]

Caesar and Pompey, George Chapman, 1602–05, Unknown, Unacted? Q1 (1631) [STC 4993]

Cambises, Thomas Preston, c.1558–69, Unknown, Court? Q1 (1570?) [STC 20287]

The Captain, John Fletcher (with Francis Beaumont?), 1609–12, King's Men, Globe/Blackfriars, F1 (1647) [Wing B1581]

The Captives, Thomas Heywood, 1624, Lady Elizabeth's Men, Cockpit, MS [MSR, ed. Arthur Brown, 1953]

The Chances, John Fletcher, *c*.1617, King's Men, Globe/Blackfriars, F1 (1647) [Wing B1581]

The Changeling, Thomas Middleton and William Rowley, 1622, Lady Elizabeth's Men, Cockpit, Q1 (1653) [Wing M1981]

A Chaste Maid in Cheapside, Thomas Middleton, 1613, Lady Elizabeth's Men, Swan, Q1 (1630) [STC 17877]

The City Madam, Philip Massinger, 1632, King's Men, Blackfriars, Q1 (1658) [Wing M1046]

The City Match, Jasper Mayne, 1637–38? King's Men, Blackfriars, F1 (1639) [STC 17750]

The Comedy of Errors, William Shakespeare, 1592–94, Strange's? Unknown, F1 (1623) [Norton]

The Conspiracy and Tragedy of Charles, Duke of Byron, George Chapman, 1607–08, Revels–Blackfriars Children, Blackfriars, Q1 (1608) [STC 4968]

The Country Girl, 'T. B.' (Anthony Brewer?), 1632–*c*.1633, King's Men? Unknown, Q1 (1647) [Wing B4425]

The Court Beggar, Richard Brome, 1639–40, Beeston's Boys, Cockpit, O1 (1653) [Wing B4870]

The Cruel Brother, William Davenant, 1627, King's Men, Blackfriars, Q1 (1630) [STC 6302]

Cupid's Revenge, John Fletcher and Francis Beaumont, 1607–08, Revels–Blackfriars Children, Blackfriars, Q1 (1615) [STC 1667]

Cupid's Whirligig, Edward Sharpham, 1607, King's Revels Children, Whitefriars, Q1 (1607) [STC 22380]

Cymbeline, William Shakespeare, 1609–10, King's Men, Globe, F1 (1623) [Norton]

Cynthia's Revels, Ben Jonson, 1600, Chapel Children, Blackfriars, Q1 (1601) [STC 14773]

The Dead Man's Fortune, Anon., *c*.1590–91, Admiral's Men? Unknown, MS plot [Dramatic Documents]

The Deserving Favourite, Lodowick Carlell, *c*.1622–29, King's Men, Blackfriars/Court, Q1 (1629) [STC 4628]

The Devil's Charter, Barnabe Barnes, 1606, King's Men, Globe, Q1 (1607) [STC 1466]

Dido, Queen of Carthage, Christopher Marlowe and Thomas Nashe, *c*.1588? Chapel Children, Unknown, Q1 (1594) [STC 17441]

The Distresses, William Davenant, 1639, King's Men, Blackfriars, F1 (1673) [Wing D320]

Doctor Faustus, Christopher Marlowe, 1588–89, Strange's Men? Unknown, QA (1604) [STC 17429]; QB (1616) [STC 17432]; *Marlowe's Doctor Faustus 1604–1616: Parallel Texts*, ed. W. W. Greg (Oxford: Clarendon Press, 1950)

The Double Marriage, John Fletcher and Philip Massinger, 1619–23, King's Men, Blackfriars, F1 (1647) [Wing B1581]

The Downfall of Robert, Earl of Huntingdon, Henry Chettle and Anthony Munday, 1598, Admiral's Men, Rose, Q1 (1601) [STC 18271]

The Duchess of Malfi, John Webster, 1613–14, King's Men, Blackfriars/Globe, Q1 (1623) [STC 25176]

The Dutch Courtesan, John Marston, c.1604, Queen's Revels Children, Blackfriars, Q1 (1605) [STC 17475]

Eastward Ho, George Chapman, Ben Jonson and John Marston, 1605, Queen's Revels Children, Blackfriars, Q1 (1605) [STC 4970]

Edward II, Christopher Marlowe, c.1592, Pembroke's Men, Unknown, Q1 (1594) [STC 17437]

Edward III, Anon. (Shakespeare in part), 1592–94, Pembroke's Men? Unknown, Q1 (1596) [STC 7501]

2 Edward IV, Thomas Heywood, 1592–99, Derby's Men, Unknown, Q1 (1599) [STC 13341]

The English Traveller, Thomas Heywood, 1626–27, Queen Henrietta's Men, Cockpit, Q1 (1633) [STC 13315]

Epicoene, Ben Jonson, 1609, Whitefriars Children, Whitefriars, F1 (1616) [STC 14751]

The Escapes of Jupiter, Thomas Heywood, c.1625, Unknown, Unknown, MS [MSR, ed. Henry D. Janzen, 1976 (1978)]

Every Man in His Humour, Ben Jonson, 1598, Chamberlain's Men, Curtain, Q1 (1601) [STC 14766]; F1 (1616) [STC 14751]

Every Man out of His Humour, Ben Jonson, 1599, Chamberlain's Men, Globe, Q1 (1600) [STC 14769]

The Fatal Dowry, Nathan Field and Philip Massinger, 1617–19, King's Men, Blackfriars, Q1 (1632) [STC 17646]

Fedele and Fortunio, Anthony Munday, 1583–84, Oxford's Boys? First Blackfriars? Q1 (1585) [STC 19447]

Four Plays in One, John Fletcher (with Nathan Field?) c.1612–15, Unknown, Unknown, F1 (1647) [Wing B1581]

Frederick and Basilea, Anon., 1597, Admiral's Men, Rose, MS plot [Dramatic Documents]

Friar Bacon and Friar Bungay, Robert Greene, c.1589, Queen's Men, Unknown, Q1 (1594) [STC 12267]

A Game at Chess, Thomas Middleton, 1624, King's Men, Globe, Trinity Manuscript [MSR, ed. T. H. Howard-Hill, 1990]; Archdale Manuscript [Folger Shakespeare Library, MS. V.a.231]

The Gentleman of Venice, James Shirley, 1639, 1 Ogilby's Men? Dublin?; Queen Henrietta's Men, Salisbury Court, Q1 (1655) [Wing S3468]

The Gentleman Usher, George Chapman, c.1602, Chapel Children, Blackfriars, Q1 (1606) [STC 4978]

Hamlet, William Shakespeare, 1600–01, Chamberlain's Men, Globe, Q1 (1603) [Huntington]; Q2 (1604) [Huntington]; F1 (1623) [Norton]

The Hector of Germany, W. Smith, c.1614–15, Citizens, Red Bull; Curtain, Q1 (1615) [STC 22871]

The Heir, Thomas May, 1620, Revels Company, Unknown, Q1 (1622) [STC 17713]

1 Henry IV, William Shakespeare, 1596–97, Chamberlain's Men, Theatre? Q1 (1598) [Huntington] <Q0 (1598)
2 Henry IV, William Shakespeare, 1597–98, Chamberlain's Men, Theatre? Q1 (1600) [Huntington]
1 Henry VI, William Shakespeare, 1589–90, Strange's Men, Unknown, F1 (1623) [Norton]
2 Henry VI, William Shakespeare, 1590–91, Strange's Men/Pembroke's Men, Unknown, Q1 (1594) [Huntington]; F1 (1623) [Norton]
3 Henry VI, William Shakespeare, 1590–91, Strange's Men/Pembroke's Men, Unknown, O1 (1595) [Huntington]; F1 (1623) [Norton]
Henry VIII, William Shakespeare and John Fletcher, 1613, King's Men, Globe, F1 (1623) [Norton]
The History of King Henry the Fourth, Sir Edward Dering, 1623, Amateurs at Surrenden, MS [Walton Williams and Gwynne Blakemore Evans (eds.), *The History of King Henry the Fourth, as revised by Sir Edward Dering, Bart.* (University Press of Virginia, 1974)]
The Hog Hath Lost His Pearl, Robert Tailor, 1613, 'Apprentices', Whitefriars, Q1 (1614) [STC 23658]
How a Man May Choose a Good Wife from a Bad, Thomas Heywood? c.1601–02, Worcester's Men, Boar's Head? Q1 (1602) [STC 5594]
If It Be Not a Good Play, the Devil Is in It, Thomas Dekker, 1611–12, Queen Anne's Men, Red Bull, Q1 (1612) [STC 6507]
1 The Iron Age, Thomas Heywood, 1612–13, Queen Anne's Men, Red Bull, Q1 (1632) [STC 13340]
2 The Iron Age, Thomas Heywood, 1612–13, Queen Anne's Men, Red Bull, Q1 (1632) [STC 13340]
The Island Princess, John Fletcher, 1621, King's Men, Blackfriars, F1 (1647) [Wing B1581]
Jack Drum's Entertainment, John Marston, 1600, Paul's Children, Paul's, Q1 (1601) [STC 7243]
James IV, Robert Greene, 1590–91, Queen's Men? Unknown, Q1 (1598) [STC 12308]
The Jew of Malta, Christopher Marlowe, 1589–90, Strange's Men? Unknown, Q1 (1633) [STC 17412]
John a Kent and John a Cumber, Anthony Munday, 1590 [or 1595–96?], Admiral's Men, Unknown, MS [MSR, ed. Muriel St. Clare Byrne, 1923]
Julius Caesar, William Shakespeare, 1599, Chamberlain's Men, Globe, F1 (1623) [Norton]
King John, William Shakespeare, 1595–96, Chamberlain's Men, Theatre? F1 (1623) [Norton]
King Lear, William Shakespeare, 1605, King's Men, Globe, Q1 (1608) [Huntington]; F1 (1623) [Norton]
A Knack to Know an Honest Man, Anon. (Anthony Munday? Thomas Heywood?), 1594, Admiral's Men, Rose, Q1 (1596) [STC 15028]

The Knight of Malta, John Fletcher, Nathan Field and Philip Massinger, 1618, King's Men, Blackfriars, F1 (1647) [Wing B1581]
The Knight of the Burning Pestle, Francis Beaumont (with John Fletcher?), 1607, Revels Children, Blackfriars, Q1 (1613) [STC 1674]
The Launching of the Mary, Walter Mountfort, 1633, Unknown, Unknown, MS [MSR, ed. John Henry Walter, 1933]
Lingua, or The Combat of the Tongue and the Five Senses for Superiority, Thomas Tomkis, 1607, Students, Trinity College, Cambridge, Q1 (1607) [STC 24104]
The Little French Lawyer, John Fletcher and Philip Massinger, 1619–23, King's Men, Blackfriars/Globe, F1 (1647) [Wing B1581]; F2 (1679) [Wing B1582]
Locrine, 'W. S.' (George Peele? Robert Greene?), [published 1595], Queen's Men? Unknown, Q1 (1595) [STC 21528]
Love's Cruelty, James Shirley, 1631, Queen Henrietta's Men, Cockpit, Q1 (1640) [STC 22449]
Love's Pilgrimage, John Fletcher (with Francis Beaumont?), 1616? King's Men, Blackfriars/Globe, F1 (1647) [Wing B1581]; F2 (1679) [Wing B1582]
Macbeth, William Davenant, 1664, Q1 (1674) [Wing S2930 'Macbeth, A Tragaedy. With all the Alterations, Amendments, Additions, and New Songs. As it's now Acted at the Dukes Theatre. London, Printed for *P. Chetwin* . . . 1674.']
Macbeth, William Shakespeare, 1606; adapted by Thomas Middleton 1616, King's Men, Globe; Blackfriars, F1 (1623) [Norton]; Padua Folio Copy [G. Blakemore Evans (ed.), *Shakespearean Prompt-Books of the Seventeenth Century*, vol. 1, part 2, *The Text of the Padua Macbeth* (University Press of Virginia, 1960)]
The Maid in the Mill, John Fletcher and William Rowley, 1623, King's Men, Blackfriars/Globe, F1 (1647) [Wing B1581]
The Malcontent, John Marston, c.1603–04, Chapel–Queen's Revels Children, Blackfriars; King's Men, Globe, QA (1604) [STC 17479]; QC (1604) [STC 17481]
The Massacre at Paris, Christopher Marlowe, 1593, Strange's Men, Rose, O1 (1594?) [STC 17423]
Measure for Measure, William Shakespeare, 1604, King's Men, Globe, F1 (1623) [Norton]; Padua Folio Copy [G. Blakemore Evans (ed.), *Shakespearean Prompt-Books of the Seventeenth Century*, vol. 2, *The Padua Measure for Measure* (University Press of Virginia, 1963)]
Menaechmi, William Warner (Trans. Plautus), 1592?–1594, closet, Q1 (1595) [STC 20002]
The Merchant of Venice, William Shakespeare, 1596–97, Chamberlain's Men, Theatre, Q1 (1600) [Huntington]; F1 (1623) [Norton]
The Merry Wives of Windsor, William Shakespeare, 1597, Chamberlain's Men, Theatre? F1 (1623) [Norton]
A Midsummer Night's Dream, William Shakespeare, 1595–96, Chamberlain's Men, Theatre, Q1 (1600) [Huntington]; F1 (1623) [Norton]

Money is an Ass, Thomas Jordan, c.1635? King's Revels Men? Unknown, Q1 (1668) [Wing J1047]

Monsieur Thomas, John Fletcher, 1610–16, Lady Elizabeth's Men?/King's Men? Blackfriars? Q1 (1639) [STC 11071]

The Most Virtuous and Godly Susanna, Thomas Garter, 1563–69, offered for acting, Q1 (1578) [STC 11632.5]

Much Ado About Nothing, William Shakespeare, 1598–99, Chamberlain's Men, Curtain? Q1 (1600) [Huntington]

A New Wonder: A Woman Never Vexed, William Rowley, 1611–14, Unknown, Unknown, Q1 (1632) [STC 21423]

The Night Walker, John Fletcher, c.1611, Lady Elizabeth's Men? Unknown, Q1 (1640) [STC 11072]

The Novella, Richard Brome, 1632–33, King's Men, Blackfriars, O1 (1653) [Wing B4870]

Old Fortunatus, Thomas Dekker, 1599, Admiral's Men, Rose, Q1 (1600) [STC 6517]

Orestes, Thomas Goffe, c.1613–c.1618, Students, Christ Church, Oxford, Q1 (1633) [STC 11982]

Othello, William Shakespeare, 1604, King's Men, Globe, Q1 (1622) [Huntington]; F1 (1623) [Norton]

Parasitaster, or the Fawn, John Marston, 1604–05, Queen's Revels Children, Blackfriars, Q1 (1606) [STC 17483]

The Parson's Wedding, Thomas Killigrew, 1640–41, King's Men, Blackfriars, F1 (1664) [Wing K450]

Patient Grissil, Henry Chettle, Thomas Dekker and William Haughton, 1600, Admiral's Men, Fortune, Q1 (1603) [STC 6518]

Pericles, William Shakespeare (and George Wilkins?), 1608, King's Men, Globe, Q1 (1609) [Huntington]

The Picture, Philip Massinger, 1629, King's Men, Globe/Blackfriars, Q1 (1630) [STC 17640]

The Prisoners, Thomas Killigrew, 1632–36, Queen Henrietta's Men, Cockpit, D1 (1641) [STC 14959]

The Prophetess, John Fletcher and Philip Massinger, 1622, King's Men, Blackfriars/Globe, F1 (1647) [Wing B1581]

The Revenger's Tragedy, Thomas Middleton, 1606, King's Men, Globe, Q1 (1607) [STC 24149]

Richard II, William Shakespeare, 1595, Chamberlain's Men, Theatre? Q1 (1597) [Huntington]; Q3 (1598) [STC 22309]; F1 (1623) [Norton]

1 Richard II, or Thomas of Woodstock, Anon., 1592–93? Unknown, Unknown, MS [MSR, ed. Wilhelmina P. Frijlinck, 1929]

Richard III, William Shakespeare, 1592–93, Pembroke's Men? Theatre? Q1 (1597) [Huntington]; F1 (1623) [Norton]

The Roaring Girl, Thomas Middleton and Thomas Dekker, 1611, Prince Henry's Men, Fortune, Q1 (1611) [STC 17908]

The Roman Actor, Philip Massinger, 1626, King's Men, Blackfriars, Q1 (1629) [STC 17642]

Romeo and Juliet, William Shakespeare, 1593–95, Chamberlain's Men, Theatre? Q1 (1597) [Huntington]; Q2 (1599) [Huntington]; F1 (1623) [Norton]

The Second Maiden's Tragedy, Thomas Middleton, 1611, King's Men, Blackfriars, MS [MSR, ed. W. W. Greg, 1909]

1 Selimus, Robert Greene, 1591–92, Queen's Men, Unknown, Q1 (1594) [STC 12310a; MSR, ed. W. Bang, 1908 (1909)]

2 The Seven Deadly Sins, Anon., MS plot (belonged to Strange's Men in the early 1590s? or to Chamberlain's Men *c*.1597–98?) [Dramatic Documents]

A Shoemaker a Gentleman, William Rowley, 1607–09, Queen Anne's Men, Red Bull, Q1 (1638) [STC 21422]

The Shoemaker's Holiday, Thomas Dekker, 1599, Admiral's Men, Rose, Q1 (1600) [STC 6523]

The Silver Age, Thomas Heywood, 1610–12, Queen Anne's Men, Red Bull, Q1 (1613) [STC 13365]

Sir Clyomon and Sir Clamydes, Anon., [published 1599], Queen's Men, Unknown, Q1 (1599) [STC 5450a]

Sir Giles Goosecap, George Chapman, *c*.1602, Chapel Children, Blackfriars, Q1 (1606) [STC 12050]

Sir John van Olden Barnavelt, John Fletcher and Philip Massinger, 1619, King's Men, Globe, MS [MSR, ed. T. H. Howard-Hill, 1979 (1980)]

Sir Thomas More, Anthony Munday (and Henry Chettle?), *c*.1593? or *c*.1600?; revised by Henry Chettle, Thomas Dekker, Thomas Heywood and William Shakespeare 1603–04, Unknown, Unacted? MS [MSR, ed. W. W. Greg, 1911]

The Spanish Tragedy, Thomas Kyd, 1585–87, Strange's Men, Unknown, Q1 (1592) [STC 15086; MSR, ed. W. W. Greg and D. Nichol Smith, 1948 (1949)]; Q4 (1602) [STC 15089; MSR, ed. W. W. Greg and Frederick S. Boas, 1925]; Q7 (1615) [STC 15091]

The Sparagus Garden, Richard Brome, 1635, King's Revels Men, Salisbury Court, Q1 (1640) [STC 3820]

1 St Patrick for Ireland, James Shirley, 1639–40, 1 Ogilby's Men, Dublin, Q1 (1640) [STC 22455]

The Staple of News, Ben Jonson, 1626, King's Men, Blackfriars, Folio printed in 1631 (included in F2 (1640)) [STC 14754]

2 Tamburlaine the Great, Christopher Marlowe, 1587–88, Admiral's Men? Unknown, O1 (1590) [STC 17425]

The Taming of a Shrew, Anon., 1592–93, Pembroke's Men? Theatre? Q1 (1594) [STC 23667]

The Taming of the Shrew, William Shakespeare, 1592–93, Pembroke's Men? Theatre? F1 (1623) [Norton]

The Tempest, William Shakespeare, 1611, King's Men, Blackfriars, F1 (1623) [Norton]

Thrace and Macedon, Scenario of a play set in, Sir Edward Dering? 1628, MS author plot (Folger Shakespeare Library MS X.d.206) [Joseph Quincy Adams, 'The Author-plot of an Early Seventeenth Century Play', *The Library*, 4th ser., 26 (1945–46), 17–27]

The Thracian Wonder, Anon., 1590–c.1600? Unknown, Unknown, Q1 (1661) [Wing T1078a]

'Tis Pity She's a Whore, John Ford, 1629–33, Queen Henrietta's Men, Cockpit, Q1 (1633) [STC 11165]

Titus Andronicus, William Shakespeare, 1592–94, Strange's Men/Pembroke's Men, Unknown, Q1 (1594) [Huntington]

The Traitor, James Shirley, 1631, Queen Henrietta's Men, Cockpit, Q1 (1635) [STC 22458]

Troilus and Cressida, Henry Chettle and Thomas Dekker, 1599, Admiral's Men, Rose, MS plot [Dramatic Documents]

Troilus and Cressida, William Shakespeare, 1601–02, Chamberlain's Men, Globe, Q1 (1609) [Huntington]; F1 (1623) [Norton]

1 & 2 The Troublesome Reign of John, King of England, Anon., c.1587–91, Queen's Men, Unknown, Q1 (1591) [STC 14644]

Twelfth Night, William Shakespeare, 1600–01, Chamberlain's Men, Globe, F1 (1623) [Norton]

Two Lamentable Tragedies, Robert Yarington, 1594–c.1598, Admiral's Men? Unknown, Q1 (1601) [STC 26076]

The Two Merry Milkmaids, 'I. C.' (John Cumber?), 1619–20, Revels Company, Red Bull, Q1 (1620) [STC 4281, Folger Shakespeare Library Copy 2]

The Two Noble Kinsmen, John Fletcher and William Shakespeare, 1613, King's Men, Blackfriars, Q1 (1634) [Huntington]

The Two Noble Ladies, Anon., 1619–23, Revels Company, Red Bull, MS [MSR, ed. Rebecca G. Rhoads, 1930]

Valentinian, John Fletcher, 1610–12, King's Men, Blackfriars/Globe, F1 (1647) [Wing B1581]

The Valiant Welshman, 'R. A.' (Robert Armin? Robert Anton?), 1610–15, Prince's Men, Unknown, Q1 (1615) [STC 16]

The Virgin Martyr, Thomas Dekker and Philip Massinger, 1620, Revels Company, Red Bull, Q1 (1622) [STC 17644]; *The Dramatic Works of Thomas Dekker*, ed. Fredson Bowers, 4 vols. (Cambridge University Press, 1953–61), III, 365–480

Volpone, Ben Jonson, 1606, King's Men, Globe, F1 (1616) [STC 14751]

The Walks of Islington and Hogsdon, Thomas Jordan, 1641, Red Bull Company, Red Bull, Q1 (1657) [Wing J1071]

A Warning for Fair Women, Anon., 1597–98, Chamberlain's Men, Theatre? Curtain? Q1 (1599) [STC 25089]

Westward Ho, Thomas Dekker and John Webster, 1604, Paul's Children, Paul's, Q1 (1607) [STC 6540]

What You Will, John Marston, 1601, Paul's Children, Paul's, Q1 (1607) [STC 17487]

When You See Me, You Know Me, Samuel Rowley, 1604, Prince Henry's Men, Fortune, Q1 (1605) [STC 21417]

The White Devil, John Webster, 1612, Queen Anne's Men, Red Bull, Q1 (1612) [STC 25178]

The Widow's Tears, George Chapman, 1604–05, Queen's Revels Children, Blackfriars, Q1 (1612) [STC 4994]

Wily Beguiled, Anon., 1596–1606, Paul's Children? Unknown, Q1 (1606) [STC 25818]

The Winter's Tale, William Shakespeare, 1610–11, King's Men, Globe, F1 (1623) [Norton]

The Wit of a Woman, 1604, Anon., Unknown, Unacted? Q1 (1604) [STC 25868]

Wit without Money, John Fletcher, c.1614, Lady Elizabeth's Men? Unknown, Q1 (1639) [STC 1691]

The Witch, Thomas Middleton, 1616, King's Men, Blackfriars, MS [MSR, ed. W. W. Greg and F. P. Wilson, 1948 (1950)]

The Wits, William Davenant, 1634, King's Men, Blackfriars, Q1 (1636) [STC 6309]

The Woman Hater, Francis Beaumont, 1606, Paul's Children, Paul's, Q1 (1607) [STC 1692]

A Woman Killed with Kindness, Thomas Heywood, 1603, Worcester's Men, Rose, Q1 (1607) [STC 13371]

The Woman's Prize, John Fletcher, 1610–11, King's Men? Globe?/Blackfriars? MS [MSR, ed. Meg Powers Livingston, 2007 (2008)]; F1 (1647) [Wing B1581]

Women Pleased, John Fletcher, c.1618, King's Men, Unknown, F1 (1647) [Wing B1581]

The Wonder of Women, or Sophonisba, John Marston, 1605–06, Queen's Revels Children, Blackfriars, Q1 (1606) [STC 17488]

The Wounds of Civil War, Thomas Lodge, 1586–89, Admiral's Men, Unknown, Q1 (1594) [STC 16678]

A Yorkshire Tragedy, Thomas Middleton, 1606, King's Men, Globe, Q1 (1608) [STC 22340, Folger Shakespeare Library Copy]

Other works cited

Adams, Joseph Quincy, 'The Author-plot of an Early Seventeenth Century Play', *The Library*, 4th ser., 26 (1945–1946), 17–27
Agas, Ralph, *Civitas Londinum: Facsimile from the Original in the Possession of the Corporation of the City of London* (London: Adams and Francis, 1874)
Alfield, Thomas, *A True Report of the Death and Martyrdom of M. Campion Jesuit and Priest, and M. Sherwin and M. Brian Priests, at Tyburn the First of December 1581* O1 (1582) [STC 4537]
Astington, John H., 'Gallows Scenes on the Elizabethan Stage', *Theatre Notebook*, 37 (1983), 3–9
  'Malvolio and the Dark House', in *Shakespeare Survey 41* (Cambridge University Press, 1988), pp. 55–62
  '*The Wits* Illustration, 1662', *Theatre Notebook*, 47 (1993), 122–40
Bacon, Francis, *The Essays or Counsels, Civil and Moral* (1625) [STC 1148]
Bawcutt, N. W. (ed.), *The Control and Censorship of Caroline Drama: The Records of Sir Henry Herbert, Master of the Revels 1623–73* (Oxford: Clarendon Press, 1996)
  (ed.), *Measure for Measure* (Oxford University Press, 1991)
Beaumont, Francis, and John Fletcher, *Comedies and Tragedies Written by Francis Beaumont and John Fletcher, Gentlemen*, F1 (1647) [Wing B1581]
  Fifty Comedies and Tragedies Written by Francis Beaumont and John Fletcher, Gentlemen, F2 (1679) [Wing B1582]
Beaurline, L. A. (ed.), *Love's Pilgrimage*, in Fredson Bowers (gen. ed.), *The Dramatic Works in the Beaumont and Fletcher Canon*, 10 vols. (Cambridge University Press, 1966–96), II (1970), pp. 567–695
Beckerman, Bernard, *Shakespeare at the Globe: 1599–1609* (New York: Macmillan, 1962)
  'The Use and Management of the Elizabethan Stage', in C. Walter Hodges, S. Schoenbaum and Leonard Leone (eds.), *The Third Globe: Symposium for the Reconstruction of the Globe Playhouse, Wayne State University, 1979* (Wayne State University Press, 1981), pp. 151–63
Benson, Larry D. (gen. ed.), *The Riverside Chaucer* (Oxford University Press, 1987)
Berry, Herbert, *The Boar's Head Playhouse* (Washington: Folger Shakespeare Library, 1986)

'The First Public Playhouses, Especially the Red Lion', *Shakespeare Quarterly*, 40 (1989), 133–45
'Where was the Playhouse in which the Boy Choristers of St. Paul's Cathedral Performed Plays?', *Medieval and Renaissance Drama in England*, 13 (2001), 101–16
(ed.), 'Playhouses, 1560–1660', in Glynne Wickham, Herbert Berry and William Ingram (eds.), *English Professional Theatre, 1530–1660* (Cambridge University Press, 2000), pp. 285–674
Bevington, David, *This Wide and Universal Theatre: Shakespeare in Performance Then and Now* (University of Chicago Press, 2007)
(ed.), *The Complete Works of Shakespeare*, 5th edn (New York: Pearson Education, 2004)
(ed.), *Henry IV, Part 1* (Oxford University Press, 1987)
(ed.), *The Spanish Tragedy* (Manchester University Press, 1996)
(ed.), *Troilus and Cressida* (Walton-on-Thames: Thomas Nelson and Sons, 1998)
Bowers, Fredson (ed.), *The Complete Works of Christopher Marlowe*, 2nd edn, 2 vols. (Cambridge University Press, 1981)
(ed.), *The Dramatic Works of Thomas Dekker*, 4 vols. (Cambridge University Press, 1953–61)
(ed.), *The Maid in the Mill*, in Fredson Bowers (gen. ed.), *The Dramatic Works in the Beaumont and Fletcher Canon*, 10 vols. (Cambridge University Press, 1966–96), IX (1994), pp. 569–669
Bowers, Roger, 'The Playhouse of the Choristers of Paul's, c.1575–1608', *Theatre Notebook*, 54 (2000), 70–85
Bowsher, Julian M. C., 'The Rose and Its Stages', in *Shakespeare Survey 60* (Cambridge University Press, 2007), pp. 36–48
'Twenty Years On: The Archaeology of Shakespeare's London Playhouses', *Shakespeare*, 7 (2011), 452–66
Bowsher, Julian M. C., and Patricia Miller, *The Rose and the Globe – Playhouses of Tudor Bankside, Southwark: Excavations 1988–91* (Museum of London, 2009)
Bradley, David, *From Text to Performance in the Elizabethan Theatre: Preparing the Play for the Stage* (Cambridge University Press, 1992)
Braunmuller, A. R. (ed.), *Macbeth* (Cambridge University Press, 1997)
Brissenden, Alan (ed.), *As You Like It* (Oxford University Press, 1994)
Brooke, Nicholas (ed.), *Macbeth* (Oxford University Press, 1990)
Brown, John Russell (ed.), *The Duchess of Malfi* (London: Methuen, 1964)
Bullough, Geoffrey (ed.), *Narrative and Dramatic Sources of Shakespeare*, 8 vols. (London: Routledge and Kegan Paul, 1957–75)
Burns, Edward (ed.), *King Henry VI, Part 1* (London: Thomson Learning, 2000)
Butler, Martin (ed.), *Cymbeline* (Cambridge University Press, 2005)
Calore, Michela, 'Elizabethan Plots: A Shared Code of Theatrical and Fictional Language', *Theatre Survey*, 44 (2003), 249–61
'*Enter out:* Perplexing Signals in Some Elizabethan Stage Directions', *Medieval and Renaissance Drama in England*, 13 (2001), 117–35

Carnegie, David, '"*Maluolio within*": Performance Perspectives on the Dark House', *Shakespeare Quarterly*, 52 (2001), 393–414
  'Mutinous Soldiers and Shouts [Within]: Stage Directions and Early Modern Dramaturgy', in Brian Boyd (ed.), *Words That Count: Essays on Early Modern Authorship in Honor of MacDonald P. Jackson* (University of Delaware Press, 2004), pp. 222–38
  Review of *The Thracian Wonder by William Rowley and Thomas Heywood: A Critical Edition*, edited by Michael Nolan, *Modern Language Review*, 94 (1999), 160–1
Chambers, E. K., *The Elizabethan Stage*, 4 vols. (Oxford: Clarendon Press, 1923)
Colie, Rosalie L., *Shakespeare's Living Art* (Princeton University Press, 1974)
Comito, Terry, 'Caliban's Dream: The Topography of Some Shakespeare Gardens', *Shakespeare Studies*, 14 (1981), 23–54
  The Idea of the Garden in the Renaissance (Rutgers University Press, 1978)
Corbin, Peter, and Douglas Sedge (eds.), *Thomas of Woodstock* (Manchester University Press, 2002)
Cox, John D., and Eric Rasmussen (eds.), *King Henry VI, Part 3* (London: Thomson Learning, 2001)
Craig, Hugh, 'The 1602 Additions to *The Spanish Tragedy*', in Hugh Craig and Arthur F. Kinney (eds.), *Shakespeare, Computers, and the Mystery of Authorship* (Cambridge University Press, 2009), pp. 162–80
Daalder, Joost (ed.), *The Changeling* (London: A & C Black, 1990)
Daileader, Celia R., and Gary Taylor (eds.), *The Tamer Tamed, or The Woman's Prize* (Manchester University Press, 2006)
Daniell, David (ed.), *Julius Caesar* (Walton-on-Thames: Thomas Nelson and Sons, 1998)
Davies, Sir John, and Christopher Marlowe, *Epigrams and Elegies* O1 (after 1602) [STC 6350]
Dawson, Anthony B., 'Staging Evidence', in Peter Holland and Stephen Orgel (eds.), *From Script to Stage in Early Modern England* (Basingstoke: Palgrave Macmillan, 2004), pp. 89–108
  (ed.), *Troilus and Cressida* (Cambridge University Press, 2003)
Dekker, Thomas, *The Gull's Hornbook* Q1 (1609) [STC 6500]
Delvecchio, Doreen, and Antony Hammond (eds.), *Pericles* (Cambridge University Press, 1998)
Dessen, Alan C., *Elizabethan Drama and the Viewer's Eye* (University of North Carolina Press, 1977)
  Elizabethan Stage Conventions and Modern Interpreters (Cambridge University Press, 1984)
  Recovering Shakespeare's Theatrical Vocabulary (Cambridge University Press, 1995)
Dessen, Alan C., and Leslie Thomson, *A Dictionary of Stage Directions in English Drama, 1580–1642* (Cambridge University Press, 1999)
Dusinberre, Juliet (ed.), *As You Like It* (London: Thomson Learning, 2006)

Dutton, Richard, '*The Famous Victories* and the 1600 Quarto of *Henry V*', in Helen Ostovich, Holger Schott Syme and Andrew Griffin (eds.), *Locating the Queen's Men, 1583–1603: Material Practices and Conditions of Playing* (Farnham: Ashgate, 2009), pp. 135–44
'The Revels Office and the Boy Companies, 1600–1613: New Perspectives', *English Literary Renaissance*, 32 (2002), 324–51
(ed.), *Epicene, or The Silent Woman* (Manchester University Press, 2003)
Edwards, Philip (ed.), *The Spanish Tragedy* (Manchester University Press, 1977)
Edwards, Philip, and Colin Gibson (eds.), *The Plays and Poems of Philip Massinger*, 5 vols. (Oxford University Press, 1976)
Egan, Gabriel, '"Geometrical" Hinges and the *Frons Scenae* of the Globe', *Theatre Notebook*, 52 (1998), 62–4
'The Situation of the "Lords Room": A Revaluation', *Review of English Studies*, 48 (1997), 297–309
'The Theatre in Shoreditch, 1576–1599', in Richard Dutton (ed.), *The Oxford Handbook of Early Modern Theatre* (Oxford University Press, 2009), pp. 168–85
Egan, Michael (ed.), *The Tragedy of Richard II Part One: A Newly Authenticated Play by William Shakespeare*, 4 vols. (Lewiston, NY: Edwin Mellen Press, 2006)
Elam, Keir (ed.), *Twelfth Night* (London: Cengage Learning, 2008)
Erne, Lukas, *Shakespeare as Literary Dramatist* (Cambridge University Press, 2003)
(ed.), *The First Quarto of 'Romeo and Juliet'* (Cambridge University Press, 2007)
Evans, G. Blakemore (gen. ed.), *The Riverside Shakespeare*, 2nd edn (Boston: Houghton Mifflin, 1997)
Fairbrother, Nan, *Men and Gardens* (New York: Alfred A. Knopf, 1956)
Farmer, Alan B., and Zachary Lesser, 'Vile Arts: The Marketing of English Printed Drama, 1512–1660', *Research Opportunities in Renaissance Drama*, 39 (2000), 77–165
Fitzpatrick, Tim, *Playwright, Space and Place in Early Modern Performance: Shakespeare and Company* (Farnham: Ashgate, 2011)
'Playwrights with Foresight: Staging Resources in the Elizabethan Playhouses', *Theatre Notebook*, 56 (2002), 85–116
Fitzpatrick, Tim, and Wendy Millyard, 'Hangings, Doors and Discoveries: Conflicting Evidence or Problematic Assumptions?', *Theatre Notebook*, 54 (2000), 2–23
Fitzpatrick, Tim, with Daniel Johnston, 'Spaces, Doors and Places in Early Modern English Staging', *Theatre Notebook*, 63 (2009), 2–19
Foakes, R. A., 'Henslowe's Rose/Shakespeare's Globe', in Peter Holland and Stephen Orgel (eds.), *From Script to Stage in Early Modern England* (Basingstoke: Palgrave Macmillan, 2004), pp. 11–31
Illustrations of the English Stage: 1580–1642 (Stanford University Press, 1985)
'Playhouses and Players', in A. R. Braunmuller and Michael Hattaway (eds.), *The Cambridge Companion to English Renaissance Drama*, 2nd edn (Cambridge University Press, 2003), pp. 1–52

(ed.), *Henslowe's Diary*, 2nd edn (Cambridge University Press, 2002)
(ed.), *King Lear* (Walton-on-Thames: Thomas Nelson and Sons, 1997)
(ed.), *A Midsummer Night's Dream* (Cambridge University Press, 1984)
(ed.), *Much Ado About Nothing* (Harmondsworth: Penguin Books, 1968)
Folkerth, Wes, *The Sound of Shakespeare* (London: Routledge, 2002)
Forker, Charles R., '*The Troublesome Reign, Richard II*, and the Date of *King John*: A Study in Intertextuality', in *Shakespeare Survey 63* (Cambridge University Press, 2010), pp. 127–48
(ed.), *King Richard II* (London: Thomson Learning, 2002)
Gabrieli, Vittorio, and Giorgio Melchiori (eds.), *Sir Thomas More* (Manchester University Press, 1990)
Gair, Reavley, *The Children of Paul's: The Story of a Theatre Company, 1553–1608* (Cambridge University Press, 1982)
(ed.), *Antonio's Revenge* (Manchester University Press, 1978)
The Geneva Bible: A Facsimile of the 1560 Edition, with an introduction by Lloyd E. Berry (University of Wisconsin Press, 1969)
Gibbons, Brian (ed.), *Measure for Measure* (Cambridge University Press, 1991)
Gossett, Suzanne (ed.), *Bartholomew Fair* (Manchester University Press, 2000)
(ed.), *Pericles* (London: Thomson Learning, 2004)
Graves, R. B., '*The Duchess of Malfi* at the Globe and Blackfriars', *Renaissance Drama*, n.s. 9 (1978), 193–209
Greg, W. W., *Dramatic Documents from the Elizabethan Playhouses*, 2 vols. (1931; repr. Oxford: Clarendon Press, 1969)
(ed.), *Bonduca*, Malone Society Reprints (Oxford University Press, 1951)
Gunby, David, David Carnegie and MacDonald P. Jackson (eds.), *The Works of John Webster: An Old Spelling Critical Edition*, 4 vols. (Cambridge University Press, 1995–)
Gurr, Andrew, 'The Date and the Expected Venue of *Romeo and Juliet*', in *Shakespeare Survey 49* (Cambridge University Press, 1996), pp. 15–25
'Doors at the Globe: The Gulf between Page and Stage', *Theatre Notebook*, 55 (2001), 59–71
'Maximal and Minimal Texts: Shakespeare v. the Globe', in *Shakespeare Survey 52* (Cambridge University Press, 1999), pp. 68–87
'A New Theatre Historicism', in Peter Holland and Stephen Orgel (eds.), *From Script to Stage in Early Modern England* (Basingstoke: Palgrave Macmillan, 2004), pp. 71–88
Playgoing in Shakespeare's London, 3rd edn (Cambridge University Press, 2004)
The Shakespeare Company, 1594–1642 (Cambridge University Press, 2004)
The Shakespearean Stage: 1574–1642, 4th edn (Cambridge University Press, 2009)
Shakespeare's Opposites: The Admiral's Company 1594–1625 (Cambridge University Press, 2009)
The Shakespearian Playing Companies (Oxford: Clarendon Press, 1996)
'Stage Doors at the Globe', *Theatre Notebook*, 53 (1999), 8–18
'The Work of Elizabethan Plotters and *2 The Seven Deadly Sins*', *Early Theatre*, 10 (2007), 67–87

(ed.), *The First Quarto of King Henry V* (Cambridge University Press, 2000)

Gurr, Andrew, and Gabriel Egan, 'Prompting, Backstage Activity, and the Openings onto the Shakespearean Stage', *Theatre Notebook*, 56 (2002), 138–42

Habicht, Werner, 'Tree Properties and Tree Scenes in Elizabethan Theater', *Renaissance Drama*, n.s. 4 (1971), 69–92

Halio, Jay L., 'Handy-Dandy: Q1/Q2 *Romeo and Juliet*', in Jay L. Halio (ed.), *Shakespeare's 'Romeo and Juliet': Texts, Contexts, and Interpretation* (University of Delaware Press, 1995), pp. 123–50

(ed.), *King Henry VIII* (Oxford University Press, 1999)

(ed.), *The Merchant of Venice* (Oxford University Press, 1993)

Hammond, Antony, 'Encounters of the Third Kind in Stage-Directions in Elizabethan and Jacobean Drama', *Studies in Philology*, 89 (1992), 71–99

Harbage, Alfred, *Annals of English Drama, 975–1700*, revised by S. Schoenbaum, and Sylvia Stoler Wagonheim, 3rd edn (London: Routledge, 1989)

Harris, John, and A. A. Tait, *Catalogue of the Drawings by Inigo Jones, John Webb and Isaac de Caus at Worcester College Oxford* (Oxford: Clarendon Press, 1979)

Harris, John, and Gordon Higgott, *Inigo Jones: Complete Architectural Drawings* (New York: The Drawing Center, 1989)

Hattaway, Michael, *Elizabethan Popular Theatre: Plays in Performance* (London: Routledge and Kegan Paul, 1982)

(ed.), *As You Like It* (Cambridge University Press, 2000)

(ed.), *The Knight of the Burning Pestle* (London: Ernest Benn, 1969)

(ed.), *The Third Part of King Henry VI* (Cambridge University Press, 1993)

Herford, C. H., and Percy Simpson (eds.), *Ben Jonson*, 11 vols. (Oxford: Clarendon Press, 1925–52)

Higgott, Gordon, 'Reassessing the Drawings for the Inigo Jones Theatre: A Restoration Project by John Webb?', paper based on a lecture given at a conference at Shakespeare's Globe, 13 February 2005

Hildy, Franklin J., 'Keeping up with the Jones', *Around the Globe*, 30 (Summer 2005), 26–7

'Reconstructing Shakespeare's Theatre', in Franklin J. Hildy (ed.), *New Issues in the Reconstruction of Shakespeare's Theatre* (New York: Peter Lang, 1990), pp. 1–37

Hill, Thomas, *The Gardener's Labyrinth* (1577) [STC 13485]

Hill, Tracey, *Anthony Munday and Civic Culture: Theatre, History and Power in Early Modern London* (Manchester University Press, 2004)

Hillebrand, Harold N. (ed.), *Troilus and Cressida: A New Variorum Edition of Shakespeare*, supplemented by T. W. Baldwin (Philadelphia: J. B. Lippincott, 1953)

Hirrel, Michael J., 'Duration of Performances and Lengths of Plays: How Shall We Beguile the Lazy Time?', *Shakespeare Quarterly*, 61 (2010), 159–82

Holland, Peter (ed.), *A Midsummer Night's Dream* (Oxford University Press, 1994)

Honigmann, E. A. J., 'Re-enter the Stage Direction: Shakespeare and Some Contemporaries', in *Shakespeare Survey 29* (Cambridge University Press, 1976), pp. 117–25

Horace, *The Odes and Epodes*, with an English translation by C. E. Bennett (London: William Heinemann, 1914)

Horsman, E. A. (ed.), *Bartholomew Fair* (Harvard University Press, 1960)

Hosley, Richard, 'The Gallery over the Stage in the Public Playhouse of Shakespeare's Time', *Shakespeare Quarterly*, 8 (1957), 15–31

  'The Playhouses', in Clifford Leech and T. W. Craik (gen. eds.), *The Revels History of Drama in English*, 8 vols. (London: Methuen, 1975–83), III (1975), pp. 197–235

  'The Staging of Desdemona's Bed', *Shakespeare Quarterly*, 14 (1963), 57–65

  'Was There a Music-Room in Shakespeare's Globe?', *Shakespeare Quarterly*, 13 (1960), 113–23

  (ed.), *A Critical Edition of Anthony Munday's Fedele and Fortunio* (New York: Garland, 1981)

Howard, Jean E., *Shakespeare's Art of Orchestration: Stage Technique and Audience Response* (University of Illinois Press, 1984)

Howard-Hill, T. H. (ed.), *Sir John van Olden Barnavelt*, Malone Society Reprints (Oxford University Press, 1980)

Hoy, Cirus (ed.), *The Double Marriage*, in Fredson Bowers (gen. ed.), *The Dramatic Works in the Beaumont and Fletcher Canon*, 10 vols. (Cambridge University Press, 1966–96), IX (1994), pp. 95–220

Humphreys, Arthur (ed.), *Julius Caesar* (Oxford University Press, 1984)

Hunter, G. K., 'Were There Act-Pauses on Shakespeare's Stage?', in Standish Henning, Robert Kimbrough and Richard Knowles (eds.), *English Renaissance Drama: Essays in Honor of Madeleine Doran and Mark Eccles* (Southern Illinois University Press, 1976), pp. 15–35

  (ed.), *Malcontent* (London: Methuen, 1975)

Ichikawa, Mariko, *Shakespearean Entrances* (Basingstoke: Palgrave Macmillan, 2002)

Ioppolo, Grace, *Dramatists and Their Manuscripts in the Age of Shakespeare, Jonson, Middleton and Heywood: Authorship, Authority and the Playhouse* (London: Routledge, 2006)

  '"The foule sheet and ye fayr": Henslowe, Daborne, Heywood and the Nature of Foul-Paper and Fair-Copy Dramatic Manuscripts', *English Manuscript Studies 1100–1700*, 11 (2002), 132–53

Jackson, MacDonald P., 'The Date and Authorship of *Thomas of Woodstock*: Evidence and Its Interpretation', *Research Opportunities in Renaissance Drama*, 46 (2007), 67–100

  'Deciphering a Date and Determining a Date: Anthony Munday's *John a Kent and John a Cumber* and the Original Version of *Sir Thomas More*', *Early Modern Literary Studies*, 15.3 (2011), 2.1–24

  'Parallels and Poetry: Shakespeare, Kyd, and *Arden of Faversham*', *Medieval and Renaissance Drama in England*, 23 (2010), 17–33

  'Shakespeare and the Quarrel Scene in *Arden of Faversham*', *Shakespeare Quarterly*, 57 (2006), 249–93

  'Shakespeare's *Richard II* and the Anonymous *Thomas of Woodstock*', *Medieval and Renaissance Drama in England*, 14 (2002), 17–65

Jewkes, Wilfred T., *Act Division in Elizabethan and Jacobean Plays: 1583–1616* (1958; repr. New York: AMS Press, 1972)
Jonson, Ben, *The Works of Benjamin Jonson*, F1 (1616) [STC 14751]
Jonsonus Virbius Q1 (1638) [STC 14784]
Jowett, John, 'Henry Chettle and the First Quarto of *Romeo and Juliet*', *Papers of the Bibliographical Society of America*, 92 (1998), 53–74
  'Henry Chettle and the Original Text of *Sir Thomas More*', in T. H. Howard-Hill (ed.), *Shakespeare and 'Sir Thomas More': Essays on the Play and Its Shakespearian Interest* (Cambridge University Press, 1989), pp. 131–49
  (ed.), *Sir Thomas More* (London: Methuen, 2011)
Kastan, David Scott (ed.), *Doctor Faustus: A Two-Text Edition (A-Text, 1604; B-Text, 1616), Contexts and Sources, Criticism* (New York: W. W. Norton, 2005)
  (ed.), *King Henry IV, Part 1* (London: Thomson Learning, 2002)
Kathman, David, 'London Inns as Playing Venues for the Queen's Men', in Helen Ostovich, Holger Schott Syme and Andrew Griffin (eds.), *Locating the Queen's Men, 1583–1603: Material Practices and Conditions of Playing* (Farnham: Ashgate, 2009), pp. 64–75
  'Reconsidering *The Seven Deadly Sins*', *Early Theatre*, 7 (2004), 13–44
  '*The Seven Deadly Sins* and Theatrical Apprenticeship', *Early Theatre*, 14 (2011), 121–39
Kiefer, Frederick, 'Curtains on the Shakespearean Stage', *Medieval and Renaissance Drama in England*, 20 (2007), 151–86
King, T. J., *Shakespearean Staging, 1599–1642* (Harvard University Press, 1971)
Kinney, Arthur F., 'Authoring *Arden of Faversham*', in Hugh Craig and Arthur F. Kinney (eds.), *Shakespeare, Computers, and the Mystery of Authorship* (Cambridge University Press, 2009), pp. 78–99
Kirkman, Francis, *The Wits, or Sport upon Sport* O1 (1662) [Wing W3218]
Knavery in All Trades: or, The Coffee-House Q1 (1664) [Wing T220]
Knutson, Roslyn, 'The Start of Something Big', in Helen Ostovich, Holger Schott Syme and Andrew Griffin (eds.), *Locating the Queen's Men, 1583–1603: Material Practices and Conditions of Playing* (Farnham: Ashgate, 2009), pp. 99–108
  'Two Playhouses, Both Alike in Dignity', *Shakespeare Studies*, 20 (2002), 111–17
Lancashire, Anne (ed.), *The Second Maiden's Tragedy* (Manchester University Press, 1978)
Lawrence, W. J., *Pre-Restoration Stage Studies* (Harvard University Press, 1927)
Levenson, Jill L. (ed.), *Romeo and Juliet* (Oxford University Press, 2000)
Lever, J. W. (ed.), *Measure for Measure* (London: Methuen, 1965)
Lindley, David, *Shakespeare and Music* (London: Thomson Learning, 2006)
Livingston, Meg Powers (ed.), *The Woman's Prize*, Malone Society Reprints (Manchester University Press, 2008)
Long, John H., *Shakespeare's Use of Music: The Final Comedies* (University of Florida Press, 1961)

Long, William B., '"Precious Few": English Manuscript Playbooks', in David Scott Kastan (ed.), *A Companion to Shakespeare* (Oxford: Blackwell, 1999), pp. 414–33

MacIntyre, Jean, 'Additional to "Production Resources at the Whitefriars Playhouse, 1609–1612"', *Early Modern Literary Studies*, 3.3 (1998), 8.1–3

'Production Resources at the Whitefriars Playhouse, 1609–1612', *Early Modern Literary Studies*, 2.3 (1996), 2.1–35

Mackintosh, Iain, 'Inigo Jones – Theatre Architect', *TABS*, 31 (1973), 99–105

Mahood, M. M., *Playing Bit Parts in Shakespeare* (London: Routledge, 1998)

Marcus, Leah S. (ed.), *The Duchess of Malfi* (London: A & C Black, 2009)

Mares, F. H., ed., *The Alchemist* (Harvard University Press, 1967)

(ed.), *Much Ado About Nothing* (Cambridge University Press, 1988)

Marshall, Cynthia (ed.), *Shakespeare in Production: As You Like It* (Cambridge University Press, 2004)

Martin, Randall (ed.), *Henry VI, Part Three* (Oxford University Press, 2001)

Massai, Sonia, 'Shakespeare, Text and Paratext', in *Shakespeare Survey 62* (Cambridge University Press, 2009), pp. 1–11

McEachern, Claire (ed.), *Much Ado About Nothing* (London: Thomson Learning, 2006)

McMillin, Scott, 'Building Stories: Greg, Fleay, and the Plot of *2 The Seven Deadly Sins*', *Medieval and Renaissance Drama in England*, 4 (1989), 53–62

The Elizabethan Theatre and 'The Book of Sir Thomas More' (Cornell University Press, 1987)

McMillin, Scott, and Sally-Beth MacLean, *The Queen's Men and Their Plays* (Cambridge University Press, 1998)

McMullan, Gordon (ed.), *King Henry VIII* (London: Thomson Learning, 2000)

Melchiori, Giorgio (ed.), *King Edward III* (Cambridge University Press, 1998)

Mulryne, J. R. (ed.), *The Spanish Tragedy* (London: A & C Black, 1989)

Munro, Lucy (ed.), *The Tamer Tamed* (London: A & C Black, 2010)

Nashe, Thomas, *Pierce Pennilesss His Supplication to the Devil* Q1 (1592) [STC 18371]

Nicol, David, 'The Date of *The Thracian Wonder*', *Notes and Queries*, 253 (2008), 223–5

Nolan, Michael (ed.), *The Thracian Wonder by William Rowley and Thomas Heywood: A Critical Edition* (Salzburg: Institut für Anglistik und Amerikanistik, Universität Salzburg, 1997)

Oliver, H. J. (ed.), *'Dido Queen of Carthage' and 'The Massacre at Paris'* (London: Methuen, 1968)

Orgel, Stephen, *The Authentic Shakespeare, and Other Problems of the Early Modern Stage* (New York: Routledge, 2002)

'Macbeth and the Antic Round', in *Shakespeare Survey 52* (Cambridge University Press, 1999), pp. 143–53

(ed.), *The Tempest* (Oxford University Press, 1987)

(ed.), *The Winter's Tale* (Oxford University Press, 1996)

Orrell, John, 'Beyond the Rose: Design Problems for the Globe Reconstruction', in Franklin J. Hildy (ed.), *New Issues in the Reconstruction of Shakespeare's Theatre* (New York: Peter Lang, 1990), pp. 95–134

    The Human Stage: English Theatre Design, 1567–1640 (Cambridge University Press, 1988)
    'The Theaters', in John D. Cox and David Scott Kastan (eds.), *A New History of Early English Drama* (Columbia University Press, 1997), pp. 93–112
    The Theatres of Inigo Jones and John Webb (Cambridge University Press, 1985)
The Oxford English Dictionary, prepared by J. A. Simpson and E. S. C. Weiner, 2nd edn, 20 vols. (Oxford University Press, 1989)
Palmer, Barbara D., 'On the Road and on the Wagon', in Helen Ostovich, Holger Schott Syme and Andrew Griffin (eds.), *Locating the Queen's Men, 1583–1603: Material Practices and Conditions of Playing* (Farnham: Ashgate, 2009), pp. 27–39
Partridge, Edward B. (ed.), *Bartholomew Fair* (University of Nebraska Press, 1964)
Pasqualigo, Luigi, *Il Fedele* O1 (Venice, 1576) [Folger Shakespeare Library Copy]
Peacham, Henry, *Thalia's Banquet* O1 (1620) [STC 19515]
Pitcher, John (ed.), *The Winter's Tale* (London: A & C Black, 2010)
Potter, Lois (ed.), *The Two Noble Kinsmen* (Walton-on-Thames: Thomas Nelson and Sons, 1997)
Purkis, James, 'Foul Papers, Promptbooks, and Thomas Heywood's *Captives*', *Medieval and Renaissance Drama in England*, 21 (2008), 128–56
Rabkin, Norman, *Shakespeare and the Common Understanding* (New York: Free Press, 1967)
Reynolds, G. F., '"Trees" on the Stage of Shakespeare', *Modern Philology*, 5 (1907), 153–68
Richmond, Hugh Macrae, *Shakespeare's Theatre: A Dictionary of His Stage Context* (London: Continuum, 2002)
Rose, Mark, *Shakespearean Design* (Harvard University Press, 1972)
Rowland, Richard, '"Speaking some words, but of no importance"?: Stage Directions, Thomas Heywood, and *Edward IV*', *Medieval and Renaissance Drama in England*, 18 (2005), 104–22
    Thomas Heywood's Theatre, 1599–1639: Locations, Translations, and Conflict (Farnham: Ashgate, 2010)
Schanzer, Ernest (ed.), *The Winter's Tale* (Harmondsworth: Penguin, 1969)
Schlueter, June, and James P. Lusardi, 'Offstage Noise and Onstage Action: Entrances in the Ophelia Sequence of *Hamlet*', in Hardin L. Aasand (ed.), *Stage Directions in 'Hamlet': New Essays and New Directions* (Fairleigh Dickinson University Press, 2003), pp. 33–41
Shakespeare, William, *Mr. William Shakespeare's Comedies, Histories, and Tragedies*, F1 (1623) [*The Norton Facsimile: The First Folio of Shakespeare*, prepared by Charlton Hinman, 2nd edn (New York: W. W. Norton, 1996)]
Shapiro, Michael, *Gender in Play on the Shakespearean Stage: Boy Heroines and Female Pages* (University of Michigan Press, 1994)
Shirley, Frances Ann, *Shakespeare's Use of Off-stage Sounds* (University of Nebraska Press, 1963)
Sidney, Sir Philip, *An Apology for Poetry* (1595) [STC 22534]

Smith, Bruce R., *The Acoustic World of Early Modern England: Attending to the O-Factor* (University of Chicago Press, 1999)
Smith, Emma (ed.), *The Spanish Tragedy* (London: Penguin Books, 1998)
Smith, Irwin, *Shakespeare's Blackfriars Playhouse: Its History and Its Design* (London: Peter Owen, 1964)
Snyder, Susan, and Deborah T. Curren-Aquino (eds.), *The Winter's Tale* (Cambridge University Press, 2007)
Spevack, Marvin (ed.), *Julius Caesar* (Cambridge University Press, 1988)
Steele, Kelly Christine, 'Terra Incognita: A Theoretical Reconstruction of the Whitefriars Stage', unpublished PhD thesis, University of Birmingham (2009)
Stern, Tiffany, 'Behind the Arras: The Prompter's Place in the Shakespearean Theatre', *Theatre Notebook*, 55 (2001), 110–18
  Documents of Performance in Early Modern England (Cambridge University Press, 2009)
  'Epilogues, Prayers after Plays, and Shakespeare's *2 Henry IV*', *Theatre Notebook*, 64 (2010), 122–9
  Making Shakespeare: From Stage to Page (London: Routledge, 2004)
  'Re-patching the Play', in Peter Holland and Stephen Orgel (eds.), *From Script to Stage in Early Modern England* (Basingstoke: Palgrave Macmillan, 2004), pp. 151–77
  '"A small-beer health to his second day": Playwrights, Prologues, and First Performances in the Early Modern Theater', *Studies in Philology*, 101 (2004), 172–99
Stevenson, Warren, *Shakespeare's Additions to Thomas Kyd's 'The Spanish Tragedy': A Fresh Look at the Evidence Regarding the 1602 Additions* (Lewiston, NY: Edwin Mellen Press, 2008)
Stewart, Stanley, *The Enclosed Garden: The Tradition and the Image in Seventeenth-Century Poetry* (University of Wisconsin Press, 1966)
Swander, Homer, 'No Exit for a Dead Body: What to do with a Scripted Corpse?', *Journal of Dramatic Theory and Criticism*, 5 (1991), 139–52
Taylor, Gary, 'The Date and Auspices of the Addition to *Sir Thomas More*', in T. H. Howard-Hill (ed.), *Shakespeare and 'Sir Thomas More': Essays on the Play and Its Shakespearian Interest* (Cambridge University Press, 1989), pp. 101–29
  'The Structure of Performance: Act-Intervals in the London Theatres, 1576–1642', in Gary Taylor and John Jowett, *Shakespeare Reshaped: 1616–1623* (Oxford: Clarendon Press, 1993), pp. 3–50
Taylor, Gary, and John Lavagnino (gen. eds.), *Thomas Middleton and Early Modern Textual Culture: A Companion to the Collected Works* (Oxford: Clarendon Press, 2007)
Thompson, Ann (ed.), *The Taming of the Shrew*, updated edn (Cambridge University Press, 2003)
Thompson, Ann, and Neil Taylor (eds.), *Hamlet* (London: Thomson Learning, 2006)
Thomson, Leslie, 'Marlowe's Staging of Meaning', *Medieval and Renaissance Drama in England*, 18 (2005), 19–36

'"*Pass over the stage*" – Again', in Lena Cowen Orlin and Miranda Johnson-Haddad (eds.), *Staging Shakespeare: Essays in Honor of Alan C. Dessen* (University of Delaware Press, 2007), pp. 23–44

'Playgoers on the Outdoor Stages of Early Modern London', *Theatre Notebook*, 64 (2010), 3–11

'A Quarto "Marked for Performance": Evidence of What?', *Medieval and Renaissance Drama in England*, 8 (1995), 176–210

'Staging on the Road, 1586–1594: A New Look at Some Old Assumptions', *Shakespeare Quarterly*, 61 (2010), 526–50

'Window Scenes in Renaissance Plays', *Medieval and Renaissance Drama in England*, 5 (1990), 225–43

'"With patient ears attend": *Romeo and Juliet* on the Elizabethan Stage', *Studies in Philology*, 92 (1995), 230–47

Thomson, Peter, *Shakespeare's Theatre*, 2nd edn (London: Routledge, 1992)

Tilley, Morris Palmer, *A Dictionary of the Proverbs in England in the Sixteenth and Seventeenth Centuries* (University of Michigan Press, 1950)

Turner, Robert Kean (ed.), *The Little French Lawyer*, in Fredson Bowers (gen. ed.), *The Dramatic Works in the Beaumont and Fletcher Canon*, 10 vols. (Cambridge University Press, 1966–96), IX (1994), pp. 323–459

Turner, Jr., John P. (ed.), *A Critical Edition of James Shirley's St. Patrick for Ireland* (New York: Garland, 1979)

Van Fossen, R. W. (ed.), *Eastward Ho* (Manchester University Press, 1979)

Vickers, Brian, 'Shakespeare and Authorship Studies in the Twenty-First Century', *Shakespeare Quarterly*, 62 (2011), 106–42

'Thomas Kyd, Secret Sharer', *Times Literary Supplement*, 18 April 2008, pp. 13–15

'*The Troublesome Raigne*, George Peele, and the Date of *King John*', in Brian Boyd (ed.), *Words That Count: Essays on Early Modern Authorship in Honor of MacDonald P. Jackson* (University of Delaware Press, 2004), pp. 78–116

Virgil, with an English translation by H. Rushton Fairclough, 2 vols. (London: William Heinemann, 1916)

Waith, Eugene M. (ed.), *Titus Andronicus* (Oxford University Press, 1984)

(ed.), *The Two Noble Kinsmen* (Oxford University Press, 1989)

Warren, Roger (ed.), *Cymbeline* (Oxford University Press, 1998)

Warren, Roger, and Stanley Wells (eds.), *Twelfth Night* (Oxford University Press, 1994)

Weil, Herbert, and Judith Weil (eds.), *The First Part of King Henry IV* (Cambridge University Press, 1997)

Weimann, Robert, *Author's Pen and Actor's Voice: Playing and Writing in Shakespeare's Theatre* (Cambridge University Press, 2000)

Wells, Stanley, 'Staging Shakespeare's Ghosts', in Murray Biggs, Philip Edwards, Inga-Stina Ewbank and Eugene M. Waith (eds.), *The Arts of Performance in Elizabethan and Early Stuart Drama* (Edinburgh University Press, 1991), pp. 50–69

Wells, Stanley, and Gary Taylor (gen. eds.), *William Shakespeare: The Complete Works* (Oxford: Clarendon Press, 1986)

Wells, Stanley, and Gary Taylor with John Jowett and William Montgomery, *William Shakespeare: A Textual Companion* (Oxford: Clarendon Press, 1987)

Werstine, Paul, 'The Continuing Importance of New Bibliographical Method', in *Shakespeare Survey 62* (Cambridge University Press, 2009), pp. 30–45

Whitworth, Charles (ed.), *The Comedy of Errors* (Oxford University Press, 2002)

Wiggins, Martin, 'When Did Marlowe Write *Dido, Queen of Carthage*?', *Review of English Studies*, 59 (2008), 521–41

Wilders, John (ed.), *Shakespeare in Production: Macbeth* (Cambridge University Press, 2004)

Williams, George Walton (ed.), *The Island Princess*, in Fredson Bowers (gen. ed.), *The Dramatic Works in the Beaumont and Fletcher Canon*, 10 vols. (Cambridge University Press, 1966–96), V (1982), 539–670

(ed.), *The Woman Hater*, in Fredson Bowers (gen. ed.), *The Dramatic Works in the Beaumont and Fletcher Canon*, 10 vols. (Cambridge University Press, 1966–96), I (1966), pp. 145–259

Williams, George Walton, and Gwynne Blakemore Evans (eds.), *The History of King Henry the Fourth, as revised by Sir Edward Dering, Bart.* (University Press of Virginia, 1974)

Wright, James, *Historia Histrionica* Q1 (1699) [Wing W3695]

Yeandle, Laetitia, 'Sir Edward Dering of Surrenden Dering and his "Booke of Expences" (1617–1628)', *Archaeologia Cantiana*, 125 (2005), 323–44

Zitner, Sheldon P. (ed.), *Much Ado About Nothing* (Oxford University Press, 1994)

Index

Admiral's Men (first), 46
Admiral's Men (formed in 1594), 6, 46, 187n.45
Agas, Ralph, 101
Alchemist, The, 94, 152
Alfield, Thomas, 173n.16
Alleyn, Edward, 6
All's Well That Ends Well, 97–8, 152
Alphonsus, King of Aragon, 143
Antonio's Revenge, 9, 48, 137, 188n.54
Antony and Cleopatra, 13, 71
Appius and Virginia, 19
Arden of Faversham, 130, 143
As You Like It, 25, 124–5, 147
Astington, John H., 29–30, 93, 140, 172n.6
Atheist's Tragedy, The, 31

Bacon, Francis, 113
Baldwin, T. W., 108
Bartholomew Fair, 31, 161n.49
Battle of Alcazar, The, 118
Beckerman, Bernard, 20, 64, 149
Beeston, William, 12
Believe as You List, 32
Berry, Herbert, 8, 161n.45, 190n.20
Bevington, David, 170n.53, 182n.16
Bible, 103, 108, 114, 116
Blackfriars Playhouse (first), 9, 173n.15
Blackfriars Playhouse (second), 9–10, 12, 26, 32, 39, 48, 55, 65, 68, 69, 94, 152
Boar's Head Playhouse, 8
Bonduca, 38–9, 141
book-keeper, 13, 14, 32, 33, 36, 132, 134, 135, 173n.11, 174n.29, 183n.17; *see also* Edward Knight
Bowers, Fredson, 134
Bowsher, Julian M. C., 4, 6
Brayne, John, 2
Brennoralt, 111–12, 120, 122, 124
Brooke, Arthur, 104
Brown, John Russell, 44, 45
Buc, Sir George, 39

Buchell, Arend van, 4
Burbage, James, 2, 9
Burbage, Richard, 101
Burns, Edward, 190n.26
Butler, Martin, 108

Caesar and Pompey, 143
Calore, Michela, 170n.54
Cambises, 188n.49
Captain, The, 59
Captives, The, 13, 16, 45–6, 132, 135, 183n.17
Carnegie, David, 49, 169n.43
Chamberlain's Men, 6, 9, 163n.72
Chances, The, 61, 66
Chapel Children (operated at first Blackfriars), 9, 192n.31
Chapel Children (operated at second Blackfriars 1600-1603), 9
Changeling, The, 60, 135, 145, 147, 154, 157
Chaste Maid in Cheapside, A, 5, 53
Chaucer, Geoffrey, 106
City Madam, The, 32–3, 134
City Match, The, 37
Cockpit (Phoenix) Playhouse in Drury Lane, 11, 12, 13, 26
Colie, Rosalie L., 104
Comedy of Errors, The, 41, 86, 183n.17
Comito, Terry, 103, 104
Condell, Henry, 26
Conspiracy and Tragedy of Charles, Duke of Byron, The, 56
Country Girl, The, 177n.10
Court Beggar, The, 61–2
Crane, Ralph, 36, 44, 67, 179n.26
Cruel Brother, The, 56
Cupid's Revenge, 34–5, 96, 152
Cupid's Whirligig, 48, 92
Curtain Playhouse, 4, 104, 114
Cymbeline, 23, 108, 119
Cynthia's Revels, 46

Daileader, Celia R., 171n.57
Daniell, David, 63
Davenant, William, 11
Davies, Sir John, 26
Dead Man's Fortune, The, 132
Dekker, Thomas, 26
Derby's Men (patronised by William Stanley, 6th Earl of Derby, Lord Strange), 187n.45
Dering, Sir Edward, 186n.35
Deserving Favourite, The, 168n.34
Dessen, Alan C., 19, 57, 73, 120, 165n.4, 170n.55, 177n.12, 188n.54
Devil's Charter, The, 7, 19–20, 142
Dido, Queen of Carthage, 143–4
Distresses, The, 58
Doctor Faustus, 30, 35, 68, 162n.68, 183n.17, 190n.24
Double Marriage, The, 64–5, 173n.11
Downfall of Robert, Earl of Huntingdon, The, 3, 167n.25
Duchess of Malfi, The, 14, 44, 45, 72, 130, 148–9
Dutch Courtesan, The, 41
Dutton, Richard, 15, 180n.33

Eastward Ho, 9, 49
Edward II, 142
Edward III, 110–11, 124, 183n.17
2 Edward IV, 55, 138, 188n.54
Edwards, Philip, 137
Egan, Gabriel, 72, 159n.9
English Traveller, The, 187n.46
entr'acte music, 22, 55, 69, 173n.15
Epicoene, 89–92
epilogue, 15, 145, 146, 147, 150
Erne, Lucas, 15, 178n.15
Escapes of Jupiter, The, 185n.32
Evans, G. Blakemore, 186n.35
Evans, Henry, 9
Every Man in His Humour, 75–7, 81
Every Man out of His Humour, 4, 14

Fairbrother, Nan, 103
Farmer, Alan B., 32
Farrant, Richard, 9
Fatal Dowry, The, 135
Fedele and Fortunio, 57–8, 179n.28
Fitzpatrick, Tim, 7, 92–4, 159n.17, 180n.35
Foakes, R. A., 7, 22, 117, 181n.39, 182n.4, 185n.31
Forker, Charles R., 52
Forman, Dr Simon, 191n.30
Fortune Playhouse, 6–7, 35, 133
Four Plays in One, 66
Fowler, Richard, 133
Frederick and Basilea, 18
Friar Bacon and Friar Bungay, 117–18, 138–9

Gabrieli, Vittorio, 123, 190n.25
Gair, Reavley, 8, 9
Game at Chess, A, 87
Gentleman of Venice, The, 120, 122
Gentleman Usher, The, 77
Globe Playhouse, 5–6, 7, 10, 26, 32, 45, 55, 56, 68, 70, 72, 100, 128, 136, 148, 152
  New Globe, 35, 71
Gossett, Suzanne, 166n.10
Graves, R. B., 45
Gray's Inn, 86
Greg, W. W., 38
Gurr, Andrew, 12, 14, 15, 16, 20, 168n.34, 175n.31, 192n.39

Habicht, Werner, 117, 187n.48
Hall, Edward, 185n.33
Hamlet, 13, 15, 74–5, 96, 129–30, 136, 147–8, 180n.35
Hammond, Antony, 21
Hattaway, Michael, 163n.73, 163n.77
Hector of Germany, The, 115–16, 119, 124, 142
Heir, The, 106–7, 120, 122
Heminges, John, 26
1 Henry IV, 70, 133
2 Henry IV, 180n.34, 184n.27
Henry V, 15
1 Henry VI, 57, 118–19, 141
2 Henry VI, 24, 109–10, 123–4, 185n.33
3 Henry VI, 20–1, 94–6, 130, 141
Henry VIII, 34
Henslowe, Philip, 4, 6, 8, 22, 23, 35, 117, 158n.3, 163n.73
Herbert, Sir Henry, 32, 37
Herford, C. H., 171n.59
Higgott, Gordon, 11
Hildy, Franklin J., 12
Hill, Thomas, 101, 102, 123
Hirrel, Michael J., 14
Hog Hath Lost His Pearl, The, 177n.7
Holinshed, Raphael, 185n.33, 186n.34
Holland, Peter, 22
Honigmann, E. A. J., 166n.7
Hope Playhouse, 8
Horace, 149
hortus conclusus, 103, 104
Hosley, Richard, 17–18, 55–6, 67–8, 160n.36, 167n.18, 172n.9, 173n.15
How a Man May Choose a Good Wife from a Bad, 87–8
Humphreys, Arthur, 23, 63
Hunter, G. K., 175n.39

If It Be Not a Good Play, the Devil Is in It, 161n.49
intervals, 66, 133, 134–5, 157; *see also* entr'acte music

Ioppolo, Grace, 161n.47
Iron Age, 1 The, 20
Iron Age, 2 The, 8, 133, 145–6, 147
Island Princess, The, 85–6

Jack Drum's Entertainment, 9, 133
Jackson, MacDonald P., 176n.4, 191n.29
James IV, 86–7
Jew of Malta, The, 3, 133
John a Kent and John a Cumber, 55
Jones, Inigo, 11
Jones/Webb drawings, *see* Worcester College drawings
Jonsonus Virbius, 53
Jowett, John, 173n.16, 178n.15, 187n.45
Julius Caesar, 23, 63–4, 88, 100–1, 125–8, 154

Kathman, David, 163n.72, 170n.52
Kiefer, Frederick, 189n.9
King John, 37, 185n.34
King Lear, 74, 135, 148
King's Men, 9, 22, 55, 152, 171n.57, 187n.45
Kirkman, Francis, 54
Knack to Know an Honest Man, A, 77
Knavery in All Trades, 132–3
Knight, Edward, 32, 33, 38
Knight of Malta, The, 178n.21
Knight of the Burning Pestle, The, 61, 193n.42
Knutson, Roslyn, 191n.28

Lady Elizabeth's Men, 132
Lancashire, Anne, 178n.20
Launching of the Mary, The, 173n.10
Lawrence, W. J., 190n.24
Lesser, Zachary, 32
Levenson, Jill L., 178n.15
Lever, J. W., 184n.25
Lindley, David, 172n.3
Lingua, 192n.35
Little French Lawyer, The, 37–8, 40–1, 66, 73–4, 97, 134
Livingston, Meg Powers, 171n.57
Locrine, 141–2
Lodge, Thomas, 25, 188n.51
Long, William B., 13
Love's Cruelty, 176n.4
Love's Pilgrimage, 33–4, 58–9, 77–8
Lusardi, James P., 74

Macbeth (by Davenant), 191n.30, 193n.45
Macbeth (by Shakespeare), 66–7, 74, 142–3, 149, 165n.6
MacIntyre, Jean, 10, 180n.35
Mackintosh, Iain, 11

MacLean, Sally-Beth, 169n.51, 179n.25, 191n.28
Mahood, M. M., 52
Maid in the Mill, The, 134
Malcontent, The, 26, 68–9, 133
Mares, F. H., 181n.41
Marshall, Cynthia, 124
Massacre at Paris, The, 77, 177n.14
Massai, Sonia, 191n.28
Master of the Revels, 14, 15; *see also* George Buc, Henry Herbert
Mayne, Jasper, 53
McMillin, Scott, 163n.72, 169n.51, 179n.25, 187n.45, 191n.28
Measure for Measure, 46–7, 97, 154, 184n.25
Melchiori, Giorgio, 123, 190n.25
Menaechmi, 41
Merchant of Venice, The, 24, 69–70, 88–9
Merry Wives of Windsor, The, 180n.34
Middle Temple, 51, 112
Midsummer Night's Dream, A, 22–3, 134, 189n.1
Miller, Patricia, 6
Money is an Ass, 53
Monsieur Thomas, 62–3
Moseley, Humphrey, 14
Most Virtuous and Godly Susanna, The, 185n.34
Much Ado About Nothing, 113–14, 123
Munday, Anthony, 57
Munro, Lucy, 171n.57

Nashe, Thomas, 181n.39
New Wonder, A, 170n.55
Night Walker, The, 60–1
Nolan, Michael, 172n.4
Novella, The, 59–60, 163n.68

Old Fortunatus, 46, 117
Orestes, 146–7
Orgel, Stephen, 14, 25
Orrell, John, 6, 11, 12, 161n.45
Othello, 30, 136
Oxford's Boys, 173n.15
Oxford's Men, 8

Palmer, Barbara D., 170n.53
Parasitaster, or the Fawn, 11, 135
Parson's Wedding, The, 53
part, actor's, 15, 16
Pasqualigo, Luigi, 57, 179n.28
Patient Grissil, 7
Paul's Playhouse, 8–9, 26, 48, 55
Peacham, Henry, 93–4
Pericles, 70, 88, 153
Picture, The, 56
Plutarch, 23, 125

plots, 16, 18, 19, 132, 187n.42
Prisoners, The, 133–4
Prophetess, The, 173n.11

Queen Anne's Men, 8, 187n.45
Queen's Men (Queen Elizabeth's players), 47, 170n.52, 179n.25, 180n.39

Red Bull Playhouse, 8, 172n.9
Red Bull (Revels) Company, 132
Red Lion Playhouse, 2
Revenger's Tragedy, The, 18–19
Reynolds, G. F., 186n.36
Richard II, 30–1, 52–3, 57, 70–1, 80–1, 101–2, 130, 176n.4, 182n.12, 184n.24
1 Richard II, or Thomas of Woodstock, 176n.4
Richard III, 24, 132
Richmond, Hugh Macrae, 71
Roaring Girl, The, 163n.75
Roman Actor, The, 56
Romeo and Juliet, 15, 58, 79–80, 81–2, 89, 104–5, 119–20, 136–7, 153, 161n.49, 167n.25, 181n.46
Rose, Mark, 182n.15
Rose Playhouse, 2–4, 68, 118
Rowland, Richard, 179n.29

Salisbury Court Playhouse, 12, 26
Schanzer, Ernest, 25
Schlueter, June, 74
Second Maiden's Tragedy, The, 39–40, 44–5, 84, 178n.16
1 Selimus, 131–2
Seven Deadly Sins, 2 The, 19, 163n.72
Shapiro, Michael, 147
Shoemaker a Gentleman, A, 172n.9
Shoemaker's Holiday, The, 121–2
Sidney, Sir Philip, 120–1
Silver Age, The, 8, 87
Simpson, Percy, 171n.59
Sir Clyomon and Sir Clamydes, 47–8
Sir Giles Goosecap, 167n.25
Sir John van Olden Barnavelt, 36–7, 140–1
Sir Thomas More, 122–3, 139–40, 141
Spanish Tragedy, The, 30, 115, 119, 137–8, 140
Sparagus Garden, The, 184n.24
Spevack, Marvin, 63
1 St Patrick for Ireland, 144
stage keepers/attendants, 30, 78, 132, 134
Staple of News, The, 134
Steele, Kelly Christine, 10
Stern, Tiffany, 15–16, 147, 191n.28
Strange's Men, 158n.3, 163n.72, 187n.45
Street, Peter, 6
Sussex's Men, 180n.39
Swan Playhouse, 4–5, 53, 55, 72, 89

2 Tamburlaine the Great, 20, 144
Taming of a Shrew, The, 88
Taming of the Shrew, The, 69, 78, 88, 184n.21
Tarlton, Richard, 93–4, 180n.39
Taylor, Gary, 17, 171n.57, 187n.45, 189n.11
Tempest, The, 23
Theatre Playhouse, 2, 4, 5, 69, 104
Thomson, Leslie, 57, 73, 85, 165n.4, 170n.53, 177n.12
Thomson, Peter, 89
Thrace and Macedon, Scenario of a play set in, 116–17
Thracian Wonder, The, 53, 54, 172n.4
tiremen, 132, 134
'Tis Pity She's a Whore, 130, 163n.69
Titus Andronicus, 68
Traitor, The, 120, 122, 178n.16
Troilus and Cressida (by Chettle and Dekker), 18
Troilus and Cressida (by Shakespeare), 20, 39, 83, 108–9
Troublesome Reign of John, 1 & 2 The, 185n.34
Turner, Robert Kean, 38, 41
Twelfth Night, 29–30, 49–51, 82–3, 107, 110, 112, 124, 153
Two Lamentable Tragedies, 140, 141
Two Merry Milkmaids, The, 14
Two Noble Kinsmen, The, 105–6, 118, 121
Two Noble Ladies, The, 132, 143

Valentinian, 42–3
Valiant Welshman, The, 143
Vickers, Brian, 191n.29
Virgil, 108
Virgin Martyr, The, 8, 31–2, 143, 162n.68
Volpone, 78–9

Waith, Eugene M., 105
Walks of Islington and Hogsdon, The, 37
Warning for Fair Women, A, 55, 118
Webb, John, 12
Webster, John, 26, 68
Weimann, Robert, 147
Werburgh Street Theatre, Dublin, 192n.34
Westward Ho, 177n.8
What You Will, 9
When You See Me, You Know Me, 168n.37
White Devil, The, 112–13
Whitefriars Children, 180n.33
Whitefriars Playhouse, 10, 48, 171n.57, 180n.35
Widow's Tears, The, 37, 110
Wiggins, Martin, 192n.31, 192n.32
Williams, George Walton, 186n.35
Wily Beguiled, 121
Winter's Tale, The, 25, 167n.18
Wit of a Woman, The, 87

Wit without Money, 41
Witch, The, 67
Witt, Johannes de, 4, 72
Wits, The, 48, 92–3
Woman Hater, The, 41–2
Woman Killed with Kindness, A, 19
Woman's Prize, The, 66, 170n.57
Women Pleased, 31

Wonder of Women, or Sophonisba, The, 56
Worcester College drawings, 10, 11–12, 174n.25
Worcester's Men, 8, 187n.45
Wounds of Civil War, The, 46
Wright, James, 161n.45

Yeandle, Laetitia, 186n.35
Yorkshire Tragedy, A, 43